PRAISE FOR
KISSES *from* KATIE

"*Kisses from Katie* is another wonderful reminder that 'big' things for the kingdom do not come from age or experience but as an overflow of a deeper love within. I highly encourage you to read this captivating account of obedience to God's call, and I challenge you to consider what you are doing to 'care for the least of these.'"

  —Dr. Wess Stafford, president and CEO, Compassion International

"Katie Davis has the story that makes radio talk show hosts stop in their tracks and say with deep disbelief, 'No, she didn't.' But, yes, she did! Katie Davis is the young dynamo of the gospel, bringing love and joy not just to her children but to an entire village and region. She is an inspiration and a testament to what God will do when one is willing to be used."

  —Hugh Hewitt, host of *The Hugh Hewitt Radio Show*

"I was blown away when I first heard of Katie's incredible story. I'm excited many others will now have the opportunity to be inspired and challenged by it."

  —Scott Harrison, founder/CEO of charity: water

"I was profoundly moved, challenged, and convicted as I read *Kisses from Katie,* and I came away wanting to know Jesus the way that Katie does. This is an honest and compelling account of one young woman's journey of obedience to a Jesus who loves the whole world, especially the forgotten and the marginalized."

  —Mike Erre, author of *Why the Bible Matters* and *The Jesus of Suburbia*

"A breathtaking journey into the sorrow and beauty of abandon to Jesus Christ. Katie Davis is young, still learning daily how best to serve. Yet her reckless, Peter-like love calls the bluff of a Christianity that refers to Jesus as 'Lord' with only partial intent of doing what He says. This is not a book to read if you wish for your comfort, convenience, and control to remain undisturbed. But if you stand willing to act upon belief, here you will encounter the full heartache and joy that await any person who ventures near to God's heart through adoption and other ways of loving the orphan in distress."

—Jedd Medefind, president, Christian Alliance for Orphans

"*Kisses from Katie* will be one of those books you cannot put down. It will literally transform everything about you and guide the way for you to take your ordinary life and fashion it into something extraordinary."

—Tom Davis, author of *Red Letters, Fields of the Fatherless,* and *Priceless*

"As I read Katie's book, I felt like I was reading Amy Carmichael. As Amy did in her life, Katie shows Jesus to be amazingly wonderful not only in what she writes but also in how she selflessly cares for the fatherless. If you want to love Jesus more and better understand His love for the least of these, read *Kisses from Katie*. She is for our generation what Amy was for hers: a hero in fulfilling God's call to care for orphans."

—Dan Cruver, director, Together for Adoption,
and author of *Reclaiming Adoption*

"Katie Davis is an inspiration to me as a wife, mom, and follower of Christ. Her devotion to the Lord and her love for His children challenge me to give sacrificially, serve selflessly, and live out my salvation with radical abandon!"

—Heather Platt, adoptive mother and wife of David Platt, author of *Radical*

KISSES
from KATIE

A Story of Relentless Love and Redemption

KATIE DAVIS
with BETH CLARK

HOWARD BOOKS
A DIVISION OF SIMON & SCHUSTER, INC.

New York   Nashville   London   Toronto   Sydney   New Delhi

Howard Books
A Division of Simon & Schuster, Inc.
1230 Avenue of the Americas
New York, NY 10020

First Howard Books hardcover edition October 2011

HOWARD and colophon are trademarks of Simon & Schuster, Inc.

For information about special discounts for bulk purchases,
please contact Simon & Schuster Special Sales at 1-866-506-1949
or business@simonandschuster.com.

The Simon & Schuster Speakers Bureau can bring authors to your live event.
For more information or to book an event, contact the Simon & Schuster Speakers Bureau at 1-866-248-3049 or visit our website at www.simonspeakers.com.

Designed by Davina Mock-Maniscalco

Journal entry backgrounds © iStock

Manufactured in the United States of America

20 19

Library of Congress Cataloging-in-Publication Data

Davis, Katie.
    Kisses from Katie / Katie Davis, with Beth Clark.
        p.   cm.
    1. Davis, Katie, 1988-   2. Orphans—Services for—Uganda.   3. Orphans—Uganda—Social conditions.   4. Orphanages—Unganda.   5. Church work with orphans—Uganda.
6. Social work with children—Uganda.   I. Clark, Beth, 1967–   II. Title.
HV1347.D38 2011
362.73092—dc22   2011011683
[B]

ISBN 978-1-4516-1206-6
ISBN 978-1-4516-1210-3 (ebook)

For Jesus. Every word, every breath is for you.

And for my girls, Prossy, Margaret, Agnes, Zuula, Mary, Hellen, Tibita, Sarah, Scovia, Joyce, Sumini, Jane, Grace, and Patricia, for teaching me more about His unfailing love each and every day.

CONTENTS

ACKNOWLEDGMENTS

For these dearest ones, thank you seems so insufficient, yet I humbly offer my deepest gratitude to . . .

My incredible children: Thank you for making me a mother. For the gift that is each one of you and each moment spent with you. Thank you for being willing to have a few more nights of roll eggs than usual. You are the very best children a mom could ever ask for, and I love you to forever and back again.

Mom, Dad, and Brad: Thank you for believing in me, no matter what, for always pushing me to follow my dreams, and for dreaming with me. Mom and Dad, you taught me how to love, how to live with strength, kindness, grace, and joy. The way you continue to give of yourselves to me and to my daughters humbles me. Brad, my strong shoulder and greatest encourager, I am so proud to call you my brother and best friend. I love you all.

Beth, Curtis, and Karen: Thank you for pouring your time and hearts into this book. This is a reality only because of you. What a precious gift from God that He put all of you in my life for such a time as this! Thank you for your friendship.

The Howard team: Thank you for believing in the message of our story. Thank you for your hard work, your wisdom, and your incredible patience with me as I missed every single deadline. I never could have asked for or dreamed of such gracious people to work with.

Shana, Renee, and Matt: Thank you for reading this manuscript long before it was a book and believing it could be. For all the advice, all the wisdom, all the wiped-away tears and shared-in laughter, not just now but always. You know I could go on. You are three of the greatest gifts He has graced me with; thank you for being my friends, thank you for being family.

My friends and family, and the beautiful people of Uganda: Thank you for sharing your lives and hearts with me and allowing me to write about our relationships. Without you, there is no story.

All who prayed: Everyone who brought dinner, watched the girls for the day, ran errands, called long distance with encouragement, came with late-night cookies, and kept the fridge stocked with Diet Coke. You are too many to name, but your prayers and kindness have carried me—lifted my arms and refreshed my soul. Thank you.

My Beautiful One who created all of this: My thank-you is far too minuscule to express my gratitude that You, who could do this all by yourself, would choose to include me in your plan. I can only beg that this grace, so undeserved, would be to great effect for You.

FOREWORD

People who really want to make a difference in the world usually do it, in one way or another. And I've noticed something about people who make a difference in the world: They hold the unshakable conviction that individuals are extremely important, that *every life matters*. They get excited over one smile. They are willing to feed one stomach, educate one mind, and treat one wound. They aren't determined to revolutionize the world all at once; they're satisfied with small changes. Over time, though, the small changes add up. Sometimes they even transform cities and nations, and yes, the world.

People who want to make a difference get frustrated along the way. But if they have a particularly stressful day, they don't quit. They keep going. Given their accomplishments, most of them are shockingly normal and the way they spend each day can be quite mundane. They don't teach grand lessons that suddenly enlighten entire communities; they teach small lessons that can bring incremental improvement to one man or woman, boy or girl. They don't do anything to *call* attention to themselves, they simply *pay* attention to the everyday needs of others, even if it's only one person. They bring change in ways most people will never read about or applaud. And because of the way these world-changers are wired, they wouldn't think of living their lives any other way.

This realization came to me on my first day in a small village near Katie's home in Jinja, Uganda. My driver took me from Entebbe airport to the village because that's where Katie happened to be when we arrived. The place is called Masese (pronounced *Ma-SESS-ay*). It is a place of intense poverty; it's filthy and it smells like raw sewage rotting in the hot sun, often made worse by the distinct odor of homemade moonshine. To drive through Masese is to witness one gut-wrenching scene after another, and Katie absolutely loves it because she loves the people who live there.

Masese is located at the foot of a hill. On top of that hill is a school where the ministry Katie directs supplies food to the school students and, by special arrangement with the school officials, to the children of the village too, even if they are not enrolled in the school. The school was my first stop in Uganda and I could easily tell the schoolchildren apart from the village children. Certainly, the students' uniforms distinguished them, but so did their cleanliness, their shoes, and the fact that their noses weren't running and their mouths weren't bleeding.

Many of the village children appeared to be sick, but one little girl, who looked to be two or three years old, stood out more than the rest. Her tiny body seemed barely able to carry her enormous belly, and her dirty skin was dotted with unidentifiable bumps that each resembled a wart, a blister, and the kind of sore that appears with chicken pox, all in one lesion. A wound that was part scab, part raw and oozing covered about half of her little mouth. I watched Katie walk over to this fragile child, pick her up gently, assess her needs almost instantly, and begin asking other children questions about her.

"Who is this child?"

"What is her name?"

"Where is her home?"

"Where is her mother?"

At first, no one seemed to know the answers, but word must have spread that "Auntie Kate" wanted to know about this child, because soon the little girl's aunt approached Katie to say that her name was Napongo, her mother had gone to Kampala and had been away for months. Her father had gone somewhere else (*gone* is a word far too often associated with fathers in Uganda). The aunt, who must have been twelve or thirteen years old, was responsible for the little girl.

Within a few minutes, I was being jolted along the uneven road from the Masese school in Katie's sixteen-passenger van with the fragile little girl, her aunt, and four of Katie's fourteen children. We were headed to the home of Katie's friend Renee to give Napongo a bath because Renee's was the closest place Katie knew that had clean running water.

I watched in awe, and a bit of disgust, as the little girl stood motionless in the tub as Katie ran water from a portable showerhead and sprinkled it on her wrists. I silently wondered why she didn't move a little faster with the bathing process and then it dawned on me: Perhaps the little girl had never been in a bathtub. Having her entire body sprayed with the showerhead could have terrified her. Katie was dripping water on her own wrists, and then on the little girl's, to help her feel safe and at ease.

Napongo barely moved as Katie tenderly ran a bar of soap over her. The clean, clear water that came out of the showerhead became dark red as it rolled off her into the drain. And then, in a move that surprised Katie and me, the aunt walked into the bathroom, took the soap from Katie, and began to scrub the little girl. I was afraid the child would burst into tears, but still she stood without squirming or squealing or raising any of the objections toddlers typically raise.

Katie and I watched quietly, both of our minds filled with the same question: "How can it be that this aunt, who isn't clean herself and lives in squalor in a dirty village, knows the importance and urgency of cleanliness for this child?" She was washing the little girl with determination and concentration, as though she understood that this activity was vital to the child's well-being. More than likely, this auntie had really wanted Napongo to be clean and well all along, but simply didn't have the means to help her.

When the child had been bathed to her aunt's satisfaction, Katie wrapped her in a towel and carried her to a nearby bed. She knelt in front of her and began to remove jiggers from her feet. *Jigger* was not a word I'd heard before. In Uganda, jiggers are everywhere and they cause much trouble. They are small insects that burrow painlessly into a person's skin and create a tiny egg sac, leaving a little bump that appears as inflammation. While having jiggers doesn't hurt until they have practically infested an area of the body, having them removed can be excruciating. But the child didn't wince, scream, or jerk in any way as Katie removed the jiggers and cut away dead skin around them. She simply sat silently as a few tiny tears made their way slowly down her face.

I backed into a corner, thinking that if I fainted, I wouldn't fall backward; I would simply slide down the wall. I told myself it was fatigue from jet lag, and it was—partly. And partly it was a mixture of disgust, sadness, and shock over the child's willingness to so quietly endure this painful procedure.

Under normal circumstances, I might have been tempted to think the little girl was too sick to recover. But because I knew she was in Katie's care, I had every reason to believe she'd be just fine.

I knew the stories. I'd read all of Katie's blog, her chronicle of her life and work in Uganda, starting in 2007. I knew that if anyone could give a little girl the love and attention she needed, it would be Katie. I was aware that Katie would not only tend to the child for part of an afternoon but for days or months to come if necessary.

Not unexpectedly, about ten days later, Katie saw Napongo in Masese. She was not improving as Katie had hoped. Certainly, she looked better than she had when I first saw her. The wounded place on her mouth had healed completely, probably because her young aunt applied the antibiotic ointment Katie gave her, as instructed. But the child's belly was still enormous and tight. The sores all over her body remained. Ugandans recognized the disease and had a name for it, but no one anywhere could translate that name into English.

So, for the remainder of my stay in Uganda, Napongo lived at Katie's house with the rest of us. She received nourishing meals and vitamins, plus the affection and care of fourteen sisters. On her first Sunday there this child, who literally wore dirty tatters and went barefoot every day because she had no other option, had a brand-new sundress and a pair of shoes to wear when she went to church for the very first time.

One of the moments with Napongo etched most deeply in my mind took place when Katie took her to be tested for HIV. Katie and I, with all fourteen girls and Napongo, piled into the van and went to Renee's house because Renee had HIV-testing supplies. Napongo sat on the kitchen counter. I once again stood in close proximity to the wall—just in case. This child who had so stoically endured the painful removal of her jiggers began to shriek as the needle pierced her veins. The sound was like a vise grip on my heart as I watched drops of her young blood fall on the paper testing strip. Katie, Renee, and I, along with a couple of other friends, waited nervously, fully aware of what the test results would mean to Napongo's life and future.

And then, after a weighty sigh, Renee announced with a whisper, "She's positive."

The kitchen was silent.

Today, Napongo's mother has returned from Kampala and has learned to love and care for her in a whole new way. With Katie's help, Napongo is receiving regular HIV treatments, infusing new life into the body that was wasting away only a few months ago. She attends preschool, and she runs and laughs and dances and giggles—as four-year-old girls are supposed to do. Katie and her family visit Napongo often, amazed and overjoyed by the way her life has turned around.

Napongo's story is only one. Many others in Katie's community can tell of times when she took notice of their situations and stopped to provide as much help and compassion as humanly possible. During my short stay in Uganda, I witnessed a steady stream of people who dropped by Katie's house or stopped her on the street for various reasons. One woman, a neighbor, came at night. She had a fever and wasn't feeling well. Katie quickly put on a pair of latex gloves and pricked her finger to test for malaria. Over the next few days, someone dropped by to ask Katie for a letter of reference to help him obtain a visa to the United States. Someone came to speak to her about his schooling. A neighbor stopped by to share her struggles with her health and finances. As Katie cared for each one and did what she could do to assist or encourage, I realized that there are no statistics in Katie's world. There are only people, and *every life matters*.

You'll see that over and over again throughout these pages. It's not only the way Katie lives, it's also the way you can live if you choose to do so. Human suffering and need are everywhere. Katie is not a superhero; she's really just an ordinary woman who wanted more than anything to obey God and say yes to whatever He asked of her. It just so happened that a great adventure awaited her when she did, and she now finds herself in the midst of a remarkable story that is unfolding in jubilant ways, in heartbreaking ways, and in courageous ways every day.

God has been writing a story in Uganda for a long time. He's used lots of people to accomplish what He has wanted to do there over the years. Some of them have given their lives for His purposes in this country, and though we don't know them, we honor them. Others are giving their lives to participate in all God is doing in this land today, as we write this book. They are both Ugandan natives and citizens of countries far away; they are Katie's friends and colleagues; they are ordinary people who love an extraordinary God; they are part of Katie's story and part of God's ongoing story here.

If you are ordinary but hungry to obey God, may you find inspiration and encouragement in these pages. May you find the strength to say yes and be launched into your very own amazing story.

—Beth Clark

INTRODUCTION

I never meant to be a mother. I mean, I guess I did; not right now, though. Not before I was married. Not when I was nineteen. *Not* to so, so many little people. Thankfully, God's plans do not seem to be affected much by my own.

I never meant to live in Uganda, a dot on the map in East Africa, on the opposite side of the planet from my family and all that is comfortable and familiar. Thankfully, God's plans also happen to be much better than my own.

You see, Jesus wrecked my life. For as long as I could remember, I had everything this world says is important. In high school, I was class president, homecoming queen, top of my class. I dated cute boys and wore cute shoes and drove a cute sports car. I had wonderful, supportive parents who so desired my success that they would have paid for me to go to college anywhere my heart desired. *But* I loved Jesus.

And the fact that I loved Jesus was beginning to interfere with the plans I once had for my life and certainly with the plans others had for me. My heart had been apprehended by a great love, a love that compelled me to live differently. I had grown up in a Christian home, gone to church, and learned about Jesus all my life. Around the age of twelve or thirteen, I began to delve into the truths of Scripture. As I read and learned more and more of what Jesus said, I liked the lifestyle I saw around me less and less. I began to realize that God wanted more from me, and I wanted more *of* Him. He began to grow in me a desire to live intentionally, and different from anyone I had ever known.

Slowly but surely I began to realize the truth: I had loved and admired and worshiped Jesus without doing what He said. This recognition didn't happen overnight; in fact I believe it was happening in my heart long before I even knew it. It was happening as I explored the possibility of overseas volunteer work, it was happening as I took my first three-week trip to Uganda, it was happening as I fell in love with a beautiful country full of gracious, joyful people and immense poverty and squalor that begged me to do more. It was happening in so many ways, and I couldn't deny it. I wanted to actually *do* what Jesus said to do.

So I quit my life.

Originally, my quitting was to be temporary, lasting just one year before I went to college and returned to normal, American teenager life. But after that year, which I spent in Uganda, returning to "normal" wasn't possible. I had seen what life was about and I could not pretend I didn't know. So I quit my life again, and for good this time. I quit college; I quit cute designer clothes and my little yellow convertible; I quit my boyfriend. I no longer have all the things the world says are important. I do not have a retirement fund; I do not even have electricity some days. But I have everything I know is important. I have a joy and a peace that are unimaginable and can come only from a place better than this earth. I cannot fathom being happier. Jesus wrecked my life, shattered it to pieces, and put it back together more beautifully.

During the first few months I lived in Uganda, in fall of 2007, I wrote, "Sometimes working in a Third World country makes me feel like I am emptying the ocean with an eyedropper." Today, it often still feels that way. I have learned to be okay with this feeling because I have learned that I will not change the world. Jesus will do that. I can, however, change the world for one person. I can change the world for fourteen little girls and for four hundred schoolchildren and for a sick and dying grandmother and for a malnourished, neglected, abused five-year-old. And if one person sees the love of Christ in me, it is worth every minute. In fact, it is worth spending my life for.

Many days, I am still overwhelmed by the magnitude of the need and the incredible number of people who need help. Many days I see the destitute, disease-ridden children lining the streets in the communities I serve and I want to scoop up every single one of them, take them home with me, and feed and clothe and love them. And I look at the life of my Savior, who stopped for one.

So I keep stopping and loving one person at a time. Because this is my call as a Christian. I can do only what one woman can do, but I will do what I can. Daily, the Jesus who wrecked my life enables me to do so much more than I ever thought possible.

People often ask if I think my life is dangerous, if I am afraid. I am much more afraid of remaining comfortable. Matthew 10:28 tells us not to fear things that can destroy the body but things that can destroy the soul. I am surrounded by things that can destroy the body. I interact almost daily with people who have deadly diseases, and many times I am the only person who can help them. I live in a country with one of the world's longest-running wars taking place just a few hours away. Uncertainty is everywhere. But I am living in the midst of the uncertainty and risk, amid things that can and do bring physical destruction, because I am running from things that can destroy my soul: complacency, comfort, and ignorance. I am much more terrified of living a comfortable life in a self-serving society and failing to follow Jesus than I am of any illness or tragedy.

Jesus called His followers to be a lot of things, but I have yet to find where He warned us to be safe. We are not called to be safe, we are simply promised that when we are in danger, God is right there with us. And there is no better place to be than in His hands.

For as long as I can remember, one of my favorite Bible verses has been Psalm 37:4: "Delight yourself in the LORD and He will give you the desires of your heart." I used to believe it meant that if I did what the Lord asked of me, followed His commandments, and was a "good girl," He would grant all my desires and make my dreams come true. Today, this is still one of my favorite passages of Scripture, but I have learned to interpret it in a totally different way. It is not about God making *my* dreams come true but about God changing my dreams into *His* dreams for my life.

Today I am living the desires of my heart and I cannot imagine being happier; I cannot imagine living any other life than the one that unfolds before me day by day. But believe me, I am by no means living *my* plan. I thought that I wanted to go to college with my high school boyfriend, get married, have a successful career and children, settle into a nice house down the road from my parents, and live happily ever after. Today I am a single woman raising a houseful of girls and trying to teach others the love of Jesus in a land that is a far cry from my hometown and my culture. This is not a life that I dreamed up on my own or even knew I desired. I am watching God work, and as I "delight myself in the Lord" by doing what He asks of me and by saying yes to the needs He places in front of me, He is *changing* the desires of my heart and aligning them with the desires of His. As I go with Him to the hard places, He changes them into the most joyful places I could imagine.

It sounds beautiful, adventurous, even romantic in ways, right? It is beautiful. And the crazy thing is, it is so simple. Don't misunderstand; it is *not easy*. But it is simple in that each and every one of us was ultimately created to do the same thing. It will not look the same. It may take place in a foreign land or it may take place in your backyard, but I believe that we were each created to change the world for *someone*. To serve *someone*. To love *someone* the way Christ first loved us, to spread His light. This is the dream, and it is possible. Some days it is excruciatingly difficult, but the blessings far outweigh the hardships.

I have absolutely no desire to write a book about myself. This is a book about Christ. This is a book about a Christ who is alive today and not only knows but cares about every hair on my head. Yours too. I cannot really even pretend to fathom that, but I know it is true. I know this is true because I have seen it so profoundly in the very short amount of life that I have lived. I have seen it in extraordinary miracles and in moments so mundane that they are easily overlooked. And that is why I am writing this book. I am writing on the chance that a glimpse into the life of my family and me, full of my stupidity and God's grace, will remind you of this living, loving Christ, and what it means to serve Him. I am writing with the hope that as you cry and laugh with my family you will be encouraged that God still uses flawed human beings to change the world. And if He can use me, He can use you.

1

FALLING IN LOVE—WITH A COUNTRY

Sometimes it hits me like a brick to the head: My life is kind of insane. I am twenty-two years old; I have fourteen children, eleven
of whom are currently being homeschooled. We so often have extra
people staying with us—dying grandmothers, destitute refugees, or
severely malnourished children—that I am forever doing a head count
before I begin making meals. Most days, though, bumping along these
red dirt roads in my sixteen-passenger van full of singing (or screaming) children, neighbors, and occasionally our pet monkey, seems
completely normal—so much so that I have a hard time writing about
it. To me, there is nothing very spectacular about this everyday craziness; it is just the result of following Jesus into the impossible, doing
the little I can and trusting Him to do the rest.

Moving to the other side of the world and having a large family
was never my dream or even my idea. But as I look back, I can see
that God spent my whole life preparing me for the life He had
planned for me—the people He placed in just the right places at just
the right times, and circumstances I could never fathom would eventually be for His glory. For years before I went to Uganda, I had fanta-
sized about doing something incredible for God and others; what I

have learned is that I can do nothing incredible, but as I follow God into impossible situations, He can work miracles in and through me.

I first mentioned it—the idea of doing something outside the norm—to my parents in a serious way on my sixteenth birthday. To celebrate, my parents took me to eat my favorite food, sushi, at my favorite restaurant. It was a lighthearted occasion until I made a nervous comment that changed the mood completely: "I think I will spend a year doing mission work after I finish high school and before I go to college."

The smiles on my parents' faces gave way to blank stares and looks of confusion. The happy chatter at the dinner table ceased and my comment seemed stuck in the atmosphere. Silence.

I might as well have said I wanted to play quarterback in the NFL or fly to the moon. To them, taking a year to do mission work was about that far-fetched. It was completely unheard of in the Davis family and, I knew, probably unacceptable. My father had always been adamant about his desires for my life, desires rooted in his love for me and in his concern for my safety and well-being. As most parents do, both my mom and my dad wanted to do everything they could to guarantee me a successful, comfortable life, and they felt the best way to secure a "good" future for me was to provide me with a college education that would prepare me for a career.

A few minutes after I mentioned taking a year off to have some kind of adventure besides college, my parents recovered from their shock and responded in the best possible way; they didn't say no. They simply said they were not sure about the idea, but they would think about it. I was convinced in my heart that my desire was right. I was ready to go; it was up to God to convince my parents.

Sporadically over the next eighteen months, I remembered this conversation and searched the Internet for the word *orphanage* so I could investigate volunteer opportunities. I never had Uganda specifically in mind. As my senior year in high school grew closer, I began applying to volunteer at several orphanages I had found online. A home for babies in Uganda was the first to respond and say they were in need of volunteers. I was excited and my parents agreed to allow me to go over winter break during my senior year, hoping I would "get it out of my system." Their only requirement was that I find an adult to travel with me.

My parents may have been more clever than I gave them credit for. Of course, finding an adult who could take three weeks away from a job in the United States—and who wanted to spend that vacation time, including Christmas, in Africa with me—proved impossible. So I begged my mother to accompany me. When she realized how much I wanted to go and saw that I wasn't giving up on the idea, she said she would think about it. She soon realized this trip was not a whim but something about which I was deeply passionate, and because she is a woman who genuinely wants her children to be happy and fulfilled, she reluctantly agreed to the adventure. Before long, her reluctance turned into anxious enthusiasm and she became excited to be the person who would share this dream with me.

In December 2006, my mom and I were on our way to Uganda, where we would spend three weeks volunteering in a home for abandoned or orphaned babies. During those three weeks, I lost part of my heart to a place I'd never been before. I fell in love with Uganda as soon as I arrived. After I woke up the first morning of our stay, I looked around and saw glistening bright white smiles against ebony faces; I heard happy voices, lilting language, and gentle laughter. I saw strength and depth of character in people's eyes. I found Uganda to be a beautiful land filled with beautiful people.

Jinja, the city nearest to the village where I live today, sits nestled against the shore of Lake Victoria and at the source of the Nile River. Views of the lake and the river took my breath away when I saw them for the first time, and the explosion of color I saw as bumpy, vibrant, red dirt roads traversing the lush green landscape captivated me.

The people who called this fascinating country home astounded me with their gracious kindness and gentle ways. I watched, wide-eyed, as cattle, goats, and chickens roamed freely through the villages while curious children wandered among the shacks and makeshift businesses (such as little stores that sell canned drinks or washbasins or airtime for cellular telephones). In the town, I saw the kind of everyday life that happens in every society, in its own way, take place as people shopped along Jinja's main streets, did their banking, or met friends and chatted on the sidewalk. When I went to the villages, I witnessed men and women shucking corn, cooking, talking among themselves, or simply sitting beside the road quietly taking in the happenings of village life.

Whether I was in the town or out in a village, children were everywhere. When they saw a person with a different color of skin, they giggled and shouted. Some ran toward me with glee, others shrieked and fled at the sight of a foreigner. Those who weren't afraid of me grabbed my hands eagerly, as though we had been friends forever. It was easy for me to fall in love with them and with their country, its enormous beauty juxtaposing extreme poverty.

Most of our time was spent working at the babies' home feeding, changing, teaching, and playing with the many children there. The children as well as the women who worked in the orphanage inched their way into my heart, leaving their little handprints all over it. I would never be the same.

I left Uganda in tears at the end of our trip, the country and the people now a part of me. I cried all the way back to Tennessee and knew that someday I would return. I was forever ruined for comfort, convenience, and luxury, preferring instead challenge, sacrifice, and risking everything to do something I believed in. I realized it as I bathed babies and changed diapers in the babies' home, as I met older children and threw stones into the river with them, and as I did everything I could do to meet the basic human needs so evident around me. My heart had found its joy as I served the beautiful people the world calls "poor" but who seemed so rich in love to me. I have no doubt that God was preparing a longing in my heart for Uganda many years before I could even find this country on a map; there is no other explanation for the instant love I felt for this place and these people. Though the red soil eventually wore off the soles of my feet, Uganda never left my heart and was never far from my mind.

Upon my return to the United States to finish my last semester of high school I must admit I had become a bit obsessed with Uganda. I glanced at the clock during class to figure out what time it was there and daydreamed about what my friends in Uganda were doing. I talked about Uganda so much that I'm sure all my friends in the States wanted to tell me kindly to shut up. I knew I *had* to get back.

During my trip to Uganda, I met a pastor who had founded and ran an orphanage on the outskirts of Jinja. He was planning to open a kindergarten there and had asked me to be the teacher. The idea seemed a bit preposterous, as I had little experience teaching anything other than Sunday school, but he insisted I was the one for the job. Once I returned home, I realized I was prepared to do whatever I could to get back to my beloved Uganda, even if it meant suddenly becoming a kindergarten teacher.

By the end of my senior year, after many conversations and ample opportunities to see that I was serious about returning to Uganda, my parents had finally agreed to my postponing college for one year. I promised to spend only one year in Uganda and, when that year was finished, to return to the States and enroll in college. In the meantime, though, I had agreed to teach kindergarten in a small slum village outside of Jinja, Uganda. Though many of my friends and much of my family did not understand my desire to be so far away for so long, no one could dampen my enthusiasm. Every once in a while I felt nervous, but more often than not I could hardly contain my excitement for this yearlong adventure.

My dad, still unhappy that I was not going to college, never lost his fatherly concern for me. As a father who had worked to provide everything his only daughter had ever needed or wanted, he had many misgivings about the adventure I was determined to undertake. In fact, he refused to allow me to move so far away from home and stay for almost a year in a place he had never visited. So he decided to go with me to Uganda and stay for a week so he could survey every aspect of the place that so captivated me and make sure I was safe.

The morning my dad and I left, I remember waking up in my beyond-comfortable bed in my parents' house, in our upscale neighborhood. In this place where most ladies paid good money to have their hands and their lawns perfectly manicured and many people had no desire whatsoever to go to East Africa, I ate my last piece of peanut butter on toast as all my friends flooded the only home I had ever known to say good-bye one last time, all of us sobbing. Saying good-bye to my best friends, the boyfriend I was in love with and hoped to marry someday, and my little brother for almost a year nearly ripped my heart out. Part of me wondered how I could leave all this behind, but the other part of me was so ready to do it.

The trip from the United States to Uganda is long, no matter which route a person travels. It is long through Amsterdam, long through London, long through the Middle East. I spent parts of the trip giddy with excitement and parts of it crying as I realized how long it would be before I saw my family or best friends again.

My dad spent the entire first week of my year in Uganda trying to convince me to get on the plane back to the States with him at the end of the week. He didn't like the dirty conditions he saw; he didn't like the evidence of disease in so many places; and he didn't like the way some men looked at or spoke to a young white woman. He hated leaving me in this country so strange to him, but he could also see how happy I was there, and by the time he left, he knew that my heart was content and he was going home alone.

The next few weeks were full of joy and frustration. I slowly settled into my room, no bigger than three-by-six feet, in the back of the pastor's house. His home was on the orphanage compound, where 102 children, ages two to eighteen, lived.

I can't really explain in words the love I felt for these children or why I felt it. I think many people would have looked at them and seen only their filthy clothes, the ringworm on their heads, or the mucus that ended up in a crust around their nostrils. They would have looked around at the dormitories of the orphanage with its smooth, hard cement floor where rats and cockroaches made themselves at home and been a bit disgusted. By the grace of God, though, I didn't see these things.

The truth is, I saw myself in those little faces. I looked at them and felt this love that was unimaginable and knew that this is the way God sees me. The children would run to me with gifts of stones or dirt and I saw myself, filthy and broken, offering my life to the God of the universe and begging Him to make it into something beautiful. I sit here in a broken world, small and dirty at His feet, and He who sits so high chooses to commune with me, to love me anyway. He blinds Himself to my sin and my filth so that He can forge a relationship with me. And this is what He did for me with these precious children. He blinded me to the filth and disease, and I saw only children hungry for love that I was eager to share with them. I adored them, not because of who I was, but because of who He is. I just sat right down on that cold, hard floor and snuggled my nose into their dirty necks and kissed their fungus-covered heads and didn't even see it. I was *in love*.

From the moment I got there, I was busy, happy, and exhausted from rocking babies, reading to toddlers, playing with preschool-aged children, and entertaining the five- and six-year-olds. I spent mornings teaching kindergarten and spent most of my afternoons with the two- to six-year-olds at the orphanage because the older children attended school during the day and didn't return to the orphanage until about 5:00 P.M.

I had come to Uganda loaded with paper, crayons, counting charts, and picture books, prepared to teach the twelve or fourteen kindergarten-aged children who lived at the orphanage. As I was in transit from the States, however, the pastor had decided he felt led to open the school up to the slum community surrounding the orphanage, and the villagers were quick to jump at the opportunity for an inexpensive education.

Imagine my surprise, then, when I showed up to teach twelve children and 138 pairs of eyes stared back at me, a sea of 138 brown little faces crammed into the barn-turned-classroom (which smelled exactly like a barn and not at all like a classroom), all ready and eager to learn. As I made my way through the maze of little bodies sitting on wobbly benches, the room was silent. Finally, someone was unable to contain a giggle any longer, piercing the quiet with joy. Some of the other students started laughing, too, while others began to cry. The children didn't know what to do; they had never been to school before. And none of them spoke English. Some, never having seen a white person, trembled with fear and were hesitant to even look at me. Others, so intrigued by this new kind of person, cautiously petted my hair, tugged on my arms, and carefully examined my blue veins through my translucent skin.

My students were respectful and obedient, but the language barrier, combined with the sheer number of them, made teaching anything seem almost impossible. I spent the first week just trying to come up with a good system of communication. "This is a ball," I would say slowly, enunciating every syllable. "Dees ees a boll," their squeaky voices echoed back. We would spend all morning repeating this exercise, only to have someone come up to me at the end of the day holding a pencil and proudly proclaim, "Dees ees a boll!"

The language issues came as a bit of a surprise because I hadn't dealt with them while working at the babies' home during my three-week stay in Uganda. The babies' home was located in the city of Jinja and many people there spoke English, so my mom and I never had trouble communicating. Besides, technically, English is the official language of Uganda, but the truth is that very few people outside the major cities speak English, certainly not in the small villages outside Jinja, such as the one in which I was living and working. What I learned during that time, though, is that love knows no language. Although we were not able to speak to one another, we found many other ways of communicating; the children seemed to know I loved them, and I knew they loved me too.

God did eventually send a wonderful translator and three marvelous Ugandan women to teach beside me. I am certain that I learned much more from my students and fellow teachers than they did from me.

As much as I learned from others, there were certain aspects of adapting to a new culture that I simply had to figure out as I went along, things like how to calculate quickly how many Ugandan shillings equaled one American dollar or trying to ride sidesaddle on a *piki*. (A *piki* is a motorcycle and serves as the primary mode of transportation for many people in and around Jinja. Many men have their own businesses as *piki* drivers. They can be found congregating in groups in the middle of downtown Jinja or hailed, like taxis in the United States, along the side of the road.)

Days were spent learning to communicate, laughing hysterically with my students, and trying to laugh at the frustrations that came with this new job. Afternoons were spent with the children at the orphanage playing tic-tac-toe and hangman in the dirt, having my hair tugged in all different directions, and getting covered in the red dust that I was learning would never wear off my feet.

One of my greatest joys was the orphanage's time of praise and worship to God with all 102 children who lived there. During this time, which lasted for about an hour before the children went to bed, they sang with all their hearts, laughed, cried, and prayed in a language I couldn't understand. They were simply being with Jesus and I could feel God's presence there more strongly than I ever had before. I marveled at God's huge love for us as I cradled little babies late into the night—that even these children, the least of these, were created by Him specifically for a very special purpose.

There were many moments of great joy: singing of Jesus' love with the older children as we took a walk to the river to throw stones, cuddling with babies from the orphanage in my twin bed at five in the morning, jumping for joy in church with people so full of God's love that they could not hold still. However, there were still many moments when my patience was challenged. Through the frustrations, God taught me to laugh at myself, my ways of doing things, and what used to be important to me. He taught me that when doing my best was still not enough, that was when He took over; and because of His great grace and love, even in the frustrating moments I was filled with an inexplicable happiness and peace, my daily proof that I was living my purpose.

I laugh now to think how stressed out I was about geckos in my bed, children eating erasers, and learning to cook beans on an open fire, wash my laundry by hand with bar soap, or bathe outside in a bucket. Every day, though, as I looked around at beautiful, expectant faces with huge coffee-brown eyes hungry for the love of Jesus, I knew that I was here just to love, and the rest I would figure out in time.

Sometimes, in the midst of all the loving, praising the Lord, and energy and laughter the children around me seemed to exude, I forgot that these children had been orphaned, that they had horrible sorrow and tremendous pain in their pasts. One day, I was reminded.

Six-year-old Derek, a shy little boy with the face of an angel, fell and bumped his head. He looked so determined not to cry—here children are taught to be "big" and tough—but against his best efforts, tears began to flow. I pulled him into my lap, and almost as quickly as they had started the tears stopped. But what was left, the sorrow in those eyes beyond the tears, I will never forget. The eyes that peered out of that six-year-old face were a hundred years old and had seen more tragedy in their short lifetime than most ever will. I was filled with grief for this beautiful boy. I cradled in my arms a child who had seen his parents and siblings killed and had more than likely been forced to kill others himself in the war in northern Uganda. This child had known what it meant to be truly starving, to be totally lost, to be utterly hopeless.

And in that same moment of sadness, I was blown away by the greatness of our Lord, by the fact that God in all His mighty plans had cared enough for this child, had cared enough for me, to put us together in that moment. The God who created the heavens and the earth knew that on a rainy day in Uganda a little boy would bump his head, and the pain would be deeper than just that bump. God had put me in just the right place and given me the privilege of loving this child, gently rubbing his back and holding his hand, in a way he had not been loved in a long time, if ever. By the grace of God, I was blessed with the gift of being able to hold and hug this child, eventually tickling him until those sorrowful eyes brightened a little, and Derek threatened to erupt with laugher. We sat there like that for quite some time, and Derek never spoke. When I asked him if he wanted to go play now, he shook his head and looked at me with a face that read "No, can I stay here forever," and when we finally got up for dinner, those big brown eyes were full of gratitude. God reminded me again that day that I have *one* purpose, in Uganda and in life, and that is to *love*. I could ask for no greater assignment.

Even though God reminded me in powerful ways at times, like on that day with Derek, that I was called to Uganda, there were still times in those early days when I wondered *Why me? Why would God choose me to do this?* But as I think through my life, I see how blessed and loved I have been. I think it is only normal that God would ask, even require, me to share this love with others who may not know it. Luke 12:48 says, "From everyone who has been given much, much will be demanded; and from the one who has been entrusted with much, much more will be asked." And I have been given so much.

So this is why my everyday, crazy, chaotic life seems so normal. It is simply an ongoing, ever-changing result of what it looks like to try to love like Christ in my life. This is the spot on the map where God has asked me to do the things I do—like pour out my heart for children who are hungry or alone, to try to help people leave harmful work and learn skills that will help them care for their families, or to assist women who are struggling to raise their children alone. This is the place where I am supposed to follow Jesus, obey Him, and make my best effort, with His gracious help, to treat people with dignity and care for them unconditionally. To say yes to each and every thing He asks of me, to each person He places in front of me.

ONE DAY...

Saturday, September 29, 2007

Sometimes working in a Third World country makes me feel like I am emptying the ocean with an eyedropper. And just when I have about half a cup full of water it rains: More orphaned children from the north migrate to where I live, more abandoned and dead babies are found, more people are infected with HIV. It is enough to discourage even the most enthusiastic and passionate person. And yet the discouragement lasts only a moment and God tells me to keep going. That He loves me. That He loves these people. That He will never leave or forsake any of us, not one. That my work is important—to Him.

I spent the day today at the wedding of my friend Lydia. It was a beautiful celebration not only of the love two people can have for each other but also of the love God has for us. At the reception, there was cake and singing and dancing, just as there

would be at any American wedding. One thing
that wasn't like an American wedding,
however, was the congregation of street
children at the gate, all longing to join the
party inside. I immediately felt suffocated
inside the gates of the extravagant party.
So for most of the reception you could find
me outside with the raggedy, dirty street
children dancing and laughing and cuddling.
Most people were slightly appalled that I
was associating with these children—the
outcasts of society. Many of the fancily
dressed guests at the wedding even came
and told me that I probably shouldn't associ-
ate with these children, let alone kiss them
and let them bury their faces in my hair.

"They are street children!" the people
would cry, as if it was some kind of sin, as if
the children could help it. We had so much
fun, though. The children ate up every bit of
attention I could give, danced as close to me
as they possibly could, and lavished me with
love. We spun and laughed until we ached
and had to collapse in the grass outside of

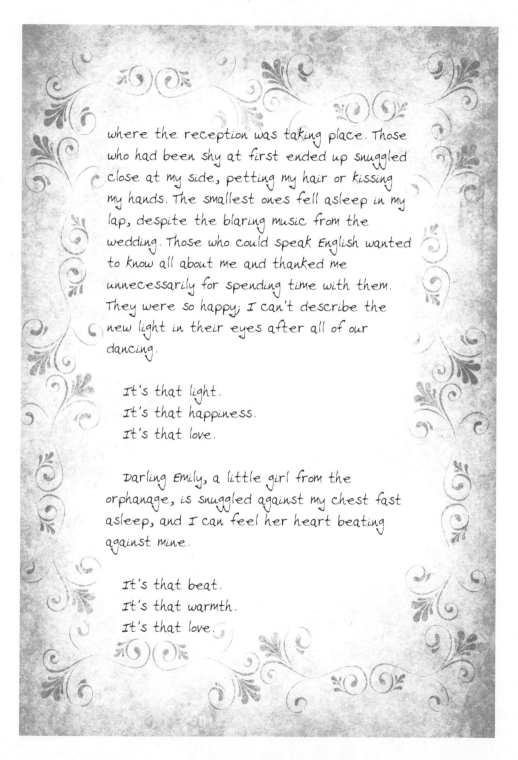

where the reception was taking place. Those who had been shy at first ended up snuggled close at my side, petting my hair or kissing my hands. The smallest ones fell asleep in my lap, despite the blaring music from the wedding. Those who could speak English wanted to know all about me and thanked me unnecessarily for spending time with them. They were so happy; I can't describe the new light in their eyes after all of our dancing.

It's that light.
It's that happiness.
It's that love.

Darling Emily, a little girl from the orphanage, is snuggled against my chest fast asleep, and I can feel her heart beating against mine.

It's that beat.
It's that warmth.
It's that love.

That love is the reason I just keep filling up my little eyedropper, keep filling it up and emptying my ocean one drop at a time. I'm not here to eliminate poverty, to eradicate disease, to put a stop to people abandoning babies. I'm just here to love.

2

IN THE CRUCIBLE OF CONTRADICTION

October 6, 2007

The classroom where I teach is between the animal feeding grounds and the pit latrines, so my classroom is constantly filled with the smell of waste, animal and human.

The weather is stifling here. The moment I step out of my icy shower, I begin to sweat.

I sleep under a mosquito net to avoid getting bitten by mosquitoes infected with malaria and other diseases, but I still can't avoid ants and crickets in my bed.

In my bathroom lives a rat the size of a house cat and there are a few bats in the shower. This morning I almost grilled a lizard in my toaster.

Fred, my piki man, is almost always late, sometimes runs into cows, runs out of gas, or forgets to warn me of impending potholes.

When it rains, the awful roads turn into muddy swamps, making it nearly impossible to go anywhere.

For lunch and dinner we eat *posho*, which is corn flour boiled in water until it is thick and pasty. It tastes a little worse than Elmer's glue.

Sometimes, the children are so dirty they actually reek; it is impossible to touch them without becoming filthy.

With the wind blowing red dust everywhere, it is impossible not to be filthy anyway.

A rooster crows around five to wake me up each morning—that is, if I haven't already been up all night with a sick baby or getting sick myself.

And to you, these sound like complaints. They are not; this is me, rejoicing in the Lord, because you see…

I love my tiny classroom. I love the hot sun on my face. I love my bed, cozy under my net after a long day. I love my home sweet home, all its creatures included. I love Fred, my *piki* man. I love my long walks home, day or night, rain or shine. I love the beating, cleansing Ugandan rain. I love my Ugandan meals, prepared with such love and generosity. I love to be hugged and touched and jumped on and cuddled by these precious children. I love the cool, dusty breeze in my hair. I love every African sunrise, the cool and calm of a new morning. I love each and every day, each and every moment that I spend in this beautiful country; I rejoice in each breath I take.

If I had to summarize in one word my first weeks and months in Uganda, it would be *contradiction*. The physical environment of Uganda is one huge paradox: amazing, breathtaking beauty juxtaposed against immense poverty and desolation. My life—especially my emotions—hung in the balance between absolutely loving my new life in Uganda and battling severe loneliness. Not a single person around me understood *anything* about my life, my culture, or my background. Their frame of reference was so different from mine that even the most detailed explanation hardly helped them understand or relate. Most of the people around me didn't speak my language, nor did I speak theirs. This communication vacuum left me feeling isolated and forced to work much harder to build meaningful relationships. In addition, everyone around me was either much older or much younger than I was; I had no peers. And for someone who had landed in Uganda fresh out of the American high school experience, where I'd had many good friends, the absence of people my age caused me to feel even more alone.

During my early days here, I was learning so much—everything from how to eat foods I'd never seen before to how to communicate through hand signals and facial expressions with people whose language I did not know. My horizons were being expanded in the most amazing ways; my perspectives were changing every day; and my faith was being challenged and stretched. All of this was so exciting to me. I didn't want to admit that, in the midst of such a wonderful and invigorating experience, I sometimes felt tangible pangs of loneliness when I thought about how many miles away I was from the people I loved. I spent many hours curled up in a ball on my lumpy twin bed, sweltering, often in the dark, and crying—partly because I was overwhelmed and feeling inadequate and partly because I missed my family or my boyfriend. Sometimes, I cried because I was simply exhausted.

Even though I cried often, there were four words I absolutely did not want to hear from anyone at home, especially those who had

questions and misgivings about my being in Uganda: "I told you so." I
didn't want anyone to know that I sometimes longed for my familiar
home while I reveled in the newness of a country so unlike anywhere
I'd ever been, that I missed my old friends terribly even as I was making wonderful new ones. I didn't want to tell friends and family that I
could dance and sing and play with children all day long yet collapse
in tears at night in the privacy of my small room. I could praise God
with all my joyful heart and then later pour out my heart to Him with
frustration and weeping when no one could hear.

The contradiction comes when I realize that *all* these experiences
and emotions were real. The happiness that gave me chill bumps was
as deep as my loneliness. My sense of certainty about being exactly
where God wanted me was solid, but just as firm was the fact that I
wondered at times what on earth I was doing here. The frustration
that threatened to overtake me on some occasions was just as deep
and true as the unbounded joy I felt at other times. I loved my new
life; I truly loved it. But compared to the life I had been living, *it was
hard.*

There were many moments when the only way I could keep going
was to try my best not to look back but to look only forward, relying
on God's perfect plan. Like so many other things, this wasn't always
easy, but it was the key to conquering the mountains of difficulty that
arose on the landscape of my life.

Despite the obstacles, I felt a surprising level of comfort living in
Uganda most of the time. I felt I was born to be there, and in many
ways, living there seemed more natural than living in my native country. I had the unexplainable feeling, a settled *knowing*, that I was
where I was made to be. I knew deep in my soul that I was home.

Ugandan culture was so foreign to my own and I was scolded
many times for things that seemed innocent before I understood what
was expected of me: walking into a house with my shoes on or feeding
leftover food to the dogs was considered rude and unacceptable in
this new culture. On one particularly frustrating occasion, I showed

up for lunch with dirty hands and was chastised for that; then I arrived slightly late for lunch with the same people the next day because I took time to wash my hands, and the hostess yelled at me for that.

Things that seemed so simple were insanely challenging in my new environment. For example, I didn't have any idea how to prepare a freshly caught fish for dinner or what was a fair price for a pineapple in the local market, so someone had to tell me. I also had no idea how to prepare fresh beans, a Ugandan staple, for dinner. In America, I simply bought a can of beans at a grocery store, emptied them into a pot on the stove, and ate them several minutes later. This is not the way to cook beans that *don't* come out of a can! "Mama Cook," the woman who prepared meals at the orphanage, had told me I needed to boil the beans, and that sounded easy enough. I had no idea how long the boiling of fresh beans could take, so I put the pot on the fire around six the first night I cooked them, fully expecting to eat at seven. They were finally ready around midnight.

While the orphanage I was living at had electricity, it rarely worked. The power often went out for days or weeks at a time. Many of my nights were spent sitting in my tiny room with a candle handwriting 138 worksheets for the next day's school lessons, since there was no such thing as a copy machine where I was staying.

Many times, as I looked at the candle illuminating my room on those dark and sometimes lonely nights, He reminded me that I could light candles in the hearts of others as long as I let Him fill my heart first. He reminded me that I was indeed the light of the world and I was to shine before those around me so that they would glorify Him (see Matthew 5:14). In the soft glow of candlelight one black night in my room, I opened my journal and began to write:

My candle is lit; I am on fire for God, for this place, for these people. My purpose here is to spread His light. One candle can

light up my entire room. Jesus can light up
this entire nation, and my flame can be a
part of that. I am blown away that my God,
who could do this all by Himself, would choose
to let me be a little part of it.

I spent many nights without power in the place where I lived, and yet that's where I saw the power of one life, one candle in one woman's heart.

Everything seemed to be such a paradox: One minute, I was squatting over a pit latrine in the middle of a village, pressing my lips tight together to avoid the rancid smell and keep giant flies and cockroaches from flying into my mouth, and the next I would be staring out over the Nile River, deeply inhaling the fresh breeze. Materially speaking, the people who began to fill my life were the poorest I had ever met and yet they overflowed with the riches of the heart. They lived in houses of sticks or stones and mud; they slept on hard dirt floors. But they did not blame God for this or ask Him for more. They knew their circumstances were due to the brokenness of this world and they simply praised Jesus for keeping them alive through it all. They believed in His goodness. They lived with love and passion, caring for one another and for me and deeply appreciating the simplest gifts life had to offer: the happy giggles of children, the smile and warm greeting of a friend, the beauty that surrounded them, a chance to work when possible, a helping hand when needed most.

In my mind, these people had every reason to be despondent and downcast, but they were the most joyful human beings I could imagine. I learned so much from them as they made my frustrations seem small and petty and taught me just to rejoice in the simple pleasures God had surrounded me with. Once I could do this, I embraced extreme exhilaration; I felt closer to God, to myself, and to the people and more alive than ever before.

Through all the challenges and contradictions and through the gracious people all around me, God was opening my eyes to a whole new world and way of living and most important to a whole new way of living out the Gospel. Every day I have spent in Uganda has been beautifully overwhelming; everywhere I have looked, raw, filthy, human need and brokenness have been on display, begging for someone to meet them, fix them. And even though I realize I cannot always mend or meet, I can enter in. I can enter into someone's pain and sit with them and *know*. This is Jesus. Not that He apologizes for the hard and the hurt, but that He enters in, He comes with us to the hard places. And so I continue to enter.

As I continued to enter the lives of new friends God had given me and walk in the midst of a new culture, I realized that He was using the contradictions that surrounded me to change my point of view. In the beginning, I would have described it as God turning my world upside down, but now I know that He was actually turning it right side up! I thought of the life I left behind, in which I would have easily dropped $100 on a pair of shoes. Now I looked around and realized that $100 could provide a starving family with food for months. I thought of how, after a long, hard day in my previous life, I would have crashed on the couch with a pint of ice cream, a good sappy movie, and my closest girlfriends. Here, at the end of a long, hard day, there was nothing to do but cry out to Jesus for the strength to go on.

I loved my new life. It was wonderful in so many ways, but I would be lying if I said I didn't miss the comforts and the people of my old one desperately. My human flesh still sometimes wanted to go to the mall and spend a ridiculous amount of money on a cute pair of shoes. Sometimes I wanted to sit on my mom's kitchen counter chatting with my friends and eating brownies. Sometimes I just wanted to turn off my brain and watch mindless television. I wanted to go on dates with my boyfriend. Sometimes I wanted to hop into my convertible, go to the grocery store, and pick out any kind of food that my heart desired. Most days, I wished I could wake up under my down comforter in a house with my loving family, not all by myself. Sometimes I just wished I could hang out with my little brother and his buddies, eating junk food and laughing late into the night. Sometimes I wanted to spend hours upon hours talking with my best friends about boys and fashion and school and life. I wanted to go to the gym; I wanted my hair to look nice; I wanted to be allowed to wear jeans. I wanted to be a normal teenager living in America, sometimes.

But I wanted other things more. *All* the time. I wanted to be spiritually and emotionally filled every day of my life. I wanted to be loved and cuddled by a hundred children and never go a day without laughing. I wanted to wake up to a rooster's crow and open my eyes to see lush green trees that seemed to pulse with life against a piercing blue sky and the rusty red soil of Uganda. I wanted to be challenged endlessly; I wanted to be learning and growing every minute. I wanted to be taught by those I teach, and I wanted to share God's love with people who otherwise might not know it. I wanted to work so hard that I ended every day filthy and too tired to move. I wanted to feel needed, important, and used by the Lord. I wanted to make some kind of difference, no matter how small, and I wanted to follow the calling God had placed on my heart. I wanted to give my life away, to serve the Lord with each breath, each second. At the end of the day, no matter how hard, I wanted to be right here in Uganda.

Opportunities to make someone else's life better were so much more attractive to me than the thought of the comforts I once knew. The longer I stayed, the more I realized that deep fulfillment had begun to swallow my every frustration. No matter how many contradictions I struggled with, how difficult certain situations were, no matter how lonely I got, no matter how many tears I cried, one truth remained firmly grounded in my heart: I was in the center of God's will; I was doing what I was created to do.

ONE DAY...

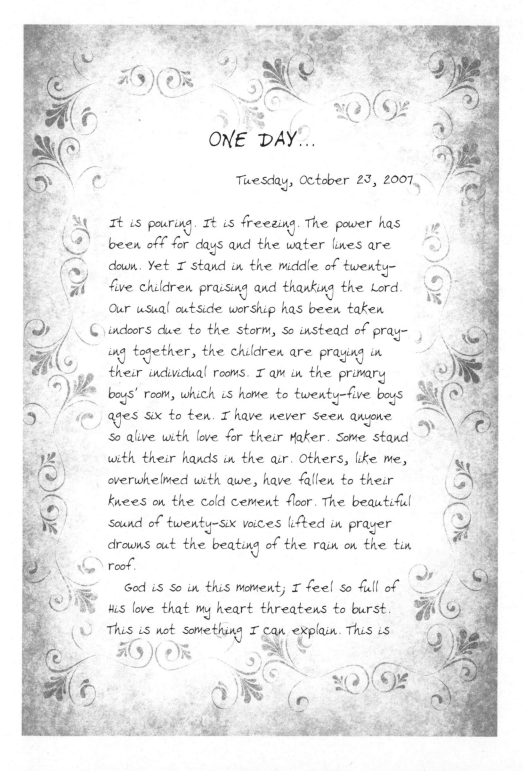

Tuesday, October 23, 2007

It is pouring. It is freezing. The power has been off for days and the water lines are down. Yet I stand in the middle of twenty-five children praising and thanking the Lord. Our usual outside worship has been taken indoors due to the storm, so instead of praying together, the children are praying in their individual rooms. I am in the primary boys' room, which is home to twenty-five boys ages six to ten. I have never seen anyone so alive with love for their Maker. Some stand with their hands in the air. Others, like me, overwhelmed with awe, have fallen to their knees on the cold cement floor. The beautiful sound of twenty-six voices lifted in prayer drowns out the beating of the rain on the tin roof.

God is so in this moment; I feel so full of His love that my heart threatens to burst. This is not something I can explain. This is

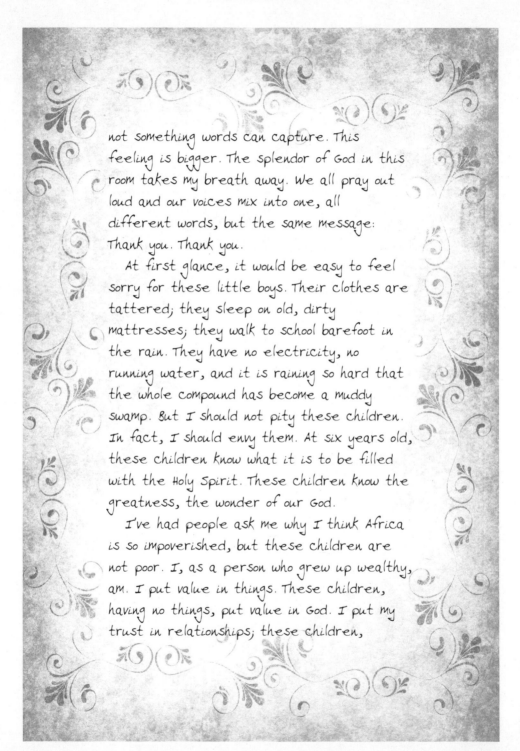

not something words can capture. This feeling is bigger. The splendor of God in this room takes my breath away. We all pray out loud and our voices mix into one, all different words, but the same message: Thank you. Thank you.

At first glance, it would be easy to feel sorry for these little boys. Their clothes are tattered; they sleep on old, dirty mattresses; they walk to school barefoot in the rain. They have no electricity, no running water, and it is raining so hard that the whole compound has become a muddy swamp. But I should not pity these children. In fact, I should envy them. At six years old, these children know what it is to be filled with the Holy Spirit. These children know the greatness, the wonder of our God.

I've had people ask me why I think Africa is so impoverished, but these children are not poor. I, as a person who grew up wealthy, am. I put value in things. These children, having no things, put value in God. I put my trust in relationships; these children,

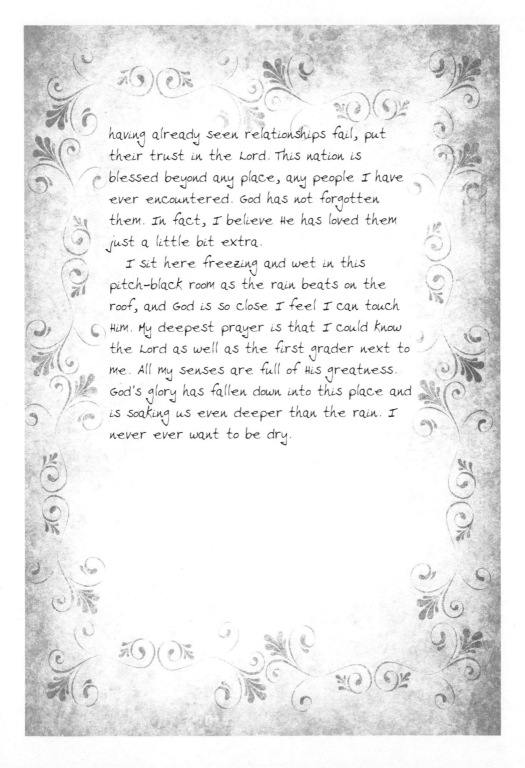

having already seen relationships fail, put their trust in the Lord. This nation is blessed beyond any place, any people I have ever encountered. God has not forgotten them. In fact, I believe He has loved them just a little bit extra.

I sit here freezing and wet in this pitch-black room as the rain beats on the roof, and God is so close I feel I can touch Him. My deepest prayer is that I could know the Lord as well as the first grader next to me. All my senses are full of His greatness. God's glory has fallen down into this place and is soaking us even deeper than the rain. I never ever want to be dry.

3

ENOUGH TO GO AROUND

As the overwhelming contradictions became more and more apparent to me, they also began to bother me in a way I could no longer ignore.

The plight of people had posed a problem for me for as long as I could remember. Somehow, as a young child, I was aware that there was a world beyond the comfort of my own neighborhood. My parents had taught me that my family and I, and the people around us, were some of the "blessed ones." I understood that people all over the world were hungry and poorly clothed and living in ramshackle huts or under bridges. And these realities broke my heart.

Now the human tragedy that had captured my attention as a child was weighing on my heart in a greater way. The people who had once been anonymous in their suffering were now my friends.

When I thought about the children, these little ones who were my students and my new friends, and those back in America, the contrasts were unimaginable. For example, I remembered many years of the first day of school. As I entered each new grade, my parents bought me a brand-new "back-to-school" outfit. I had new school supplies, every item on a typically extensive list from my teacher. I was so excited to take them to school! But what I loved most was a new box of crayons—perfectly shaped points, with nice paper wrappers, in every color I could imagine. For a young schoolgirl, new crayons were bliss.

In the United States, the back-to-school season is a retail event—just as much as Easter or Halloween. Stores are filled with brightly colored notebooks, backpacks and lunch boxes, and stacks of pens and pencils and paper. All but the least fortunate students have a significant stash of new belongings with which to start school each year. But in Uganda, a tablet is expensive. A new pen or pencil is a treasure. Many children don't get excited about going to school because even if they have the money for school fees, they may not be able to buy their supplies.

As I thought about the discrepancies between the culture I came from and the one I now lived in, I could not stop thinking about my life and the lives of many of my friends in the States—and being appalled by our luxuries when people on our same planet were living in such poverty and need. I began to realize huge flaws and gaps in my faith, a wide chasm between what I proclaimed to believe and how I was actually living.

I had to do something.

I didn't know what to do. In fact, I didn't know much at all, but I quickly became convinced that I could not simply live in a room in an orphanage in Uganda and teach kindergarten. As much as I enjoyed what I was doing, I had to do more to help the people around me.

There were so many needs to be filled, so many issues to be addressed. There's more HIV than medicine to treat it: There's a growing population of children who need a warm bed and a hot meal because their parents have died; there's a need for basic education in matters of hygiene and sexual behavior, education that could reduce disease and improve the quality of everyday life. I could have chosen anything and done something about it—and that would have helped. But I wanted to be strategic, and I wanted to do something with the power to bring significant, long-term, positive change to individuals, families, and the village where I lived.

I remember the day well. With such great pride the tiny, barefoot and bald, coffee bean–colored little girl showed me, her teacher, the closet-sized room she calls home. With great excitement she introduced her new *mzungu* (white) teacher to her mother who, upon seeing a white person for the first time, shrieked with glee and examined me closely. Immediately a feast of rice and *matoke* (boiled, unripe plantains), Ugandan staples and probably all this family had to eat for the day, was prepared. A younger sibling ran to get a mat woven out of banana fibers for the teacher to sit on, but everyone else sat on the dirt floor. The family did not apologize for the fact that there was no table or chairs for the meal, or the fact that all seven of us could hardly fit comfortably in the house. They fed me like a queen and wished they could give me something more.

They rejoiced in what the Lord had given them, this tiny house and a few kilograms of food for the day, and they were happy to share. I wondered what could happen if the rich of the world would share with the poor the way this darling family had shared with me: without holding back, giving their all and believing that the Lord would provide more as needed. I was learning so much from my students. I was learning from these people who seemed to have nothing and yet had everything they needed in their hearts full of trust and grace.

Every day after school, I walked my kindergarten students home, just as I had walked that little girl home on that particular day. Day after day, I witnessed poverty that was unimaginable. Hungry, naked, fly-covered children lay in the dirt crying for a mother who would never come because HIV had taken her life. I met parents who made cakes of mud and salt to fill their children's bellies because drought made it impossible to grow food. I met grandmothers who worked from before the sun came up until long after it disappeared beyond the horizon to find enough food for the eight orphaned children they had been left to care for.

As I walked my students home, I also met other children along the way, school-age boys and girls who, for some reason, were not attending classes. I saw others who had come to school for the first few weeks and not returned. In the limited Luganda I had picked up, I tried to ask these children why they would not attend school. What I learned was shocking to me: Their guardians, be it an aunt or uncle, mother, father, or grandparent, could not afford the mere US $20 the school charged to cover operating costs for a three-month term.

I learned that sending children to school is one of the greatest living expenses a Ugandan family has, and most families have multiple children. School fees far exceed, by about four times, the cost of water or electricity, which most families do without anyway. These realities apply to children who have parents; many children don't, so going to school is not even a possibility for them. I thought about these things as I lay in bed at night exhausted, devastated, and angry that people were living (and dying) like this while I had lived such an extravagant life for the past eighteen years. As abject poverty confronted me every day, I felt deeply convicted about one thing: God did not make too many people and not enough resources to go around. Because we were living in His world, there *had* to be a solution.

Everywhere I looked in the Bible, from the beginning of the Old Testament to the end of Revelation, people who believe in God are supposed to share with the poor. Helping the poor is not something God asks His people to do; it is something that, throughout all generations, He instructs us to do. Several passages settled into my heart in a weighty, urgent way as I read them over and over again. Every time I read these words, I came to the same conclusion: God wanted me to help the people around me who needed help. This is why His Word says in Deuteronomy 24:19–22:

> When you are harvesting in your field and you overlook a sheaf, do not go back to get it. Leave it for the alien, the fatherless and the widow, so that the Lord your God may bless you in all

the work of your hands. When you beat the olives from your trees, do not go over to the branches a second time. Leave what remains for the alien, the fatherless and the widow. When you harvest the grapes in your vineyard, do not go over the vines again. Leave what remains for the alien, the fatherless and the widow. Remember that you were slaves in Egypt. That is why I command you to do this.

And this is why, when people who had known Jesus went about establishing His church on earth, they emphasized the fact that God's people are to be generous and kind to others, so no one suffers need or lack. The Book of Acts makes this plain (2:44–45; 4:32–35):

All the believers were together and had everything in common. Selling their possessions and goods, they gave to anyone as he had need. All the believers were in one heart and mind. No one claimed that any of his possessions was his own, but they shared everything they had. With great power the apostles continued to testify to the resurrection of the Lord Jesus, and much grace was upon them all. There were no needy persons among them. For from time to time those who owned lands or houses sold them, brought the money from the sales and put it at the apostles' feet, and it was distributed to anyone as he had need.

Clearly, from God's perspective, those who are blessed with riches are supposed to share with the poor, meaning that those who don't have the resources to get what they need can do so, to the point that the poor aren't so poor anymore. I looked around, though, and these new friends of mine were still destitute. I wondered what the western world was missing and why so many Christians didn't seem to be doing what God so obviously wants us to do where the needy are concerned.

My conviction that I had to do something to help, coupled with my newfound understanding of school fees, made it easy for me to know what to do. The first step to helping this village was to get the children whose caretakers had defaulted on school fees back into school, or to get children who had never had the opportunity to go to school into school for the first time. If these children couldn't get an education, they would grow up to live the same kind of lives their parents and grandparents were living—unable to secure a job and unable to send their own children to school, thus continuing the cycle of poverty. I knew that I myself could not change the village or the country of Uganda, but *educated children could.*

I quickly figured out that I knew some people in the States who had leftover "olives from their trees" and "wheat from their fields," people who would be willing to share their resources to put some of these sweet children into school.

The fee to send one child to school for one term is very little to people who live in the First World. In fact, a child can go to school for one term for anywhere between US $10 and $50, an amount some families spend on weekend entertainment—and an amount that is astronomical and impossible for most families in Uganda.

Lots of people I knew in the United States had a little extra to spare three times a year, but a single mother working two jobs in Uganda may make 80,000 shillings in two months. For that mother, this means half a year's salary can send one of her children to school.

Lack of education, as I see it, is one of Uganda's greatest burdens and providing opportunities for schooling is one of its greatest needs. According to the *CIA World Factbook* and other sources, the population of Uganda in January 2011 was 33,398,682. Approximately 50 percent of those people are under the age of fourteen. The average life expectancy in Uganda is slightly more than fifty-two years of age and the median age in Uganda is fifteen.[1] So Uganda is a nation of young people. Roughly half its citizens are adolescents, and there are few elderly people to pass on useful skills or simple life lessons to the young generation.

Many of these young people are my friends. They are boys and girls I know personally because I laugh with them when they are happy and dry their tears when they're sad or afraid. I feed them and bathe them and bandage their wounds. They are not anonymous, they are not statistics; they are people I love and people God loves. He wants the best for them, and so do I.

Obviously the key to eternal life for these children is Jesus, but the key to a better life here and now is education. Children must learn to read and write, to add and subtract and multiply. They must learn about science and social studies and everything else school offers in order to be productive citizens in the future. Their nation needs them to move it forward, not hold it back. It needs them to be equipped to provide good leadership and support in positions of government, medicine, technology, social services, and other areas of society. Uganda truly has the potential to live up to its moniker, "the pearl of Africa," if today's children can gain the knowledge and experience they need to usher their country into a bright future.

My friend Patrick had just lost his job and was going to be unable to pay school fees for his daughters in the upcoming term. I met Patrick when I worked at the orphanage. He is a quiet, respectful, hardworking man, but the first word that comes to mind when I think of him is *dignified*. He is extremely intelligent but one of the humblest people I know. He is a devoted husband and father and a faithful man of God. He would do absolutely anything for his children—if he could. He wanted desperately to send his daughters to school, but because he did not have a job during that time, even though he was eager to work, he could not afford to do so. Previously he and his wife had been using every penny they made just to pay their daughters' school fees, so other things, like uniforms and school supplies, were not luxuries these girls had.

I dug into my small savings account and for slightly more than

$60 per child I was able to pay for everything. So for the first time in their lives these girls who wore the same dresses to school every day were able to have uniforms like all the other children at the school. Instead of taking notes on scraps of newspaper, they had notebooks. When I had finished paying the headmaster for everything, we called the girls into the office and gave them their new uniforms, books, and pencils. They put the new red dresses on right away. I have never seen anyone so happy or grateful. They were down on their knees thanking me; their father beamed with pride. And all of this for less than my family spent on groceries each week.

I knew I had to make it possible for other children to feel this happy and for my friends and family at home to feel as joyful and useful as I felt. I lay in bed under my mosquito net that night, listening to the crickets chirp and dreaming of sending more children to school, teaching them the truth not only of a bigger world but of Jesus who loves and cares for them, who sees and knows them personally. I wanted to share with my wealthy friends the truth of the tragedy that was taking place on the other side of the world and the truth that we could do something to change it. I didn't exactly know how to go about this, but what I did know was the smiles on those girls' faces when they found out they would be able to continue going to school. I knew the gratitude of guardians who worked day and night to provide for their children and still could not afford school. I knew the faithfulness of the Lord who had brought me to this place and opened my eyes to this need.

The Lord continued to show me more children who needed help. The next week, I walked twin girls home from school. They lived about two miles from the school and walked barefoot every day, over the rocks and mud, rain or shine. I soon found out that they lived with their three older siblings and grandmother, Maria. As we sat on her dirt steps, the grandma told me the children's stories. Their mother had come to visit when the twins were about two years old and confided in her mom that she had recently tested positive for

HIV. Feeling utterly hopeless and overwhelmed, the mother had left in the middle of the night, leaving her own mother to raise her five children.

Since then *Jja Ja* (grandmother) Maria had been doing any work she could get her hands on, working long days on a banana plantation and growing and selling her own cassava (a starchy vegetable that looks like a long, fat French fry) on the side. All this work gave her enough to send only the twins to school, with enough left over for a bit of food. I whispered to her about my plan to find sponsors for some of the children in the area and she fell to her knees. "I know that I am not alone in raising these children," she said. "You see how God takes care of me? I am not alone. Today God has sent you to answer our greatest prayer."

And standing there in the stifling African sun, I had chill bumps. That is the greatness of our God, not just that He would put me there for Jja Ja Maria, but also that He would put her there for me, an example of true faith, complete trust, and real gratitude. All the time the people in that little Ugandan village claimed that I blessed them. I know, though, that they blessed me more.

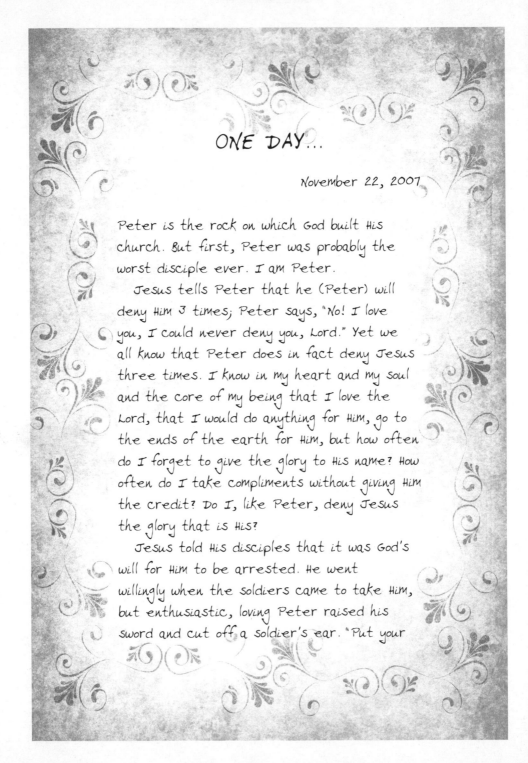

ONE DAY...

November 22, 2007

Peter is the rock on which God built His church. But first, Peter was probably the worst disciple ever. I am Peter.

Jesus tells Peter that he (Peter) will deny Him 3 times; Peter says, "No! I love you, I could never deny you, Lord." Yet we all know that Peter does in fact deny Jesus three times. I know in my heart and my soul and the core of my being that I love the Lord, that I would do anything for Him, go to the ends of the earth for Him, but how often do I forget to give the glory to His name? How often do I take compliments without giving Him the credit? Do I, like Peter, deny Jesus the glory that is His?

Jesus told His disciples that it was God's will for Him to be arrested. He went willingly when the soldiers came to take Him, but enthusiastic, loving Peter raised his sword and cut off a soldier's ear. "Put your

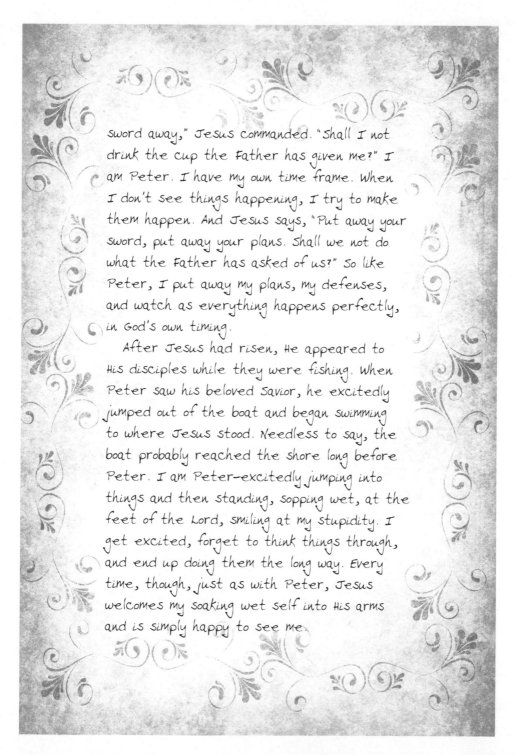

sword away," Jesus commanded. "Shall I not drink the cup the Father has given me?" I am Peter. I have my own time frame. When I don't see things happening, I try to make them happen. And Jesus says, "Put away your sword, put away your plans. Shall we not do what the Father has asked of us?" So like Peter, I put away my plans, my defenses, and watch as everything happens perfectly, in God's own timing.

After Jesus had risen, He appeared to His disciples while they were fishing. When Peter saw his beloved Savior, he excitedly jumped out of the boat and began swimming to where Jesus stood. Needless to say, the boat probably reached the shore long before Peter. I am Peter—excitedly jumping into things and then standing, sopping wet, at the feet of the Lord, smiling at my stupidity. I get excited, forget to think things through, and end up doing them the long way. Every time, though, just as with Peter, Jesus welcomes my soaking wet self into His arms and is simply happy to see me.

I am Peter who made many mistakes, but I am Peter for whom God had great plans, whom God established to do His work. Peter is the rock on which Jesus built His church. The very night when Peter foolishly jumped out of the boat, Jesus reinstated Him in the presence of the other disciples.

"Do you truly love me?" He asked. "Then feed my lambs."

"Do you really love me? Take care of my lambs."

"Peter, do you love me? Feed my sheep, and come follow Me."

For each time I deny God the glory that is His, for each time I follow my will instead of listening to His, for each time I jump ahead without first consulting my Lord, He asks, "Daughter, do you truly love me?" and I do.

"Feed my sheep." And I will. And I do.

"Come follow me." And I am, or at least I am trying.

I am Peter. I mess up. I make mistakes,

I am far from perfect, and God will use me. God will establish great things through me.

You are Peter. God already knows that you will make a mess, but His plan for you is great. Go. Feed His sheep.

4

SAYING YES

I was blessed. It wasn't because of anything I did; it was because I serve an unbelievably gracious God who will honor a willing and obedient heart. My love for the people around me was not something I could muster up myself; it was God given, it came from the overflow of the love He had lavished on me.

I hadn't come to Uganda with a degree in education; I wasn't a nurse; and I certainly didn't consider myself a missionary. I had absolutely no idea what was involved in running a ministry and frankly did not possess the business knowledge or organizational skills required to do so. I was in no way qualified, but I was available.

I have learned that something happens when one makes herself available to God: He starts moving in ways no one could imagine. God began doing things in me, around me, and through me as I offered myself to Him. I began each day saying, "Okay, Lord, what would you have me do today? Whom would you have me help today?" And then I would allow Him to show me. I would like to say that I had all kinds of great ideas about what I wanted to do and how I wanted to do it. I would like to say my ministry was born out of a carefully thought-out plan. These things simply aren't true, though. I was walking through life one moment at a time, blown away by what God could do through me if I simply said yes.

My heart was on fire with a passion to say yes to God's every re-quest—to do more to help the people around me. Starting a ministry in Uganda wasn't something I had in mind when I came here, but it seemed the only logical next step as people approached me needing help and I said yes to meeting their needs. As I prayed about what to do next and sought counsel from friends and family, I realized the only way to really be able to meet all the needs I wanted to meet in this community—to pay for children's school, keep their bellies full, offer medical assistance, and most important teach them about Christ's love for them—would be to start some kind of nonprofit orga-nization.

I felt nervous and excited as I realized this was God's next step for me. I knew that starting this organization meant I would probably spend a great deal of my life in this place and represented a major, long-term commitment to Uganda. I was anxious because it felt so permanent, so concrete, but it was a commitment I knew God wanted me to make. So I started the complicated process of investi-gating what I needed to do and enlisted my parents (who by now were becoming more supportive of my life in Uganda) to help with the pa-perwork stateside. In addition to that, they were busy raising funds to help send children to school.

The beginnings of a school sponsorship program were well under way. It was already happening thanks to the generosity of people my parents knew in the States. We simply needed to formalize the organi-zation. Even though my parents had many concerns about my being in a Third World country and were still determined for me to earn a college degree, they could not deny my passion for the work in Uganda. Because of their love for me, they were selfless enough to help me start a ministry. They loved me enough to help me live my dream, even if it didn't match their dream for me. As my mom and dad handled the administrative aspects of establishing the ministry as an official nonprofit organization, or NGO (nongovernmental organization), I set about clearing the biggest hurdle that stood in my way: finding a physical address for my work.

Having a residential address to serve as an office is a requirement for registration as any type of ministry in Uganda. The tiny room where I lived on the orphanage compound was not an acceptable address. I began looking for a self-contained, one-room place elsewhere to meet this requirement and serve as an office space. I knew that even one room might be more than my budget could handle, but God had other plans.

I searched and searched for a small place but couldn't find one. What I did find, after weeks of looking, was not at all what I had in mind. Situated behind a sturdy fence made of concrete blocks and accessed through a heavy gate, this was no one-room studio or cottage or bungalow, but a real house, with a large porch stretching across the front and four bedrooms inside. The landlord showed it to me excitedly as I shook my head; this was not what I was looking for and surely it would cost too much. It was far bigger than what I wanted or needed, but as the landlord continued to decrease the rent, so that it was almost the same price as a one-room place, I felt the Lord nudging me to take it. I had enough money saved to afford it for a brief period of time, and my parents agreed to help me. Even people I had never met found out about my work and sent money to help meet expenses. I couldn't deny the fact that God was providing, nor could I imagine why in the world I would need a house of this size, but I knew by then to listen.

At the time, I knew I loved Uganda, felt at home here, and wanted to make a difference in this country. But my long-term plans were not clear. I had a promise to fulfill to my father—to return to the States and complete my college education. I was in love with my boyfriend, whom I had left behind in the States. Beyond that, I didn't know what the future held. I thought the house would function more as an office for the NGO and as a place for me to stay during the many trips I planned to make to Uganda.

My new house was about two miles from the orphanage where I
lived and taught kindergarten. I could walk between the places, along
a rocky railroad track that runs alongside Lake Victoria, if I wanted to
take the scenic route. Or I could hire a *piki* and bounce my way
across the pitted, dusty roads from one place to the other. In my new
place, I would be close enough to old friends that I could reach them
quickly, but I would also be far enough to have the space I needed to
start my own organization and establish an identity separate from my
work as a kindergarten teacher.

Even though I liked the idea of moving to the house in the village, it wasn't easy. I would be the only white person in the village,
and perhaps the only person who spoke English. I would be a curi-
osity to my neighbors. I was still a bit scared of the prospect of living all alone in a building so big and even spent many nights
sleeping at the orphanage after I had officially "moved." For a few
weeks, I went to the house to clean and organize during the day, but
retreated in the evenings to the comfort of my 102 little friends and
rickety metal twin bed.

I was excited to start this new adventure that God had planned
for me, but at the same time I had grown quite comfortable at the
children's home. I had made friends among the staff members and
children, whom I could count on for lavish displays of affection and
outbursts of joy every single day. Although I would continue teaching
kindergarten for the remainder of the school year, moving into the
new house meant leaving behind my constant interaction with some
of those people and some familiar aspects of my life at the children's
home. I felt I had just gotten settled and into my routine and was
being uprooted again.

The morning I moved out of the orphanage, I opened my Bible to
the story of Sarah and Abraham in Genesis and it was a source of
great encouragement as I embarked on the next phase of my life in
Uganda. God had promised Sarah and Abraham that they would be
the parents of a great nation, yet at the age of sixty-five Sarah was still

childless. She was beginning to doubt. Leaving behind her homeland, she and her husband moved hundreds of miles south to the land of Canaan, the place where God had told them he would fulfill His promise. The land was full of God's promises but barren of all things cherished and familiar.

Finally tired of waiting, Sarah tried to take matters into her own hands by letting her husband sleep with her servant, and though the outcome was a child, this was not the perfect child God had promised, the one who would make her the mother of a nation. Years later, at the age of ninety, Sarah finally gave birth to her promised child. She called him *Isaac*, meaning "The Lord has filled me with laughter." Despite her frailties, little faith, and self-reliance, God accomplished His purpose—and Sarah was filled with joy.

I knew I could have stayed at the orphanage and God would have still loved me, but I could hear His voice whispering in my heart. He had given me a new place to live and a new adventure to embrace. How could I say no?

I sensed that God was leading me to my own kind of "Canaan," a land I had never been before, a place full of His promises and barren of all things comfortable and familiar. I had to let go of my life at the children's home and let God fulfill His promise, His perfect will. I chose to believe that, like Sarah, my adventure would lead to laughter and joy.

Joy came quickly as I continued to ask God how I would use this big, new house to serve Him most effectively. When I moved into it, it felt enormous. What was I, a single woman, supposed to do with four bedrooms and three bathrooms? The answer was easy. I was supposed to share it, but with whom? Not long after I moved in, one of my new friends moved in, along with four sisters, as they had been evicted from their home and needed a place to live.

Also around this time, I made a new acquaintance who soon became a dear friend. Christine had fled from a displacement camp in Kitgum, in northern Uganda, where a brutal group of rebels called the

"Lord's Resistance Army" has been ravishing the country, raping women and children, destroying homes and villages, and murdering innocent people for over twenty years. Her family's home had been burned by soldiers working for the Lord's Resistance Army, forcing her to spend most of her childhood on the run, eventually ending up in a camp for internally displaced people.

Looking for a better life, Christine came to Jinja to join her sister, who introduced her to me through a friend. Christine and I became fast friends. Christine's beautiful, in-love-with-Jesus heart, breathtaking smile, and willingness to serve made her an easy person to adore. I know that Christine has blessed and taught me far more in our friendship than I could ever hope to return, and for that I will be eternally grateful.

When I met her, Christine was looking for work and I asked her to help me with the children who would soon start coming to my house each day for lunch and help with their homework. In exchange for her work, I would provide her with a room, meals, and a small salary. When she moved in, my house had seven occupants and didn't seem so big anymore! But after a few weeks, most of my friends moved out, leaving just Christine and me. The place seemed huge again.

My mother came to visit me for Christmas that year and it was a needed taste of home and comfort. I was thrilled to have her company and glad she had the opportunity to observe firsthand the needs I was trying to meet. She could sense the new life that was unfolding for me; she quickly perceived the ways I had grown since our last time together; and she could see that I was in my element. She went with me to meet the people and the families I had befriended. She also met children and guardians who were being impacted immensely by our new sponsorship program, and saw the results of all the work she had done behind-the-scenes to help get the program started and keep it running smoothly. She heard me speaking a new language and saw me living a lifestyle that was completely opposite from the life we lived in the United States. Before she left, she had held more babies, cared for more sick people, and fed more mouths than she ever thought she would. Mom was in awe of all the Lord had accomplished in such a short time and returned to the States with a new understanding of her daughter and the life I'd been called to live.

By the first of the year, my house was ready to be used; my door was open. My friend Oliver (Oliver is a common name for girls and women in Uganda) helped me identify the children who could benefit most from going to school, the ones she knew were most "badly off." Oliver had been around the area where I lived all her life. She seemed to know absolutely everyone. She knew who was related to whom; she knew family stories and histories; and instinctively, she knew how to separate truth from village gossip. She comes across as quiet and serious, but underneath her reserved demeanor, she is perceptive, hardworking, dependable, God-loving, and determined to make a difference in her community.

Oliver was one of my first friends and before I'd known her very long, I noticed she was spending a good bit of her free time with me. She didn't seem to want anything; she simply seemed interested in why I had come to live in her part of the world. She sensed that God wanted her to help me—and help me she did, in more ways than I can count.

Oliver's friends noticed her helping me and teased her about it. "Why do you follow around that small white girl?" they asked.

"Because God is going to do something with her here," she replied. So Oliver continued to give her time and share her wisdom with me as we worked together to identify the most needy children and give them an opportunity to go to school.

Oliver and I had planned to start by sponsoring ten children but then agreed on forty when we saw how overwhelming the need was. I asked Oliver to find the forty neediest and bring me a list of their names so my mom and I could work on finding more sponsors from the States. As I told my friends and family about it and word began to spread, people began sending money to help us. I never made a desperate fund-raising plea; people simply became aware of the need and seemed happy to help meet it. We quickly raised the funds for forty children, but then Oliver showed up with a list of around one hundred children, saying, "These are the ones who need help; you can pick your forty." And I could not choose! I decided to enroll them all and pray that God would send the funds to meet the need.

I spent my days registering children for school, a process that involves a personal meeting with the student and the headmaster. To register all of our children, I was faced with the prospect of one hundred meetings—and most of them took place on "African time," which typically runs a few hours behind "real time."

As I grew to know and love these children, I realized their needs went far beyond school. Betty was a six-year-old girl who lost both of her parents to HIV and lived with her grandfather and four young siblings. Her big ears stuck out of her shiny, bald head, and her grin showed perfectly straight little white teeth. She was shy but lovable, giggling when I cupped my white hands under her chin and told her Jesus loved her.

Michael was a twelve-year-old boy who stopped going to school when his father left abruptly. When I met him, he stayed home to take care of his mother and younger sister. Michael was a born leader with big dreams for his future but not much hope of realizing these dreams because he was not able to attend school.

Lilly's two front teeth were missing, as is the case for many seven-year-old little girls, but unlike many little girls I know, Lilly was responsible for doing all the cooking and laundry for her eight brothers and sisters and her crippled grandfather, who was her only caregiver.

Betty, Michael, Lilly, and so many more: All these children were cherished by Jesus. They were created in His image. My whole being cried out in desire for them to know this.

Most of these children ate one big meal each day, at about six in the evening. Many of them had never had a parental figure to guide and love them. I wanted to teach them about the love of their heavenly Father, but this proved difficult with children who had never felt the love of an earthly parent. I knew that in order to teach them this love, I needed to first show them. So I opened the door of my home a bit wider.

Every day, around one in the afternoon, my dirt patch of a yard began to fill with the youngest children in our sponsorship program, those in third grade and younger because the older children stay at school until later. Christine and I would be ready to serve them beans and *posho* we had cooked on a big open fire in the backyard. The next few hours were spent helping with homework, studying for the next day's classes, treating simple illnesses, bandaging wounds, and running any severe case to the clinic. On Fridays, all the children would come over. We would have lunch for the little ones, who spent the afternoon playing and doing homework until time for Bible study. Around 4:00 P.M., the older children would file in, not too tired to run and play even after a long day of school. After we had quite a bit of fun studying God's Word came dinner, when we served all one hundred children. After the evening meal, everyone was able to take a shower with running water, a luxury none of them had ever experienced. We would sing and praise Jesus at the top of our lungs and the beats of our drums would fill the quiet night. Eventually, we all collapsed from happiness and spent the night all over the floor of my home, which didn't seem at all huge anymore. In the morning, all the children received a good breakfast before they began their journeys home.

With the help of my new friend and employee, Raoul, we also started a ministry to the children in the villages because I wanted to share the love of Christ and form relationships with children we weren't able to sponsor yet. In Uganda, gathering a crowd of children isn't hard to do. Just walk into a village and lots of them will come running and smiling and holding on to your hand or a loose spot of clothing. We went from village to village, visiting a total of six, sometimes on foot and sometimes on a *piki*. In the beginning we went into the villages three times a week, but later Raoul began going every day while I cared for the children who came to my house. When we ventured into the villages, we played with the children and taught them songs, so we could all sing together at the top of our lungs. Before we left each village, I shared with them a Bible story or lesson because I was so desperate for them to know that God is real and He loves them so.

Life was busy and full, chaotic at times, but it was so wonderful. This was the joy-filled result, the promise God had made as He took me into "Canaan." Despite my frailties, self-reliance, and little faith, God was accomplishing His purpose and my days were filled with laughter.

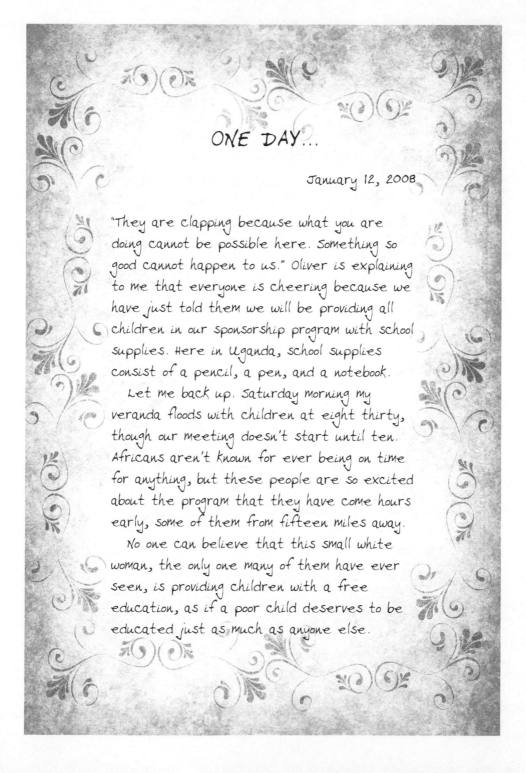

ONE DAY...

January 12, 2008

"They are clapping because what you are doing cannot be possible here. Something so good cannot happen to us." Oliver is explaining to me that everyone is cheering because we have just told them we will be providing all children in our sponsorship program with school supplies. Here in Uganda, school supplies consist of a pencil, a pen, and a notebook.

Let me back up. Saturday morning my veranda floods with children at eight thirty, though our meeting doesn't start until ten. Africans aren't known for ever being on time for anything, but these people are so excited about the program that they have come hours early, some of them from fifteen miles away.

No one can believe that this small white woman, the only one many of them have ever seen, is providing children with a free education, as if a poor child deserves to be educated just as much as anyone else.

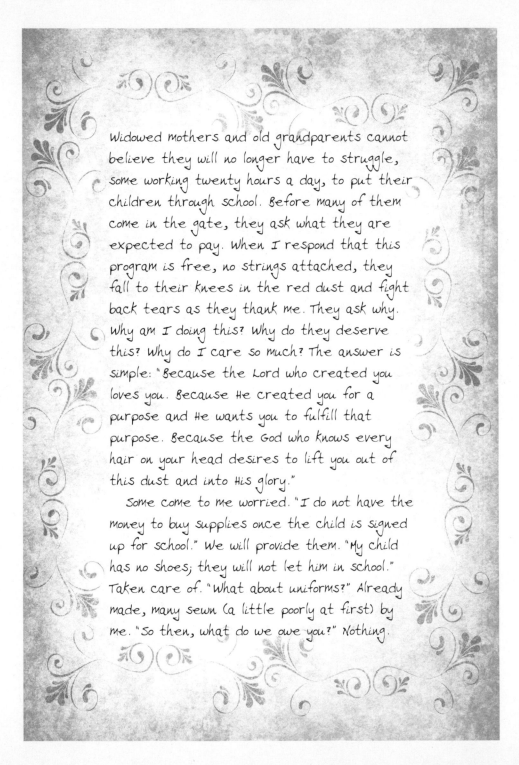

Widowed mothers and old grandparents cannot believe they will no longer have to struggle, some working twenty hours a day, to put their children through school. Before many of them come in the gate, they ask what they are expected to pay. When I respond that this program is free, no strings attached, they fall to their knees in the red dust and fight back tears as they thank me. They ask why. Why am I doing this? Why do they deserve this? Why do I care so much? The answer is simple: "Because the Lord who created you loves you. Because He created you for a purpose and He wants you to fulfill that purpose. Because the God who knows every hair on your head desires to lift you out of this dust and into His glory."

Some come to me worried. "I do not have the money to buy supplies once the child is signed up for school." We will provide them. "My child has no shoes; they will not let him in school." Taken care of. "What about uniforms?" Already made, many sewn (a little poorly at first) by me. "So then, what do we owe you?" Nothing.

That is where the cheering, shouting, dancing, and laughing come in. That is when Oliver declares, "They are so happy because this is not possible for them. They did not think this could ever happen." Well, neither did I. With God, all things are possible. In about three months, this organization has gone from a dream as I lay under my mosquito net one night to a full-blown and active nonprofit. Honestly, I'm not sure I thought it was possible either, but the Lord knew it was. One hundred and forty children are registered. On Monday morning, we will all go together to enroll them in school. They have been fitted for uniforms, which will be given to them next week with their new bag filled with supplies. As they walk home from school each day they will stop at my house for a hot, nutritious meal, a shower, study time (some days with a tutor), and prayer. All things are possible. My Lord and My Savior has been my encouragement and my strength, and here I stand on my front porch looking at over two hundred children

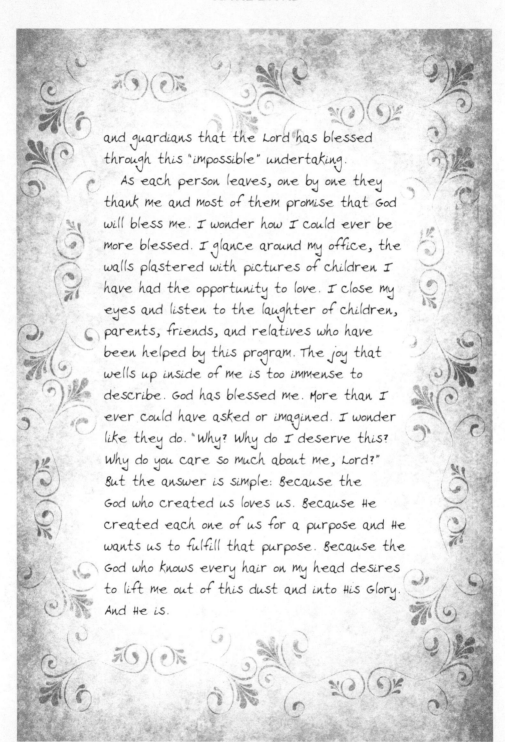

and guardians that the Lord has blessed through this "impossible" undertaking.

As each person leaves, one by one they thank me and most of them promise that God will bless me. I wonder how I could ever be more blessed. I glance around my office, the walls plastered with pictures of children I have had the opportunity to love. I close my eyes and listen to the laughter of children, parents, friends, and relatives who have been helped by this program. The joy that wells up inside of me is too immense to describe. God has blessed me. More than I ever could have asked or imagined. I wonder like they do. "Why? Why do I deserve this? Why do you care so much about me, Lord?" But the answer is simple: Because the God who created us loves us. Because He created each one of us for a purpose and He wants us to fulfill that purpose. Because the God who knows every hair on my head desires to lift me out of this dust and into His Glory. And He is.

5

"CAN I CALL YOU 'MOMMY'?"

Mommy." She said it and I knew. She was mine. I was captivated. Because Mommy is forever.

It's such a powerful name. *Mommy* means "I trust you." *Mommy* means "You will protect me." *Mommy* is for shouting when you need someone dependable and for laughing with when you are excited; *Mommy* is for crying on and cuddling with when you are sad or giggling and hiding behind when you are embarrassed. *Mommy* is the fixer of boo-boos and the mender of broken hearts. *Mommy* is a comfort place, a safe place. *Mommy* means you are mine and I am yours and we are family.

But I'm getting ahead of myself. Today someone calls me mommy several hundred times a day, but I remember vividly the first time I heard the word uttered in relation to me. The person who called me "Mommy" for the first time is now my daughter, Scovia, and though I didn't expect that I would be her mother when we met, I can't imagine life without her. I met her through a tragedy that happened at her house, when the entire structure fell on her sister Agnes.

At nine years old, Agnes had become the primary caregiver of her sisters, seven-year-old Mary and five-year-old Scovia. Their father had died of AIDS and their mother had long since disappeared. Their grandmother, who lived nearby, helped with what little she had, but often her own food was barely enough for herself. Days consisted of digging in the fields for a little something to eat and walking miles to and from the nearest well with a large plastic jug to collect the day's water. Mary kept a neighbor's baby and, in return, was provided with some food for herself. Even little Scovia went to dig for hours in the field to find food, helped fetch water, washed clothes, and cooked supper when Agnes had to stay late in the garden. Like all little girls, their hearts held hopes and dreams of the future, but the hardships of everyday life kept them focused on one day, one experience, one moment at a time.

One night as lightning cracked throughout the sky and hard rain danced on the tin roof, the girls' small house, made of sun-baked mud bricks, collapsed, crushing Agnes under a wall of sharp pieces of brick. A neighbor rushed her to the hospital, where they put her in a bed—and forgot about her. Talk of the girl who had been under the wall circulated through the community the next morning and Oliver insisted that we go see her. I couldn't see a reason not to visit her; she could certainly use some prayer.

We arrived at the hospital and found Agnes, in and out of consciousness but still smiling bright enough to light up even the gloomiest hospital in all of Uganda. No one had attempted to help her yet, not even to give her a painkiller. When I asked the head nurse why, she explained that she could not treat a patient unless she knew who would pay for the treatment. Since Agnes had no real caretaker, the nurse assumed her treatment would not be paid for. So the hospital simply didn't treat her.

This is not unusual in Uganda, where the hospital admission process is as easy as walking into a hospital and climbing into an empty bed. Those who can pay for medical attention receive it; those who can't, simply lie in a bed. In addition, many hospitals don't provide food for patients. This was the case in the hospital where Agnes was, so someone also needed to make sure she had something to eat.

I knew I could provide healthy meals for Agnes, and I also knew I could find the money to pay for whatever treatment she needed. I quickly told the nurse I would cover the costs of treating her, if only this child could get some relief. I had no idea that this commitment of $20 would turn into the commitment of a lifetime full of love and growth and joy and tears and homework and good-night kisses and more laughter than anyone can imagine.

As we headed home that day, I asked Oliver about Agnes's two sisters. She agreed we should go check on them, and upon finding them at home alone, I offered to take them to my place for lunch.

Which turned into dinner.

Which turned into bath time.

Which turned into a sleepover.

I asked Oliver to tell their neighbors and grandmother that the girls would be staying at my place until their sister was released from the hospital and we had come up with a better place for them to go. The physical resemblance between Mary and Scovia is strong; most people could quickly identify them as biological sisters. They were both shy at first. Scovia is joyful and obedient. She has a look of happy mischief in her eyes, even when she isn't being mischievous. When she laughs, which is often, she laughs from the inmost part of her being, from deep in her soul, and the laugh overtakes her whole body, making it impossible for anyone in the vicinity not to laugh along with her. She likes to jump and play, and she has energy to spare. Even though she's still a child, something about her causes observers to realize she's had experience in life. Mary is more reserved, but that doesn't mean she isn't always thinking or observing people and situations through her big, gorgeous brown eyes. In her delightful way, she's perceptive and wise beyond her years. She's focused and quite serious for her age, but still loves to dance, joke, and play with her sisters. She is understanding and quick to forgive. Mary has a generous, gentle spirit with a grateful heart and a deep love for God and the people around her. Both Scovia and Mary have hearts full of compassion, always desiring to help those around them.

The three of us—Mary, Scovia, and I—became fast friends as I took them on their first motorcycle rides and gave them their first ice-cream cones. The discovery of the bathtub complete with running water was almost more than they could handle; they must have bathed forty times that first week. We could hardly understand one another, seeing as I had learned only limited Luganda and they spoke almost no English, but still we were having way too much fun.

Meanwhile, we were spending a great deal of time at the hospital with Agnes, taking her meals and praying with her and leaving her in Oliver's care when we could not be by her side. A week later, she was discharged with the diagnosis of a broken collarbone and extensive soft tissue damage, which was excruciatingly painful and made walking difficult. She moved in with the three of us.

I quickly discovered that Agnes is a born leader. She can befriend just about anyone. She is outgoing and engaging, and she has a trustworthy quality about her. She is often ready to laugh but has a serious side that enables her to see things as they are. She is mature for her age, she knows right from wrong and is quick to set people straight. She is set in her convictions, knows what she wants, and will not easily let anyone tell her she can't have it. I was not accustomed to having such a strong personality in the house, but I was delighted.

I looked around for places these precious girls could go but found nothing satisfactory. Slowly but surely, we were becoming a family, and I would have only the very best for family. They had no living relatives capable of taking care of them. An orphanage was out of the question, in my opinion. The only option would be adoption by a family or by me.

Knowing what adoption would entail, I thought trying to accomplish it would be crazy. I found myself desperately praying that God would show me what to do. And that is when it happened. Shy, five-year-old Scovia tiptoed into my room and watched me curiously for nearly ten minutes without saying a word. And then, as though she had been pondering the question for ages, she asked, "Can I call you 'Mommy'?" And absolutely no one would have been able to say no to those big brown eyes. We *were* a family. The answer filled up my heart and then my whole self and spilled out of my mouth as naturally, as if I had always known, "Yes. I am your Mommy."

I was Scovia's Mommy, and Agnes's, and Mary's. I quickly filed the paperwork to make it legal, but the relationship was forged in our hearts even weeks before we got our stamped papers back from the courts. We adjusted quickly to this new life together and in no time it seemed that we had been family for ages. A few months later I became Mommy to two more beautiful, amazing girls. As biological sisters, twelve-year-old Prossy and nine-year-old Margaret had each other as family, but they needed more; they needed a stable home where they would be well loved. Originally, I thought once again that we would love on these sweet girls until I found somewhere better for them to go, but we all fell in love and Agnes begged that we make them a part of our family forever. How could I argue with a little girl who knew what it was not to have a loving home and who wanted to share hers with others in need?

Prossy and Margaret are tall and thin, appearing to be closer in age than the two and a half years that separate them. Prossy is sweet and quiet, respectful toward people, and deeply reverent toward God. She loves to learn and applies herself diligently to her schoolwork and her study of God's Word. She is a young woman of prayer, an individual of integrity, and a person of great promise. Prossy is a lover. Never in my life have I met a more sensitive or generous child or adult. Prossy truly grieves for those who grieve and rejoices when those around her rejoice. The simplest pleasure delights her, and just the thought of someone sad, hungry, or lonely deeply hurts her tender heart. Prossy is intuitive and uses this gift to try her very hardest to always please her family and her heavenly Father.

Margaret is simply hilarious and wonderful; joy just radiates from her. Margaret was quiet and timid at first but is anything but shy today! Margaret is spontaneous and outgoing. She has a wonderful sense of humor and a beautifully kind heart. One can never quite tell what Margaret is plotting behind her sparkling eyes. Her desire to help others laugh makes her likely to play jokes on people, but in the most good-natured way. Margaret is a wonderful listener; she makes people feel cherished and important. Everyone wants to be her friend. She is curious and inquisitive, wanting to understand the world around her and the people in it. She has big dreams for her life, and I have no doubt she will fulfill them.

As I thought about these girls—so different as individuals, but all so full of life and potential—who had moved into this house in the village with Christine and me, I could hardly believe it. Just months earlier, I had wondered what I would possibly do with my big house, but I never doubted that it was exactly the place God wanted me to have. It seemed enormous, but in less than a year, our home was filled with five precious girls. God had given this home a *family*. And with these precious souls around me, I knew that He had given me a *home*.

We relished getting to know one another and learning the ups and downs of this new family. It was incredibly challenging and beautifully wonderful all at the same time. Anyone who has ever added a person to the family knows that each new individual brings new responsibilities and dynamics.

With fostering and adoption, especially in the case of older children, there are even more challenges. My children called me "Mommy," and I so longed to be their Mommy, but building a relationship takes time, and going from being just a caregiver to Mom takes a significant period of bonding and trust building.

I wrestled with God as I thought about the hurt my children had to experience in order to become a part of my family. I had no idea what it felt like to be a nine-year-old with the responsibility of looking after my younger sisters. I couldn't imagine watching my father die and then having my mother run away, too afraid to carry the burden of my life on her own. I had no idea what it felt like to spend the first twelve years of life without knowing a parent who would cover me in love. I grieved these things for my children, and I always will. I fully trust that this is the way that God intended for their lives to unfold and that He is working all these things for their good, but there is still real pain in my heart when I think about all they have had to endure.

With each child, the pain and trauma manifested themselves in different ways and through different behaviors. I spent more time in prayer than I ever had in my life, begging God to teach me how to be a good enough mother to these priceless gifts, asking Him to guide me as I blindly dove into this blessing called adoption.

Physically, I was exhausted; I laughed to remember that I thought I had been tired before! I was thankful to have Christine to help me with the laundry, as simply learning to cook meals for more than one person was taking longer than I ever dreamed it would. I was waking up in the middle of the night to soothe someone who had a bad dream, double and triple checking that everyone had taken her medicine, brushed her teeth, and put on clean underwear. I was waking up two hours earlier to cook a real breakfast and make sure we all got to school on time. By God's grace, even in the hard moments, I knew that the job of being a mother was what God had created my heart for. We had our struggles, but at the end of the day, we were each in love with this new thing we called family in this new place we called home.

I knew that God had brought me to Uganda not just to change my heart for Him and for the poor but to make me Mommy. I am Mommy when I gather the girls into a large circle for a family meeting and when I watch them all run and play in the local swimming pool or picnic beside the Nile River. I am Mommy when several voices join together at the dinner table and say, "Thank you, Mommy, for food" (they aren't always the *same* fourteen voices, but almost invariably, several girls will express their gratitude at every meal), and when they get excited because Friday night is movie night and they want to watch *The Sound of Music* one more time. Here in my home, I am not a missionary or an aid worker; I am just a mom. I am like most other mommies—wholeheartedly dedicated and devoted to the children God has given me. I get tired and frustrated at times because I am human. But I relish my life because it is God's plan and I can't imagine anything better.

My fourteen beautiful girls call me Mommy. Four hundred children in the community where I live who have lost their mothers to starvation or disease or something else equally unimaginable call me Mommy. Because so many children are constantly shouting this word, even a lot of adults in the villages around our home call me Mommy. "Mommy to many," they say. Dignified men, store clerks, and parking attendants call me Mommy. Teachers and the doctors at the local hospital call me Mommy. I hear it in shouts as I drive down these insanely bumpy red roads; it is sung as my daughters burst through the door when they get home, it is whispered in my ear as I wake up each morning. It is hollered with joy or sobbed with longing for comfort. And every time I hear it, my heart leaps.

I am willing to bet this is how our heavenly Father feels each time we whisper His name, each time we shout it with joy or cry out in pain, every time we tell Him exactly what we need or feel:

"Father, I trust you."

"Father, you will protect me."

"You are my comfort place, my safe place."

"You are mine and I am yours and we are family."

His heart leaps and He delights in us and this is unfathomable.

ONE DAY...

Tuesday, February 19, 2008

It is a house of many cultures, many languages, and many colors. It is a house of laughter, and tears, and sometimes frustration, but mostly elation. It is a house of praise and worship and thanks. It is a house that is usually teeming with children, laughing and dancing and singing and just being kids, something many of them have never had a real opportunity to do. It's always a loud house, and it is always a grateful house. It is my house. But mostly it is God's house.

When I began renting this house last October, I didn't know exactly what I wanted to do with it. All I knew was that if the Lord had given me a house it couldn't be just for me. I knew that whatever I did, I was to use this house for the glory of my God. Well, once again, His plan for me and for my house was, is, greater than anything I could ever have asked for or imagined. My house has become a

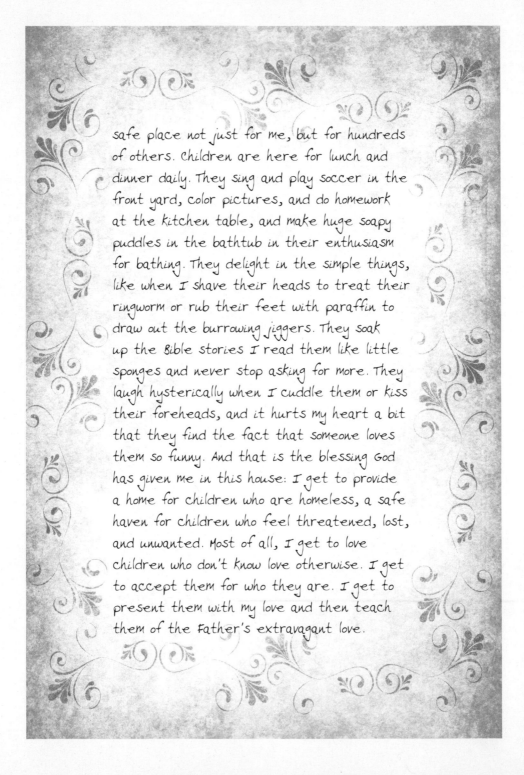

safe place not just for me, but for hundreds
of others. Children are here for lunch and
dinner daily. They sing and play soccer in the
front yard, color pictures, and do homework
at the kitchen table, and make huge soapy
puddles in the bathtub in their enthusiasm
for bathing. They delight in the simple things,
like when I shave their heads to treat their
ringworm or rub their feet with paraffin to
draw out the burrowing jiggers. They soak
up the Bible stories I read them like little
sponges and never stop asking for more. They
laugh hysterically when I cuddle them or kiss
their foreheads, and it hurts my heart a bit
that they find the fact that someone loves
them so funny. And that is the blessing God
has given me in this house: I get to provide
a home for children who are homeless, a safe
haven for children who feel threatened, lost,
and unwanted. Most of all, I get to love
children who don't know love otherwise. I get
to accept them for who they are. I get to
present them with my love and then teach
them of the Father's extravagant love.

The house full of termites and bats, the house that has taken more hours and shillings to repair than I ever could have imagined. The house I have fixed and painted and scrubbed for hours and days and weeks, the house I have sweated and cried over in desperation...

This house has become a home, not just to me but to hundreds. It holds my heart. It holds so many lessons. It is a place where children can be children, where people can know that they are important and special and loved. It is a place where people accept Christ and learn about Him and grow in Him. It is my house. But mostly, it is a house of the Lord.

6

A CHANGE OF HEART

Her name is Sumini. When I met her, a lively student in my kindergarten class, she was five years old but looked to be no more than three. She was thrilled to be learning her alphabet, and she loved to color and to sing. When she sang, her little voice was high-pitched, breathy, and filled with passion. Now, as she lay fitfully on a bed in my house, her boundless energy was drained by disease (malaria), her bright eyes dulled by hunger, and the dance in her step stilled by the crippling effects of poverty. My heart literally hurt in my chest as I watched her struggle and prayed more intensely than I'd ever prayed in my life.

As I sat up late that night trying to keep her alive one minute, one breath at a time, I had to ask myself, *Why do I have so much? And why have I always had so much? Why do my family and friends have so much? And do they even know that far, far away from the luxuries of the western world, a little songbird of a girl is fighting for her life? The roles could have so easily been reversed.* I wondered how God had chosen me to be born into such luxury when this little girl had been born into such hopelessness. I thought, *She is a girl with as many hopes and dreams as those who rest peacefully in air-conditioned houses protected by alarm systems. Yet her body is on fire with raging fever; my sheets are soaked. And right now, she has no one to care for her but me.*

My heart began to break over and over for the other children around the world who had no one to protect them, no one to speak up for them, no one to sit up with them at night and control their fevers. Who would hold them? Who would sing to them?

At some point in the night, Sumini smiled at me. In the dark, her black face blended right in with the night and all I could see was the flash of her teeth. I knew that Sumini would not die, not that night, because God had put me there to make sure of that. He had put me there to hold her. He had put me there to give her a sponge bath every hour and ibuprofen every four. He had given me the provision to afford the malaria treatment that her other family members could not. As I continued to pray over Sumini that night, God brought to mind the disciples who, when they encountered a man blind from birth, asked Jesus what the man did to deserve his condition. Jesus replied, "Neither this man nor his parents sinned, but this happened so that the work of God might be displayed in his life" (John 9:3). Disease is certainly not a sin. And poverty is not a sin; it is a condition, a circumstance that allows God's work to be displayed.

As God kept me awake to pray vigilantly for the welfare of the little girl in front of me, something changed in my heart.

I knew God wanted me to care for the poor, I had been doing it as best I could for a long time and it had become almost all I did with my life over the past eight months. It had happened so naturally, I was simply caring for those around me out of an overflow of love for Christ and the love that He had lavished upon me. I never thought I was doing anything different or unusual, just simply what He had asked. But that night as I lay praying and fighting for this precious little one, and over the next weeks and months as I poured over His Word, I realized that what I was doing was not simply my choice—it was a requirement. I wanted to give even more! I wanted to do more for the people who needed help and I wanted others to rise up and do the same. I didn't want to simply care for these people, I wanted to advocate for them. I wanted to raise more awareness for these voiceless, unseen children. I was exploding with a new enthusiasm not just to care for the orphaned and needy children but to encourage and help others do the same.

I wanted people who were warm under their down comforters to know that there were other children like Sumini out there, all alone. I wanted to tell her story.

I knew we couldn't all just pack up and move to Uganda, but I so desired to make a way for others to help, to care for these children, to do what Jesus requires. I wanted to tell them all about what I had seen and experienced so they too would know.

I saw over and over and over again in Scripture where God instructs us to do everything in our power to care for children just like these. Jesus says, "Let the little children come to me, and do not hinder them, for the kingdom of heaven belongs to such as these" (Matthew 19:14). Sumini was to be my sixth daughter. The first month she lived with us we visited many different doctors, all of whom were concerned that she might not live much longer because her spleen and liver were so enlarged due to severe malnutrition. Every time we left a doctor's office, I felt discouraged by the prognosis. Sumini, however, never had a discouraged bone in her body. She is a fighter. And she would not be beat. As it turns out, God truly did want His work to be displayed in her life, as her spleen and liver miraculously began to shrink back to normal size. With good feeding and lots of love and nurturing she once again became a healthy, happy little girl.

Sumini is tiny for her age but has a huge personality to make up for it. She is ever active. I rarely catch her walking but always running, skipping, jumping, climbing. Sumini is kind and fair. She doesn't ever want anyone to feel left out or left behind. She shares what she has and makes sure those around her always feel included and important. Sumini loves to create and is always making something new—games, pictures, food, anything. I love watching her heart transform as she learns about Jesus and contributes so much joy to our family.

As Sumini joined our family, I knew that one of God's purposes in placing me here was to grow in me, through my children, this heart for adoption. In an effort to be real, I will tell you: It was hard. Being a mother of six at age nineteen was just plain exhausting sometimes. But God continued to show me that adoption is His heart, and it was becoming mine.

Adoption is wonderful and beautiful and the greatest blessing I have ever experienced. Adoption is also difficult and painful. Adoption is a beautiful picture of redemption. It is the Gospel in my living room. And sometimes, it's just hard.

As a parent, it's hard not to know when your daughter took her first steps or what her first word was or what she looked like in kindergarten. It's hard not to know where she slept and whose shoulder she cried on and what the scar on her eyebrow is from. It's hard to know that for ten years yours was *not* the shoulder she cried on and you were not the mommy she hugged.

As a child, it's hard to remember your biological parents' death, no matter how much you love your new mom. It's hard to have your mom be a different color than you because inevitably people are going to ask why. It's hard that your mom wasn't there for all the times you had no dinner and all the times you were sick and all the times you needed help with your homework. It's hard when you have to make up your birthday. It's hard when you can't understand the concept of being a family forever yet, because your first family wasn't forever.

Adoption is a redemptive response to tragedy that happens in this broken world. And every single day, it is worth it, because adoption is God's heart. His Word says, "In love he predestined us to be adopted as his sons through Jesus Christ, in accordance with his pleasure and will" (Ephesians 1:5). He sets the lonely in families (see Psalm 68:6). The first word that appears when I look up *adoption* in the dictionary is "*acceptance.*" God accepts me, adores me even, just as I am. And

He wants me to accept those without families into my own. Adoption is the reason I can come before God's throne and beg Him for mercy, because He predestined me to be adopted as His child through Jesus Christ, in accordance with his pleasure and will—to the praise of His glorious grace.

My family, adopting these children, it is not optional. It is not my good deed for the day; it is not what I am doing to "help out these poor kids." I adopt because God commands me to care for the orphans and the widows in their distress. I adopt because Jesus says that to whom much has been given, much will be demanded (see Luke 12:48) and because whoever finds his life will lose it but whoever loses his life for *His* sake will find it (see Matthew 10:39).

God was showing me His heart and His Word in new ways right there in the life I was living through the children I was serving. Armed with this new sense of who He is and who I was as His servant, I continued trying to give myself away in every circumstance. I wanted to do God's work, let Him display Himself through my life, and change my world as much as possible every single day. Most days, that didn't include anything other people would find impressive. It simply meant being faithful to the people and the responsibilities God had given me.

I never knew what God was going to do next or whom He was going to bring into my life. I'd learned by now that sometimes people entered my life suddenly, and that just as quickly as they entered, they left. I learned to accept them, adopt them into my heart, no matter the circumstances. Some would become part of my world permanently and others would be in it for only a short season. Some of those people whose lives intersected briefly with mine made an impact that will live forever in my heart. One of those was a little girl named Brenda.

Brenda was one of the most beautiful children I have ever met. I found her at the main hospital in Jinja where my girls and I went a few times a week to pass out food to patients, pray for them, chat with them, and remind them of the love Jesus has for them. My children loved this time of serving and we always came home thanking God. When we went to the hospital, I was always moved by how great our God is in the midst of more pain than I could imagine. Sometimes a particular case touched a special place in my heart, and I knew God was calling my name, asking me to get involved. Brenda's situation was one of these.

She was no ordinary little girl. I would have guessed she, at the age of thirteen, weighed around forty pounds. She carried most of her weight in her stomach, which was hugely distended, as though she were pregnant with twins. The rest of her body was so thin I felt I could snap it in half with just a touch.

We met her on a Monday, lying limp in her rusty hospital bed, hardly able to breathe because of the pain she was in. Under her bed was a bucket containing at least four liters of blood the hospital staff had drained from her abdomen. Brenda had been to every government hospital in Uganda and no one had been able to say what was wrong, why her stomach kept ballooning as the rest of her body seemed to shrink.

Not knowing what else to do, I immediately laid my hands on her and began to pray. Within minutes my six little girls were huddled around the bed also lifting their voices to the Lord on behalf of this little girl. Different sizes, different ages, different races, speaking different languages, each of us in our own way pleaded with God for this little girl's life.

I could feel her body shaking beneath my hands as I prayed, and when I moved my hand off hers, I could see the outline of where I had touched her. My touch had made her blood come to the surface in the perfect shape of my handprint.

I returned to the hospital that evening with dinner for Brenda and her mother, who lay on the hospital floor next to her dying daughter. Overwhelmed with a sense of helplessness as soon as I walked in, I again began to pray, exalting God who was Lord in the middle of that room full of dying people, asking Him to heal where it was His will, to at least take away the pain, to wrap us all in His arms, to comfort us in the way that only He can until we come home to Him.

Over the next few days, I continued visiting Brenda several times a day, taking her food or a blanket (as I mentioned, the hospital doesn't supply these things), praying for her, and simply being with her. My girls asked about her eagerly each time I came home and each continued to pray for Brenda. Although her baffled physicians had done nothing to help her, I went to see her one day and found her condition remarkably improved. The next day, she was alert and able to have a conversation with me, and her pain seemed much less severe. The next day she was sitting and laughing, her stomach much less distended.

When I asked the doctors what they had done, they insisted they had done nothing. They believed she was better because we had touched her. I assured them that wasn't possible, but it was definitely possible that she was better because *Jesus* had touched her through someone who asked Him to do so! I believe that Jesus told His disciples to heal the sick, and I believe that Jesus works through humans as we open ourselves to Him. I had never prayed with such conviction and faith as I did during those days with Brenda, though I pray with as much fervency more frequently now. I by no means have the power to heal, but I *know* our Almighty Father does.

Then the day came when I went to the hospital again and found Brenda's room empty. Concerned about her, I asked a staff member where she was. The hospital had sent her home, because "her condition had improved significantly." The little girl I thought would die in my arms had grown steadily better and the doctors hadn't even touched her. I could believe only that Jesus did.

I may never see Brenda again. She left my life as quickly as she entered. She changed me; she strengthened my faith. I pray that she grows into a woman who loves her Maker. I pray that her sickness as a thirteen-year-old, and the miraculous healing she received, will strengthen her faith for the rest of her life.

Will Brenda remember me? When she sleeps on the blanket from my bed, will she think of the time we spent together? I don't know. But I will never forget.

My life was being filled with unforgettable experiences. Every day something happened, usually something more heartbreaking or appalling than anything I had ever encountered. I was growing accustomed to it, and I knew it was what I was created for. The sense of purpose and fulfillment I felt was nothing short of amazing, and I wanted to immerse myself in this life for the rest of my days.

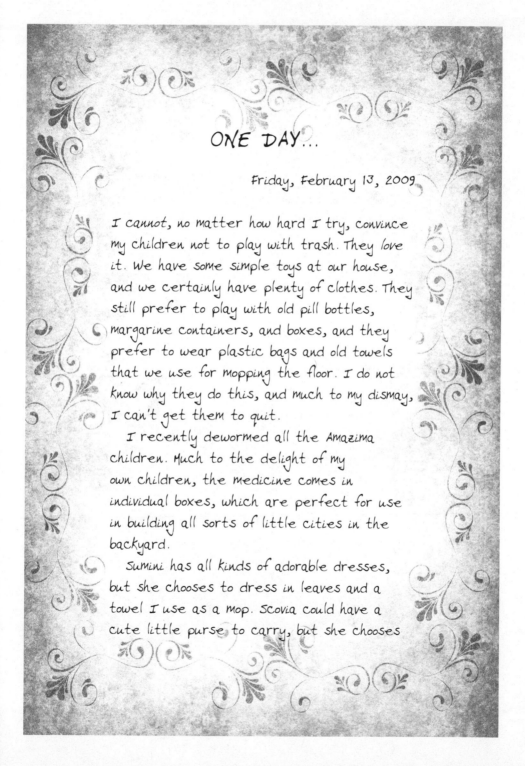

ONE DAY...

Friday, February 13, 2009

I cannot, no matter how hard I try, convince my children not to play with trash. They *love* it. We have some simple toys at our house, and we certainly have plenty of clothes. They still prefer to play with old pill bottles, margarine containers, and boxes, and they prefer to wear plastic bags and old towels that we use for mopping the floor. I do not know why they do this, and much to my dismay, I can't get them to quit.

I recently dewormed all the Amazima children. Much to the delight of my own children, the medicine comes in individual boxes, which are perfect for use in building all sorts of little cities in the backyard.

Sumini has all kinds of adorable dresses, but she chooses to dress in leaves and a towel I use as a mop. Scovia could have a cute little purse to carry, but she chooses

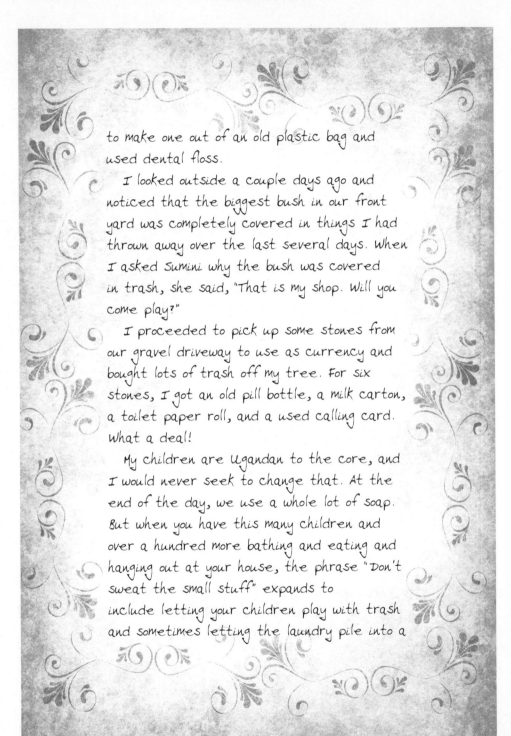

to make one out of an old plastic bag and used dental floss.

I looked outside a couple days ago and noticed that the biggest bush in our front yard was completely covered in things I had thrown away over the last several days. When I asked Sumini why the bush was covered in trash, she said, "That is my shop. Will you come play?"

I proceeded to pick up some stones from our gravel driveway to use as currency and bought lots of trash off my tree. For six stones, I got an old pill bottle, a milk carton, a toilet paper roll, and a used calling card. What a deal!

My children are Ugandan to the core, and I would never seek to change that. At the end of the day, we use a whole lot of soap. But when you have this many children and over a hundred more bathing and eating and hanging out at your house, the phrase "Don't sweat the small stuff" expands to include letting your children play with trash and sometimes letting the laundry pile into a

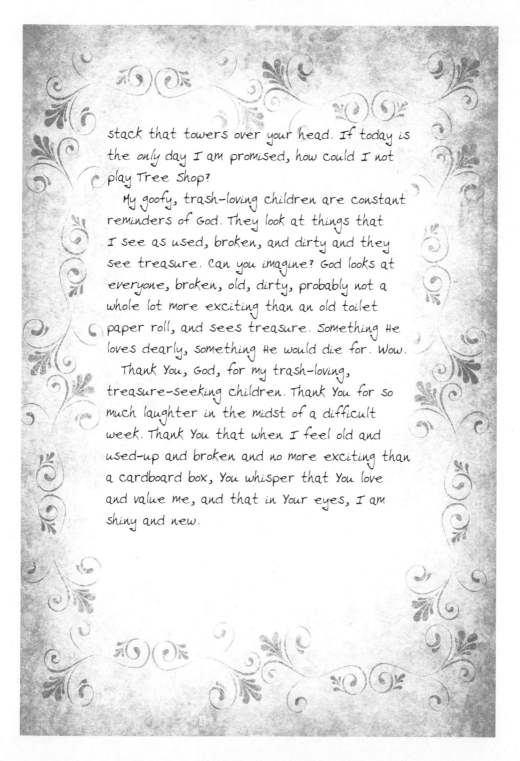

stack that towers over your head. If today is the only day I am promised, how could I not play Tree Shop?

My goofy, trash-loving children are constant reminders of God. They look at things that I see as used, broken, and dirty and they see treasure. Can you imagine? God looks at everyone, broken, old, dirty, probably not a whole lot more exciting than an old toilet paper roll, and sees treasure. Something He loves dearly, something He would die for. Wow.

Thank You, God, for my trash-loving, treasure-seeking children. Thank You for so much laughter in the midst of a difficult week. Thank You that when I feel old and used-up and broken and no more exciting than a cardboard box, You whisper that You love and value me, and that in Your eyes, I am shiny and new.

7

DEEP HUNGER, DEEP GLADNESS

The longer I stayed in Uganda and the more I grew to love being a mom, the less I wanted to return to the United States, ever. While my friends there were thinking about fraternity parties and football games, I was constantly praying about how to feed, clothe, and send to school the six beautiful little girls for whom I'd become responsible.

Using my personal savings and donations from family and friends in the States, I managed to buy the things we needed most, but finances were in short supply in our household. We didn't have a car, so we made our way around town on a *piki*. When the family consisted of Agnes, Mary, Scovia, and me, the four of us piled on one motorcycle, usually with Fred, our favorite driver. Agnes, Mary, and I sat on the back, while Scovia rode in front of Fred, gripping the handlebars. As the family grew, we had to hire more than one *piki* to carry all of us, so our family could often be seen as lots of happy girls in a small parade of motorcycles.

Even though I came from America, where everyone I knew had a car and people with several children had vans, I never considered the fact that a van would have been nice. We certainly couldn't afford one, and in a country where most people walk everywhere, we knew being able to take motorcycles meant we were living the good life!

While we have a lot more now, we never noticed or thought about the things we didn't have then. We were rich! We had all our basic needs met, which was more than most of our neighbors could say, and, more important, we had one another. We had laughter and a deep love for God and this new family He had given us.

What we lacked in funds, we compensated for in an abundance of love and joy. Many nights we ate *posho* and beans, and when we could afford to splurge, we had a popular meal of "roll eggs" (which is literally a roll of eggs with vegetables, like a thin omelet rolled into the shape of a wrap) and cassava. This luxurious meal cost about sixty cents per person in U.S. currency, but it was still a treat for us. No matter what was on our table, we sat around it chatting happily, laughing (sometimes hysterically), and grateful to be a family. Our life was almost unbelievable, and I felt like the most privileged person in the world to be living it.

But the amazing life I loved didn't come without a cost; I mean an *actual* cost. The work I was doing in Uganda cost money, and I didn't have much of that. I was learning quickly that running a ministry had at least one particular task I hadn't anticipated when I first moved to Uganda: fund-raising. For me, fund-raising has always been about more than simply raising money, it's a means of raising awareness, and in the process hopefully changing people's hearts. I enjoy being able to share with people the stories of the incredible things God is doing amid the poor in Uganda. I enjoy fund-raising, knowing the funds are going to meet such enormous needs. I feel so blessed that God has given me incredible stories to share with others.

My only aversion to fund-raising comes when it means being separated from my children. Then and now, I couldn't raise money in Uganda because money is so very scarce in this country. But it's abundant in the United States, and in the area where I grew up, people were eager to support and be part of my work in Uganda, so in the spring of 2008, I planned a trip that would serve two purposes: to visit the family I love so much and to do my best to try to raise some money.

I hadn't seen my father or my brother in almost a year, and part of me could hardly wait to throw my arms around them and simply be with them. But another part of me was ripped apart by the thought of being separated from my children. I wanted to see my biological family, but I did not want to leave Uganda and the new family God had given me. I wanted to be within only arm's reach of my beautiful daughters. I had never left Uganda as a mother before, and though I made arrangements for trusted friends to care for the girls, my heart could hardly bear the thought of being separated from them by so much time and distance.

Brentwood, Tennessee, the place where I was raised, is a suburb of Nashville, which is beautiful from the air. Blue lakes and green rolling hills are visible from the airplane window, and for people who consider that place home, a view of the landscape as the plane approaches is comforting, like a long exhale after a stressful day.

As I approached the Nashville airport to spend several weeks fund-raising there, I wasn't one of the people who exhaled. I realized I didn't really feel I was going home; I was simply returning to the place I'd been raised, going to visit my family and friends.

Eating dinner at my parents' table, sleeping in my old bed, and gabbing with my friends seemed almost surreal. I wanted to fit back into that place that I still loved and would forever call home, but it seemed impossible. Part of me was angry that the people around me seemed to take for granted even simple things, like having a meal or running water. Part of me expected at least some of my closest friends to understand what I had seen, but I found putting my experiences into words so difficult. Because sharing the realities of my new life was so hard to do, people around me found it hard to understand.

To my surprise, I discovered that I no longer fit in where I used to be so comfortable. I didn't live in this world anymore; I wasn't relieved or overjoyed to be in it again; and I wasn't comfortable there. A tiny part of me was *so* happy to collapse into the hugs of my mom, dad, and brother, but a bigger part felt so out of place.

By this time, the ministry was well on its way to becoming a legal entity. In fact, the process was almost complete. The name I'd chosen represented what I longed to see take root in the lives of everyone who came in contact with the ministry: *Amazima*, which means "truth" in Luganda.

Our stated goal was to help children experience the truth of a bigger, brighter world available to them through education and, more important, the truth of a God who created them beautifully in His image, a God who loves and values and wants the best for them. The overwhelming majority of the children around me in Uganda have never known that kind of love. What a tragedy, for that kind of love is true.

On a practical level, Amazima's way of sharing these truths was first to keep these children alive by providing them with nutritious meals and as much medical attention as possible, and on a deeper level, to teach them of the love of Christ. We wanted to teach them of Jesus who died for them, for all of us. I didn't believe it was possible to tell a child about the love of Christ without simultaneously showing her that love by feeding her, clothing her, inviting her in. If a child has never known what love is, how can we expect him to accept the love of his Savior until we first make that love tangible? I wanted these children to know life to the fullest in a relationship with Him here on earth, and life everlasting with Him in heaven later.

But the Lord had also planted in me a desire to share the *truth* He had shown me in Uganda to the people who surrounded me now in America. I wanted to share with them the truth that while their children were alive today, more than sixteen thousand other children are not, because they died of hunger-related causes in the last twenty-four hours.[1] I wanted them to know that another three thousand children in the world, mostly in Africa, will die of malaria *today*—malaria, which is both preventable and treatable.[2] I wanted to share with them the truth that many of us seemed to have over-looked—that God wanted us to care for the poor, not just care about them, but to truly *take care* of them, and many of us were not doing so. God told us to love our neighbors as ourselves, but so many of our neighbors were starving to death while our tables were filled with abundance.

Most of the people around me expected me to feel relieved to be back. Understandably, many people I saw in my hometown asked the same question: "Isn't life hard in Uganda?" Of course it was hard, in certain ways, but they didn't seem to understand that what was even *harder* was being back in the States, away from my children. There were days when I felt my soul had been ripped from my body, that my purpose had suddenly been stripped from my being. I hadn't realized what a transformation had taken place while I had been in Uganda, the spiritual richness I had experienced in material poverty and the spiritual poverty I felt now in a land of material wealth. Anyone could see that my life had changed drastically with the addition of six children, but less perceptible and more powerful was the revolution that had taken place in the core of my being. Having been changed so much in my new home and then returning to my old one came with many tears, lots of stress, the loneliness of being misunderstood, and considerable disagreement and strain in my relationship with my parents, who were still hoping I would change my mind and come back to the States to attend college as I had promised them.

During the time I spent at my parents' house, I remembered a favorite story, *The Velveteen Rabbit*. It begins with the rabbit, fluffy and beautiful, "just as a rabbit should be," but all the rabbit wanted was to be *real*. The boy who owns the rabbit loves it to tatters; his velveteen fur becomes worn and his stuffing starts to come out. "So much love stirred in his little sawdust heart that it almost burst. And into his boot-button eyes, that had long ago lost their polish, there came a look of wisdom and beauty, so that even Nana noticed it next morning when she picked him up, and said, 'I declare if that old Bunny hasn't got quite a knowing expression!'"[3]

The boy loves the bunny "so hard" that he loves his whiskers off and the pink fur on his ears turns gray. After the boy contracts scarlet fever, the doctor says the beloved, worn-out rabbit has fever germs and must be discarded, so Nana throws him out. And only then, when he is tattered and ugly, does the fairy come and make him a *real* rabbit, all sparkly and new, who can run and play with other real rabbits. He wasn't patched up or glued back together. No, he was transformed, made altogether new.

I was like that velveteen rabbit. When I first went to Uganda, I felt sparkling and beautiful, as a teenage girl from Brentwood "should" be. But now I spent my days without makeup, getting my hands dirty and doing hard but meaningful work. I was tattered and worn out. The beautiful, dirty people who populated my life had loved all the polish and propriety right off me.

I'd been hurt and scarred and banged around a bit in the past year, but God was using all those things to help me become real. My stuffing was coming out because I'd been loved to tatters. I was coming to understand that what it means to be real is to love and be loved until there is nothing left. And when there's nothing left, and we feel we're all in pieces, God begins to make us whole. He makes us real. His love sets us free and transforms us.

I don't know if I would have realized how drastically I had changed since moving to Uganda had I not returned to the States for a visit. Something about being back in an old environment caused me to see how completely different I was becoming—from my friends' lives, from my family's life, from everything I'd known in America and certainly from what I'd planned to be.

One day while in the States, I received a call from Christine in Uganda and found out that a change had taken place during my absence. The doors of my home are always open, and everyone in my family knew this and was looking for ways to share what we had with our neighbors. Christine's five-year-old cousin, Joyce, also from the war-ravaged area of northern Uganda, needed a place to live after losing all her other living relatives. Christine pleaded with me to let her stay at our home, but I didn't need much convincing—of course she must come to live with us! How could we say no, knowing the need this child had and that we had the ability to meet it, to provide her with love, a family, and a slew of sisters to play and grow with?

Though I had never met Joyce, she was now part of our family, and I couldn't wait to get home and meet her. I remember the first time I heard Joyce's voice on the phone. She was quiet at first, but then began to giggle, perhaps in response to the fact that her new sisters were giddy with excitement to know that I was on the other end of the line. At that point Joyce knew me only as a strange voice. She had no idea who "Mommy" was and why the others were so excited about me. I longed to take her into my arms and explain to her that I would be there soon and that I would love and care for her forever. I longed to speak love and tenderness over the darkest corners of her young life. But what struck me most about that first phone call with Joyce was what she said to me: "Thank you for food, Mommy. Today I am still alive."

My heart stopped. This little girl, at five years old, is simply thankful to have something to eat so she can stay alive. My mind began to race as I looked at the food piled high in my parents' kitchen: *Joyce is still alive, but so many others are not. They are dying of starvation and preventable, treatable diseases. Why, with all the wealth, technology, and resources that exist in the western world, have we not solved these problems? It is possible for children to live! And yet they are dying by the thousands. While we sit here full and content, everything we ever need right within our reach.*

As hard as it was to be in America, I knew this was why God had brought me back. This is why I had come to raise money. It wasn't to build a ministry for myself; it was to help change lives and invite other people to do it with me.

The needs I had seen in Uganda were never far from my mind; they weighed on me as a heavy, passionate burden. I needed to get back to Africa. I needed to go back to doing everything within my power to help the people around me live better lives. And I needed to get back to my girls, to reconnect with the six I was already in love with and wrap sweet Joyce in her new mommy's arms.

People I had known growing up had said, "Welcome home" when they saw me in the neighborhood. But Brentwood didn't feel like home anymore. Frederick Beuchner writes, "The place God calls us to is the place where your deep gladness and the world's deep hunger meet." I had been more than happy all my life in my home in Brentwood. But my deepest gladness and the world's deep hunger met in Uganda. My heart sang in Uganda. Everything in Uganda made me feel alive. Uganda was home, the place God was calling me, and I had to get back as quickly as possible.

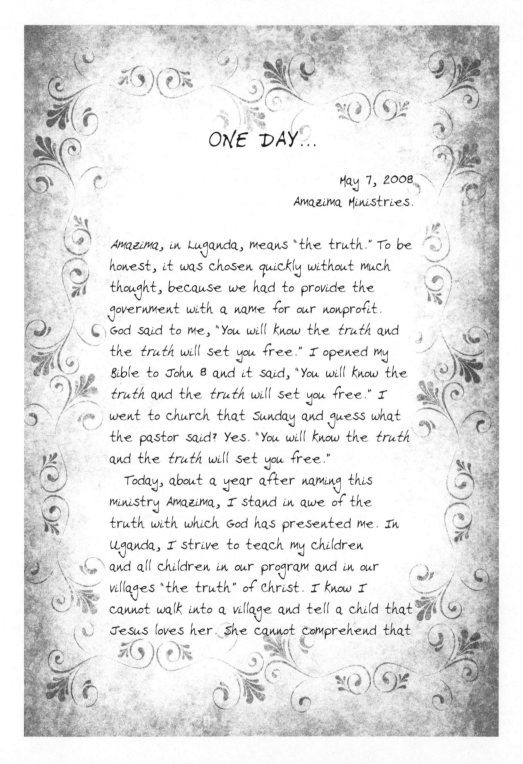

ONE DAY...

May 7, 2008
Amazima Ministries.

Amazima, in Luganda, means "the truth." To be honest, it was chosen quickly without much thought, because we had to provide the government with a name for our nonprofit. God said to me, "You will know the *truth* and the *truth* will set you free." I opened my Bible to John 8 and it said, "You will know the *truth* and the *truth* will set you free." I went to church that Sunday and guess what the pastor said? Yes. "You will know the *truth* and the *truth* will set you free."

Today, about a year after naming this ministry Amazima, I stand in awe of the truth with which God has presented me. In Uganda, I strive to teach my children and all children in our program and in our villages "the truth" of Christ. I know I cannot walk into a village and tell a child that Jesus loves her. She cannot comprehend that

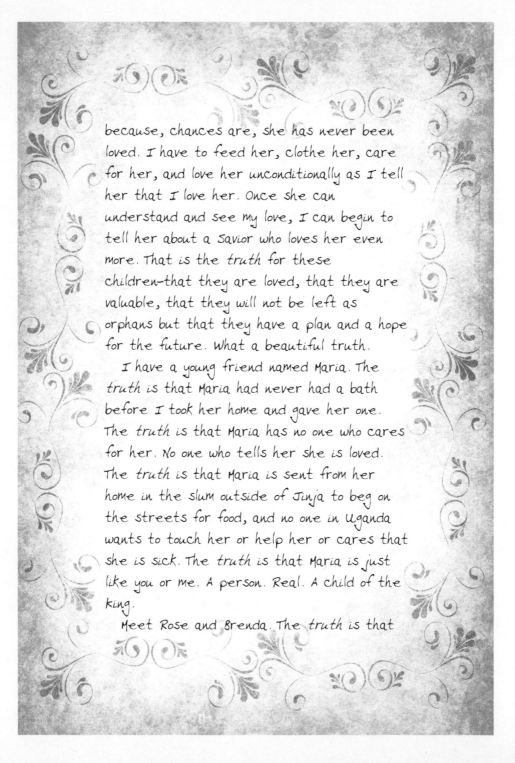

because, chances are, she has never been loved. I have to feed her, clothe her, care for her, and love her unconditionally as I tell her that I love her. Once she can understand and see my love, I can begin to tell her about a Savior who loves her even more. That is the *truth* for these children—that they are loved, that they are valuable, that they will not be left as orphans but that they have a plan and a hope for the future. What a beautiful truth.

I have a young friend named Maria. The *truth* is that Maria had never had a bath before I took her home and gave her one. The *truth* is that Maria has no one who cares for her. No one who tells her she is loved. The *truth* is that Maria is sent from her home in the slum outside of Jinja to beg on the streets for food, and no one in Uganda wants to touch her or help her or cares that she is sick. The *truth* is that Maria is just like you or me. A person. Real. A child of the King.

Meet Rose and Brenda. The *truth* is that

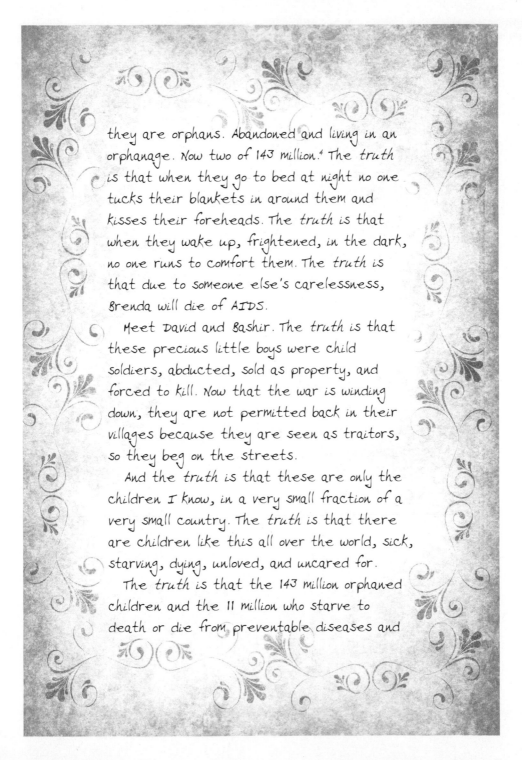

they are orphans. Abandoned and living in an orphanage. Now two of 143 million.[4] The *truth* is that when they go to bed at night no one tucks their blankets in around them and kisses their foreheads. The *truth* is that when they wake up, frightened, in the dark, no one runs to comfort them. The *truth* is that due to someone else's carelessness, Brenda will die of AIDS.

Meet David and Bashir. The *truth* is that these precious little boys were child soldiers, abducted, sold as property, and forced to kill. Now that the war is winding down, they are not permitted back in their villages because they are seen as traitors, so they beg on the streets.

And the *truth* is that these are only the children I know, in a very small fraction of a very small country. The *truth* is that there are children like this all over the world, sick, starving, dying, unloved, and uncared for.

The *truth* is that the 143 million orphaned children and the 11 million who starve to death or die from preventable diseases and

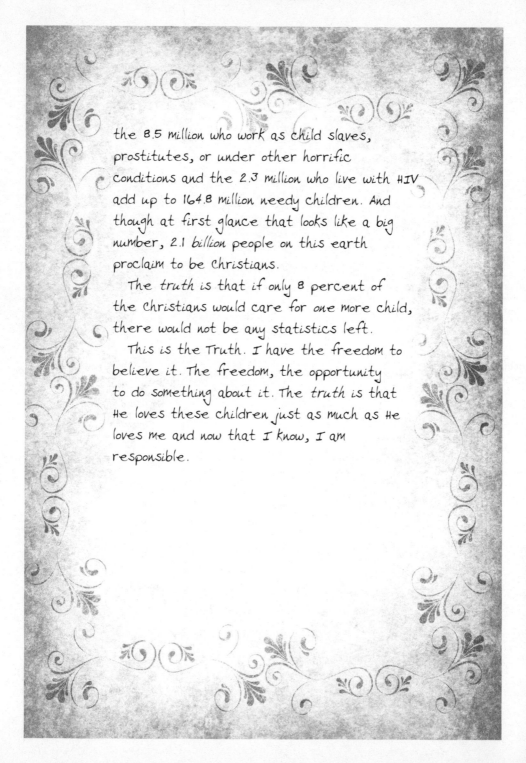

the 8.5 million who work as child slaves,
prostitutes, or under other horrific
conditions and the 2.3 million who live with HIV
add up to 164.8 million needy children. And
though at first glance that looks like a big
number, 2.1 billion people on this earth
proclaim to be Christians.

The truth is that if only 8 percent of
the Christians would care for one more child,
there would not be any statistics left.

This is the Truth. I have the freedom to
believe it. The freedom, the opportunity
to do something about it. The truth is that
He loves these children just as much as He
loves me and now that I know, I am
responsible.

8

HOW GREAT A DISTANCE
LOVE CAN BRIDGE

I was more than happy to land at Entebbe airport. I took a deep breath of the air that smells like what I can only describe as "Uganda" and let it fill me with the joy of being in the place God has called me. The simple sign, made of stone and placed beside the runway, reads to arriving passengers "Welcome to the Pearl of Africa," but to me it whispered "Welcome home."

The first two days I spent back in my house in the village began the same way, with a little brown hand rubbing my face and a soft voice saying, "Mommy. Mommy. Mommy, it's time for wake up." The second morning, Agnes looked at me and said, "There it is! It came back!"

I asked her, groggily, "What came back?"

With joy she could hardly contain, she replied, "That light that lives in your eyes!"

Yes, it was back. So was the joy that dances in my heart. I felt alive again, humbled beyond belief by how much I loved my life, ecstatic to have a large bowl of rice after a long, hot day—and wonderfully at home.

I fell in love instantly with my new daughter, Joyce. I love all children, but God puts something special in my heart when He intends
for the children to be my own. The love is different than the love I
feel for anyone else on the planet. It's the love that lets me know that
this child is indeed my daughter.

Joyce is tall, bald, and stunningly beautiful. Joyce is a caretaker;
she has a deep love for all people. She will take care of anyone she
can; babies, animals, even insects can sometimes be found being
carted lovingly around in her little hands. She always wants to make
sure that everyone around her is content, especially younger children.
She finds joy in giving love to others and is happiest when helping
someone else. She is boisterous and animated, often making up words
to tunes she knows and singing them at the top of her lungs, or running up to tackle her baby sisters or me in a wonderfully unexpected
bear hug.

Something had happened during my fund-raising trip and when I
returned to Uganda; for the first time, I didn't feel so far away from my
parents and my former life anymore. I had learned while being "home"
in America and away from "home" in Uganda just how small this earth
really is. It was as if the two worlds I had been living in had finally
merged a bit and I was discovering just how great a distance love can
bridge. God really does have the whole world sitting in the palm of His
hand. All of us are, literally, neighbors. With the simple purchase of a
plane ticket, I can get from my house in the village to my parents' living
room in twenty-four hours. And I could get back to Jinja from Brentwood in twenty-four hours as well. People tell me they miss me; they
think I am so far away. But I'm not. I'm right here, on the same earth as
everybody else, doing what I know to do to make it a little bit better.

Many people think of Uganda as another world, a place barely
connected to the societies and cultures they consider more advanced.
Certainly, differences between Africa and other parts of the world
abound. But we all have so much more in common than we have dis-
tinctions. So much more binds us together than keeps us apart.

In Uganda, as in all the nations of the earth, human beings are hungry for God; they long to live lives filled with purpose and love. They want to be able to support their families; they want to be able to work; they want to be able to give back and to be good, noble people. They want to feel important and needed and beautiful. Children want to play, eat, learn, and be loved. We are all the same. We do not live in different worlds; we live in the same world.

People are people. They all need food and water and medicine, but mostly they need love and truth and Jesus. I can do that. *We* can do that. We can give people food, water, medicine, love, truth, and Jesus. The same God created all of us for a purpose, which is to serve Him and to love and care for His people. It is universal. We can't do it in our own strength or out of our own resources, but as we follow God to wherever He is leading us, He makes the impossible happen.

People from my first home say I'm brave. They tell me I'm strong. They pat me on the back and say, "Way to go. Good job." But the truth is, I am not really very brave; I am not really very strong; and I am not doing anything spectacular. I am simply doing what God has called me to do as a person who follows Him. He said to feed His sheep and He said to care for "the least of these," so that's what I'm doing, with the help of a lot of people who make it possible and in the company of those who make my life worth living.

I was so happy to be back in my element, back with the people I loved, doing the work I enjoyed. Sometimes I felt like the "old woman who lived in a shoe," the one from the nursery rhyme: "she had so many children she didn't know what to do." There were children everywhere and there was so much exuberance I didn't know what to do.

The first weekend I was home, the children in our program spent the night at my house, about 140 of them covering every square inch of the floor. They sang a song they had practiced the entire time I was in the States: "We are the children of Amazima. We are happy to see you, Mommy. We missed you, Mommy Katie. We love you! We love you! Welcome home!" I thought my heart would burst. We spent a happy evening singing, praying, laughing until we hurt, reveling in the fact that God had brought us together.

The next morning, I noticed a rash on a little girl named Shadia. After inspecting her and her brothers and sisters I concluded it was scabies. Scabies is the kind of disease that makes a lot of people cringe. It is a contagious skin infection caused by a tiny mite that burrows under the skin and creates incredible itching. It begins as a rash, but the little bumps soon become open wounds festering on the skin. Scabies is often a result of living in filth for a long period of time, but it is also transmitted quickly by skin-to-skin contact. In this case, six of the eight children living in the home were infected.

I had visited the home where these children live. I will never forget it. Their living conditions were some of the worst I have seen. The eight children lived with their widowed aunt and their dying grandmother. These women did their best to provide, but all their hard work was rarely enough to provide the children with life's most basic necessities. They lived six miles from the nearest water hole, so they used the same water over and over. The children slept in a pile, like dogs, in a small corner of the dirt house. And yet these children were quick to dance and laugh and sing, just like children everywhere.

Now they were suffering. Their scabies was in its early form, but without treatment they would become extremely ill. I spoke to a nurse at a nearby hospital and she told me how to treat them. To cure the scabies, the children needed to bathe in warm water twice a day and then receive an application of a certain ointment. They could not share water, towels, or of course ointment.

The nurse's instructions made sense to me. It seemed a reasonable course of action, except that the children lived in abject filth. *How in the world will this family ever get enough water for all six children to have their very own bath?* I wondered. *If they do manage to get the water, how will they heat it? This family doesn't even own one towel; they certainly don't have six!*

But I had six towels. I also had running water. I had heat when the power was on and a fire in the backyard when it wasn't. I had extra sheets and strong hands that could rub ointment all over the rashes on those darling children. In addition, I was thankful to be able to help them.

So, instead of having only my seven girls in the house, in addition to Christine and me, we added six more. They were delighted to have warm baths but seemed nervous as I applied the ointment to their peeling skin. For a brief moment, I wondered, *What if I catch this disease? What kind of parent am I if I have brought these children willingly into my home and all seven of my girls get scabies?* That frightening thought fled quickly as I remembered that Jesus touched lepers and Jesus gave me my assignment in Uganda. He gave me hands that can rub healing balm on children's wounds. I was simply blessed to be able to use them.

This would be the first of many, many times we would invite disease-ridden, suffering people into our home. It would also be the first of many times that my breath would catch in my throat at the thought of exposing my children to disease. I was always quick to open my home, but a few days after realizing how sick our new friends were or being criticized by other "good" parents, fear would sneak in and I would wonder if I truly was being irresponsible.

The answer always came quickly and simply, "I sent *My* Son," the Father would breathe through my spirit. "Whoever desires to save his life will lose it, but whoever loses his life for My sake . . ." I realized I still had to be obedient to what God had asked me to do, even though He was expanding my family. I knew the desire to protect my children was God given, but that at the end of each day, this Father who loved them even more than I did would be their protector. Either He would keep them free from all harm or illness or they would get scabies, and we could afford the medicine and God would see us through it.

Over and over again, we have welcomed the sick into our lives—

into our homes, to sit with us at our kitchen table, to bathe in our showers, and to sleep in our beds. And each time, disease has touched none of us, people have been healed, God has been glorified, and my family has been tremendously blessed.

Treating the children was time and energy intensive. Bathing and dressing six children's wounds twice a day seemed like a full-time job. In addition to that, getting clean towels (without a washing machine, which I didn't have) for twelve baths a day was a chore! More than those challenges, though, was the fact that I needed to keep the infected children far enough from my girls that they would not catch scabies but avoid making our guests feel like outcasts.

We managed. Not only did the children recover, my girls never contracted scabies, nor did I. I struggled to come up with the money to pay for the children's treatments, pay the people who were helping me, and feed all of us. It was difficult. But it is in the brilliantly, gloriously, wonderfully difficult seasons that God seems to show Himself all-powerful and in control. Seeing six of His children with clean, healthy skin and renewed laughter and energy made all the effort more than worthwhile. This was one of many incidences when the Lord has shown me that the more I give of myself, the more He fills me up. The more I love, the more love I have to give.

God was teaching me the same lessons He desires to teach every single one of His children, He just chose to bring me to Uganda to do it while others can learn right where they are. My life looked different than most because I'd made different choices than most. But making different choices didn't make me superhuman. In fact, every day was filled with reminders, sometimes *painful* reminders, of my human emotions, human desires, and human limitations.

I am not one to step back from or fear much, but one situation is always certain to evoke the human emotion of fear in me. It isn't the rampant disease I encounter multiple times each day or the threat of war in a fragile nation. It is much simpler than that: a rat. One night, I had the very human need to go to the bathroom, but before I could crawl out of bed, I heard the unmistakable sound of little feet scratching around. I couldn't move. I was paralyzed with fear.

Most of the time, I am fearless; I've always been that way. But the thought, sound, or sight of a rat just does me in. So I lay there, in the sweltering darkness of my room, unable to get out of bed. I had to ask myself why I was so afraid of a relatively small animal. I'm not sure I ever answered that, but I did begin to think about how often, as human beings, we are crippled by our fears. We are afraid of change, of loss, of being hurt. We cling so tightly to what we have because we are afraid of what would happen if we didn't have these things anymore.

I remembered a story I once read:

Once there was a people who surveyed the resources of the world and said to each other: "How can we be sure that we will have enough in hard times? We want to survive whatever happens. Let us start collecting food, materials, and knowledge so that we are safe and secure when a crisis occurs." So they started hoarding, so much and so eagerly that the other peoples protested and said: "You have so much more than you need, while we don't have enough to survive. Give us part of your wealth!" But the fearful hoarders said: "No, no, we need to keep this in case of an emergency, in case things go bad for us too, in case our lives are threatened." But the others said: "We are dying now, please give us food and materials and knowledge to survive. We can't wait . . . we need it now!" Then the fearful hoarders became even more fearful, since they became afraid that the poor and hungry would attack them. So they said to one another: "Let us build walls around our wealth so that no stranger can take it from us." They started erecting walls so high that they could not even see anymore whether their enemies were outside the walls or not! As their fear increased they told each other: "Our enemies have become so numerous that they may be able to tear down our walls. Our walls are not strong enough to keep them away. We need to put bombs at the top of the walls so that nobody will dare to even come close to us." But instead of feeling safe and secure behind their armed walls they found themselves trapped in the prison they had built with their own fear. They even became afraid of their own bombs, wondering if they might harm themselves more than their enemy. And gradually they realized their fear of death had brought them closer to it.[1]

I had recently been back to the States and seen and realized this fear. A very real fear that if we gave everything away, we wouldn't have enough for ourselves. Back in my new home I saw the consequences: children starving to death, sleeping under rags and in chicken feces, withering away from disease. In our fear, even many of us who claimed to believe in Christ were failing to do what He said for the least of His people.

Fear. It's part of human nature, but it's not something we got from God. Second Timothy 1:7 says: "For God has not given us a spirit of fear, but of power and of love and of a sound mind." When I imagine God creating each one of us and planting a purpose deep in our hearts, I never imagine that purpose being mediocrity. While the Bible doesn't tell every person on earth specifically what his or her life's calling will be, it does include a lot of general direction:

"You are to find me in the least of these." Yes.

"You are to leave your earthly possessions and come follow me." Yes.

"You are to love and serve the Lord God with all your heart and love your neighbor as yourself." Yes.

"You are to go and make disciples of all nations." Yes.

"You are to entertain strangers and lepers and tax collectors." Yes.

"You are to show mercy." Yes.

"You are to live a life of mediocrity and abundance, holding on tight to your comfortable lifestyle, lest you lose it." No.

I don't think so. "Mediocrity and abundance" aren't there. However, mediocrity and abundance, comfort and ease, do seem to be safe choices for many people, myself included. In stark contrast, leaving our possessions, following Jesus when we don't have a well-defined plan, and entertaining strangers—well, that does sound a little scary. But what if, just beyond that risk, just beyond the fear is a life better than anything we have ever imagined: *life to the fullest.*

I certainly don't believe everyone should sell all of their belongings and pack a suitcase and move to Africa. I don't think people all over the planet should drop everything to go somewhere far from everything familiar and be missionaries. In fact, I believe anyone can be a missionary right where they are.

Every day, we have a choice. We can stay nestled in our safe comfortable places, as I did when the rat was in my room. We can let fear of something that really is small compared to the greatness of God cripple us. Or we can take a risk, do something to help someone else, make a person smile, change someone's world. Life to the fullest exists. It's available. All we have to do is decide to get up and embrace it.

I don't always want to help other people. Generally speaking, I do. But there are certain days when I, like everyone else in the world, simply want to do what I need to do and keep moving. It's part of being human. But so often, when we stop to be kind when we don't really want to, that's when the sacrifice becomes most rewarding.

The night in 2007 was cold and rainy. I was walking out of the supermarket on Main Street in downtown Jinja, on my way home. Then I saw him. Huddled on the street corner, drenched and shivering, was a little boy. At that moment, all I really wanted to think about was getting home, getting dry, and crawling into my warm bed. But a voice inside told me to stop.

I took the little boy inside the supermarket to dry him off a bit and bought him some biscuits and juice. I gave him my sweatshirt, a small wooden cross I carried in my pocket, and some change so he could get a ride home.

As he left, he called out, "What is your name?"

"Katie," I responded, "Auntie Katie."

"Me, I am Daniel," he shouted and disappeared into the wet, chilly night.

About a year later, I walked into the supermarket to buy food for my family and got caught in a big hug. Two small brown arms wrapped around me as a child's voice excitedly proclaimed, "Auntie Katie!"

I looked down to see Daniel. *Beaming.*

"Wait," he urged me.

He hurried to the nearest street vendor and bought me a popsicle with the little pocket change he had. He then dug his little hand in his pocket and pulled out the small wooden cross. Looking at me with a wide grin, he spoke words that pierced my heart: "I have never stopped praying for you every day."

To this day, I think of that story and stand amazed at the goodness of our God and the enormous things He can accomplish if I am obedient to His command to stop and love the person in front of me. That rainy night, I really just wanted to hop on a *piki* and go home. But I stopped, because that's what my heart told me to do. I only gave him a sweatshirt (I'm sure I have eight more). I only gave him some cheap biscuits (I can eat biscuits anytime I want to). I only gave him enough money for his ride home (probably less than the equivalent of fifty cents). But Jesus gave him hope that night. And he remembered. He didn't just remember my face; he remembered my name. He prayed for me. He prayed for my safety and for the opportunity to see me again. I blessed him just one cold night, and he blessed me every day after that for an entire year.

ONE DAY...

Wednesday, July 23, 2008

Hello from the world of scabies, babies, and much, much laughter!

Our treatment of the "scabies family," as we now endearingly call them at my house, is going along quite nicely. Actually, we have added two more to the bunch. Upon going to the children's house the other day to let their Auntie know that they will be staying with us for a while we found that baby Cyrus and older sister Falida were also infested with the little bugs. The baby has the worst case by far. So of course, they have also moved in with us. That makes fifteen children in my house. The children with scabies have to be bathed twice a day, my children have to be bathed once a day, everyone has to eat three times a day—that is twenty-three baths and forty-five meals not including me or those who help around the house. It is, without a doubt, a lot of work. But we rejoice

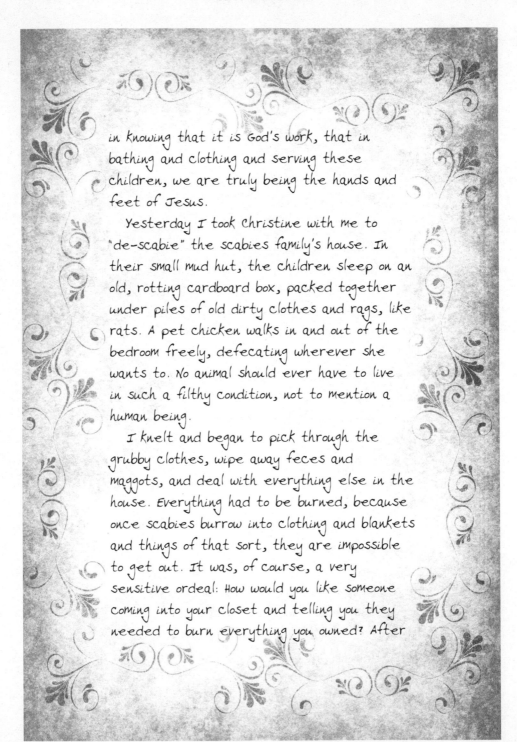

in knowing that it is God's work, that in bathing and clothing and serving these children, we are truly being the hands and feet of Jesus.

Yesterday I took Christine with me to "de-scabie" the scabies family's house. In their small mud hut, the children sleep on an old, rotting cardboard box, packed together under piles of old dirty clothes and rags, like rats. A pet chicken walks in and out of the bedroom freely, defecating wherever she wants to. No animal should ever have to live in such a filthy condition, not to mention a human being.

I knelt and began to pick through the grubby clothes, wipe away feces and maggots, and deal with everything else in the house. Everything had to be burned, because once scabies burrow into clothing and blankets and things of that sort, they are impossible to get out. It was, of course, a very sensitive ordeal: How would you like someone coming into your closet and telling you they needed to burn everything you owned? After

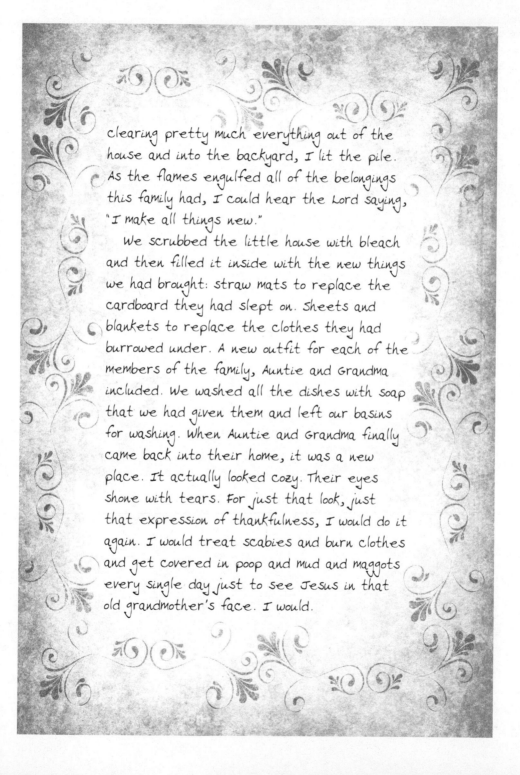

clearing pretty much everything out of the house and into the backyard, I lit the pile. As the flames engulfed all of the belongings this family had, I could hear the Lord saying, "I make all things new."

We scrubbed the little house with bleach and then filled it inside with the new things we had brought: straw mats to replace the cardboard they had slept on. Sheets and blankets to replace the clothes they had burrowed under. A new outfit for each of the members of the family, Auntie and Grandma included. We washed all the dishes with soap that we had given them and left our basins for washing. When Auntie and Grandma finally came back into their home, it was a new place. It actually looked cozy. Their eyes shone with tears. For just that look, just that expression of thankfulness, I would do it again. I would treat scabies and burn clothes and get covered in poop and mud and maggots every single day just to see Jesus in that old grandmother's face. I would.

9

EVERYTHING I NEED

My life became a balancing act. On one side, I was running a small nonprofit organization and needed amounts of money that seemed unfathomable to me. On the other side, I was learning how to be a real mother, even if my motherhood was unconventional. Both aspects were testing and growing my faith in marvelous ways, as I learned to trust God to provide material needs as well as wisdom and courage to parent the precious lives with which He had entrusted me.

I reveled in the opportunities to wipe dirty faces, paint small fingernails, and make balls out of socks so the girls would have something to play with. I didn't feel my life as a mother was much different from the lives of mothers everywhere, except that I prepared eighteen pieces of toast every morning, had seven people splashing me during bath time, and got covered with about 140 good-night kisses at the end of every day.

The seven girls who had become my family had been through so much in their young lives. I wanted to give them the world. But sometimes, when they looked at me with big, curious, expectant eyes, I wondered, *What if I can't?* If being a new mother taught me anything, it was just how inadequate I truly am and just how dependent I am on my Father to give me the strength and grace for each day.

We were, in every way, a normal family, imperfect but perfectly knit together by our Creator. Sometimes my children were late to school because I lit the toast on fire, other days they simply stayed home from school because Mom wanted to play! Sometimes we ran out of food and ate pancakes for dinner. Some days there seemed to be so many people in my house screaming and coloring on the walls and riding the dogs as though they were little horses that I felt I might just collapse. And still, in all my imperfection, their hopeful eyes would look up at me with such love and faith that I could answer their every question.

"Mommy, where does the sun go when I am sleeping?"

"Mommy, are all ladybugs girls?"

"Mommy, where do I go when I die? Do fish go there too?"

"Well, why don't fish breathe air?"

"Mommy, what makes the sky blue?"

"Mommy, why aren't you bald like me?"

"Mommy, why is your skin different from mine?"

Mommy, Mommy, Mommy . . .

One of the questions that surprised me most was this: "Mommy, if Jesus comes to live inside my heart, will I explode?"

"No!" I proclaimed as the children and I headed to the Nile River for a few of them to be baptized that day.

Then I thought about the question a bit more.

"Yes, if Jesus comes to live in your heart, you will explode." That is exactly what we should do if Jesus comes to live inside our hearts. We will explode with love, with compassion, with hurt for those who are hurting, and with joy for those who rejoice. We will explode with a desire to be more, to be better, to be close to the One who made us.

Their beautiful, dependent spirits and their never-ending list of questions reminded me of how inadequate I really was, and reminded me that I was to mirror this dependence and awe in my relationship with the Father. He was, He is everything I need.

Sometimes I sing. Sometimes I dance. Sometimes I laugh and sometimes I cry. And sometimes, I can't explain why I do what I do, except to say that the grace and goodness of God are so big that I can't contain them and the passion overflows. So I told my daughters that day, "Yes, my little ones. Jesus is coming to live inside your heart. Get ready to explode."

I made peace with feeling inadequate because the truth is, I was. I still am; we all are. I quickly became okay with being imperfect. Throughout the Bible, God chose seemingly inadequate people to do His work. Look at Mary, the mother of Christ. She probably wasn't much older, and was perhaps even younger than I, when she became a mother. I'm sure she was no more ready than I was to answer a high-pitched voice when asked all sorts of questions to which she didn't know the answers. But God had called her to parent, and so she did.

When I thought about Mary, I decided not to strive to be a perfect mother but to simply endeavor to be like she was—completely unprepared but ready to take the child God handed to her. Mary's faith was courageous and her obedience was complete. She submitted to God, regardless of the cost or the consequences. She submitted, even if it meant losing her reputation and the man she loved. Or even her life.

Mary was a mother. I am a mother. As long as God keeps giving me these precious children of His, I will continue to love them to the best of my ability. I will be an inadequate, uncertain, loving-with-everything-I-have, filled-with-more-joy-than-I-deserve mother.

God has a way of using inadequate people, and sometimes He calls us to reach a little higher or to stretch a little further, even when we feel we can't do any more. We simply trust Him. And then, He gives us everything we need to do the "more" that He is asking of us. When God asked me to bring another daughter into our family, it didn't matter that I might burn her toast from time to time. All that mattered was that I would love her.

I remember receiving the phone call that one of the children in our sponsorship program had just lost her mother. I raced to the scene. As I entered the room, my eyes scanned the small space until they rested on six-year-old Sarah, curled up on the dirt floor next to the body of her mother, weeping. In the darkness of the crowded mud hut that night, Sarah recognized me as Auntie Katie and crawled into my lap as she listened to her neighbors discuss where she would go now that her mother had passed away.

My heart ached as I held Sarah's hand the next day at her mother's funeral. Her relatives had informed her that she was to come and live with me, and while Sarah had some measure of affection for me as the woman who paid her school fees, I could not imagine that talk of a new mother brought her any comfort as relatives lowered her biological mother into the ground.

As we walked away that day, heading home to our ever-growing family, Sarah hid her eyes behind my oversized white sunglasses and flashed me the first smile I had seen from her in days. A cool breeze blew through the still hot day and my heart burst with compassion for my new little girl.

Sarah was shy and solemn those first few weeks, but slowly she began to show her spunky and inquisitive spirit. Sarah is a child full of playful whimsy and imagination with bright dancing eyes and a beautiful smile. She has a courageous and kind heart and is one of the most creative people I have had the privilege of meeting. Like my other girls, she is wise and independent beyond her years, but never misses a chance to be playful or to burst into joyful song. She is deeply loyal to her family and to God and loving to all she meets.

Sarah fit right into our family and the other girls embraced her with love, compassion, and gladness. Our family was growing at an astounding rate, and every time someone new joined us, my heart became more deeply rooted in Uganda. My growing attachment to my new home produced great tension inside me, because *all* of me wanted to just live in Uganda forever, but that didn't change the fact that I had promised my parents I would return to the United States and attend college.

I realized that I had two perfect lives: a perfect life in America with an amazing family who are my main support system, great friends who encourage and help me, a man with whom I was in love, a great education and the opportunity to continue it, and a future bright and teeming with opportunities.

I also had a perfect life in Uganda with a home, sparsely furnished but full of love and hard work, eight beautiful children who called me mommy, a stunning view of the Nile and God's splendor all around me, situations that stretch me in ways no college could, big dreams, and a future bright and teeming with opportunities. And all the time I wrestled with my two lives, wondering when the day would come when I had to choose just one. I looked around at my daughters' toys littering my room and pictures of loved ones back home posted on my walls, and I realized I had everything I could ever want, it was just in two different places. I knew that if the time came when I had to choose, I would pick this new life God had given me, but I wasn't ready to choose just yet. I wanted to keep my new Ugandan life, but I wanted to keep my American blessings too.

As August approached, I was aghast at the choice I was about to have to make. While it seemed simple enough, the promise I made my parents now ripped my heart in two. When I made it, I had *no idea* I would have a house full of daughters when the time came to fulfill it. No part of me wanted to leave them for any amount of time, but at the same time I did want sincerely to honor my mother and father and keep my promise to them.

God tells us over and over in His Word to obey our parents and I desperately wanted to respect these people who had always supported me and given me everything I needed in life. I did not understand how God could have blessed me with such a perfect new home and family and want me to leave it. I couldn't imagine leaving my children for an extended period of time, so I thought perhaps I could enroll in a university in the States and complete a semester to appease my parents, then finish my degree online from my home in Uganda.

With that "one semester and finish online" idea in my mind, I began to pack for a trip that would carry me a long, long way from my new home for an extended period of time. It was a trip that seemed so difficult I could barely breathe when I thought about it. I struggled enormously as I prepared to leave behind everything I'd grown to love and everyone I'd given my heart to. Even though I was going back to a familiar place with familiar people, and even though it would be for only a few months, everything about the immediate future was unknown. I couldn't imagine being part of the American college scene.

I knew I would return to Uganda as soon as possible, but I didn't know what would happen between now and then. I didn't know what my girls might go through in my absence or what the country might experience while I was away. I wondered what life would look like for the girls without me there with them, and what life would look like for me in a totally different world without the people I loved most. I tried not to think about what I might have to handle long distance, and I certainly couldn't bear thinking of all the times my daughters would go to sleep without a good-night kiss from me or all the times I would do the same without dozens of kisses from them.

In the weeks and days leading up to my departure, I made the best arrangements I could for the girls, our home, and Amazima. I entrusted my most precious people—my daughters—to my friend Melissa, knowing she loved them and they loved her. I also knew Melissa had the skills needed to care for all eight girls and I felt comfortable leaving them in her care—well, as comfortable as I *could* have felt. I left everything pertaining to the house in Christine's capable hands, knowing she would keep things running smoothly at home and maintain a clean, orderly, pleasant environment for the girls. She would also see that everyone had clean clothes and the most nutritious meals we could afford. I asked Oliver to oversee all aspects of Amazima while I was away, confident that she would do an excellent job. In addition, Oliver would drop by our house often to check on the girls.

I communicated emergency contingency plans to trustworthy friends and left emergency funds in a lockbox. I didn't know what else to do, on a practical level, to prepare to leave. But I don't think I ever could have prepared emotionally. I thought about the fact that several of the girls had lived without a mother for a period of time. Some had hardly known their mothers, others knew their mothers well enough to still feel the fresh pain of losing them. And now I was leaving. They would be loved and well cared for, but in a very real sense, they would also be motherless again. It was *so* hard on them, and it made me feel sick just to think about it.

The night before I left, the girls insisted that I sleep in their room. They simply wanted to be near me for as long as possible before our lengthy separation. I slept in a twin bed with little Scovia and all of us awoke at 5:00 A.M. so I could get ready to leave for the airport. It was a grueling early morning with many tears.

Several weeks earlier, when I answered yes to the question about our hearts exploding when Jesus comes to live inside them, I meant that figuratively. Now I had the feeling my heart might actually explode not because Jesus lives in it, but because of the intensity of the pain and grief I felt over leaving my daughters for months at a time. When the moment came for me to walk out of my house, to a car waiting to drive me to the airport, my heart indeed felt as if it was going to erupt and shatter. I had no choice but to trust that Jesus was in there, holding my heart together.

With travel arrangements made, a plane to catch, suitcases in hand, and clothes wet with tears from my girls, I had never faced a moment of surrender like I did when I climbed into the car to leave. It was the hardest moment of my life to that point. In simplest terms, I was going to the airport about three hours' drive from my home. But in reality I was embarking on an agonizing journey of blind faith and pure trust.

The road out of my village is bumpy. A driver has to navigate pot-holes like an obstacle course to get from my house to the main road that goes to Kampala and on to the airport at Entebbe. The farther away I got from home, the more my trust had to increase. I kept wondering if the Lord really would be everything I needed for this new and uncertain phase of my life. I couldn't imagine that my heart had the capacity for any more trust, but with every passing mile, I found that it did.

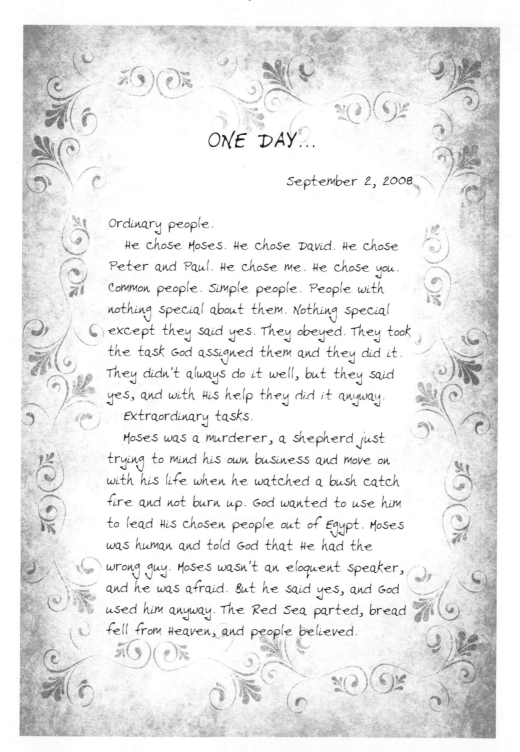

ONE DAY...

September 2, 2008

Ordinary people.

He chose Moses. He chose David. He chose Peter and Paul. He chose me. He chose you. Common people. Simple people. People with nothing special about them. Nothing special except they said yes. They obeyed. They took the task God assigned them and they did it. They didn't always do it well, but they said yes, and with His help they did it anyway.

Extraordinary tasks.

Moses was a murderer, a shepherd just trying to mind his own business and move on with his life when he watched a bush catch fire and not burn up. God wanted to use him to lead His chosen people out of Egypt. Moses was human and told God that He had the wrong guy. Moses wasn't an eloquent speaker, and he was afraid. But he said yes, and God used him anyway. The Red Sea parted, bread fell from Heaven, and people believed.

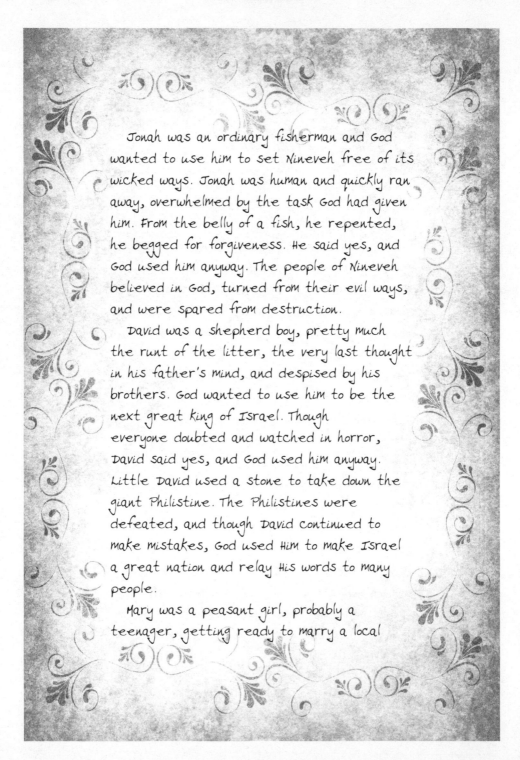

Jonah was an ordinary fisherman and God wanted to use him to set Nineveh free of its wicked ways. Jonah was human and quickly ran away, overwhelmed by the task God had given him. From the belly of a fish, he repented, he begged for forgiveness. He said yes, and God used him anyway. The people of Nineveh believed in God, turned from their evil ways, and were spared from destruction.

David was a shepherd boy, pretty much the runt of the litter, the very last thought in his father's mind, and despised by his brothers. God wanted to use him to be the next great king of Israel. Though everyone doubted and watched in horror, David said yes, and God used him anyway. Little David used a stone to take down the giant Philistine. The Philistines were defeated, and though David continued to make mistakes, God used Him to make Israel a great nation and relay His words to many people.

Mary was a peasant girl, probably a teenager, getting ready to marry a local

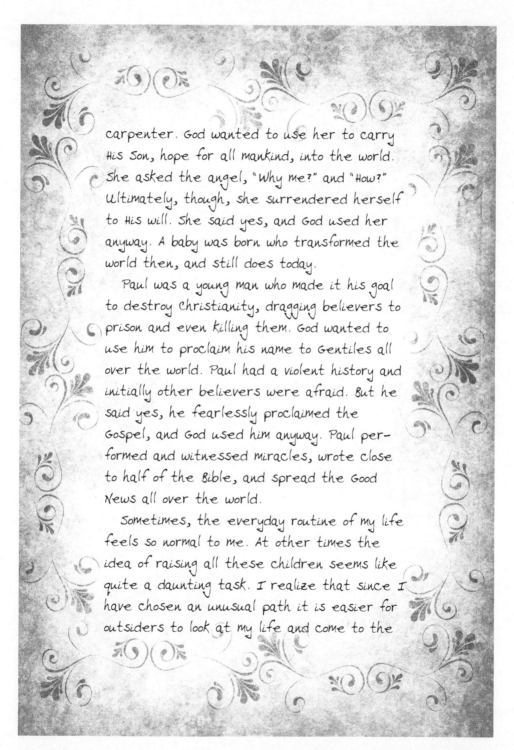

carpenter. God wanted to use her to carry His Son, hope for all mankind, into the world. She asked the angel, "Why me?" and "How?" Ultimately, though, she surrendered herself to His will. She said yes, and God used her anyway. A baby was born who transformed the world then, and still does today.

Paul was a young man who made it his goal to destroy Christianity, dragging believers to prison and even killing them. God wanted to use him to proclaim his name to Gentiles all over the world. Paul had a violent history and initially other believers were afraid. But he said yes, he fearlessly proclaimed the Gospel, and God used him anyway. Paul performed and witnessed miracles, wrote close to half of the Bible, and spread the Good News all over the world.

Sometimes, the everyday routine of my life feels so normal to me. At other times the idea of raising all these children seems like quite a daunting task. I realize that since I have chosen an unusual path it is easier for outsiders to look at my life and come to the

conclusion that it is something extraordinary. That I am courageous. That I am strong. That I am special. But I am just a plain girl from Tennessee. Broken in many ways, sinful, and inadequate. Common and simple with nothing special about me. Nothing special except I choose to say "yes." "Yes" to the things God asks of me and "yes" to the people He places in front of me. You can too. I am just an ordinary person. An ordinary person serving an extraordinary God.

10

A PROMISE TO KEEP

As my plane made its way around the world from Uganda to Nashville, I could not forget the scene that took place at my house the night before I left for the United States. Agnes, age ten, pleaded with me, "Mom, don't go to America to work and make money for us. Don't go to school so you can get a job. Stay here. We will just eat grass if we don't have money. Yes, that is what we will do. We don't need money. See?"

And she ran outside and ate a handful of grass.

Then she made a face that told me that maybe she wanted to rethink that plan. But how sweet to think that she would rather eat grass than be apart from me. I believe, had I been able to stay and love on my children every single day, I too would have been content to eat grass for the rest of my life.

But there I was, in the United States. Somehow, despite my desire to get back to Uganda, God allowed a peace that transcends all understanding to flood my soul. In the depths of my spirit, I knew all would be well with my girls. He assured me over and over that my children would be okay. Over the next months, He taught me that they were never really mine to begin with; they were simply gifts with which He had graced me. They were His. Even though my heart ached to know that I could not touch them for a while, He assured me that they would never be out of His loving embrace.

I'm sure people thought I would feel at home immediately once I arrived at my parents' house. But this simply wasn't true. I felt completely out of place, much as I had the last time I had made a visit, but this time I knew my trip would be longer; so the feeling was worse. I felt deeply conflicted because I so wanted to honor my parents and their request for me to attend college and, at the same time, I was devastated over being so far away from my girls. Though I had only parented them for a short time, the mother's love in my heart was true and God given, and a mother should never have to be so separated from her children.

I'd like to say that I was nice, polite, pleasant, and graceful about my transition back to the United States—just as a person who loves Jesus so much should be. But I wasn't. In fact, once I arrived on American soil, I was grumpy and miserable quite a bit of the time. With certain people, I struggled to have even a normal conversation without sobbing.

I tried to be "okay." I really did. I know many people, including my parents, thought I wasn't trying, but I was; I was truly doing my best. I wish now that in doing my best, I had been nicer to my parents, my brother, and my boyfriend. I also wish I'd been nicer to my roommate, a good friend from high school with whom I shared an apartment near the local university I was attending. But unfortunately, the people closest to me caught the greatest force of my sadness and frustration. In trying to do my best, I was at my all-time worst.

I tried to go to parties. I threw parties; I was really good at that in high school. I went to the gym. I did homework. I went out dancing and on dates with my boyfriend. I really tried to be the person I was before I went to Uganda, healthy and happy and well-adjusted and normal in America. But I wasn't that person anymore, and while everyone else still expected me to fit in, *I didn't.*

Not long after I arrived in the States, I poured out my heart about feeling like a stranger in my native land in my journal, and I came to a better understanding of why I felt I didn't belong there.

I have often wondered since reentering the United States why I feel such great culture shock. How can I feel such a disconnect with the place I was born, raised, and for eighteen years called home? How can I feel that my real home is a place in which I have spent just over a year? I have blamed it on many things.

American extravagance.

The grocery store that almost sends me into panic mode due to the sheer quantity and variety of foods.

People who build million-dollar homes.

The lack of understanding and a lack of thanksgiving on the part of all of us.

The ease with which we receive medical care.

The amount of stuff that just clutters our lives.

All these things make it difficult to readjust, yes. But what has been the biggest shock to my system, the huge disconnect, is that I have stepped out of my reliance on God to meet my needs. I "miss" Jesus. He hasn't disappeared, of course, but I feel so far from Him because my life is actually functioning without Him. By "functioning," I mean that if I am sick, I go to the drugstore or to the doctor. If I am hungry, I go to the grocery store. If I need to go somewhere, I get in my car. When I need some advice or guidance, I call my mom or go plop on my roommate's bed. If I want to feel happy, I get Brad, my little brother, or someone else to make me laugh.

I keep forgetting to ask God first to heal me, to fill me, to guide me, to rejoice with me. I have to set aside "time to pray" in the morning and at night instead of being in constant communication with Him. In Uganda, because I was so physically "poor," I was completely dependent on God and spiritually as wealthy as ever. As I sit here writing, I am frustrated with my own stupidity, my human willingness to step back into dependence on stuff and these places I swore I detested.

God blessed me, though, with a few people who really did "get" it, including the May family and my friends Gwen and Suzanne. The only times I was really "okay" during the whole time I was in America were when I was with the Mays, a family I worked for at the time. My job was to care for their terminally ill little boy, Dylan. Not only did I genuinely love Dylan and his family, taking care of him and helping them was the only experience that made me feel I was being useful or doing anything important. Of course, I now see that this wasn't true. Being kind to my roommate and showing Jesus to the people around me was important. But I think I was too angry with God for instructing me to obey my parents and then allowing me to fall in love with something totally different to realize that I could serve Him in useful, fulfilling ways, right where I was. I never want to forget this again.

One truth I did realize, though, was something I really thought I already knew. I did know it, on some level, but my time in America drilled it into me in a whole new way. I came to understand and believe with more passion than ever that God is in control. I mean absolute, complete, sovereign control. It sounds like a basic principle of the Christian faith, but many times people who say these words use them to encourage someone else. Sometimes it's much harder to embrace the fact that God is in control when *you* are the one with the terrible diagnosis, the empty bank account, and no job, the drug-addicted son or daughter, or all your children and the ministry you love are in Africa while you are in America.

I had to tell myself over and over again, "God is really in control." I felt as though I lived in a vacuum of aloneness and impossibility. Most people saw me as a nineteen-year-old college student. But I didn't look like, feel like, or understand what it meant to be a college student. I felt like a small, young woman who had eight children in Uganda and 150 young minds I was helping to educate there—and that's the life I understood. But few people around me seemed to be able to grasp it.

People asked me how I would provide for my family long distance as a nursing major, taking nineteen hours of courses and working fifteen hours per week. I could only offer my standard answer: "God will provide." That simple, honest answer had always proven true. Christians say this often, but sometimes we don't understand the full truth of it.

I knew exactly what "God will provide" meant. It meant that on any given day, just when I needed it, a check for $1,000 would arrive in the mail so I could pay the rent on my house and pay salaries for my employees. It meant that the next week, He would inspire someone to send a check that would help with the electric bill and that just as we ran out of food, someone would send money to help stock the cupboard again.

I found it strange when people looked doubtfully at me when I said "God will provide." I knew He would; I'd seen Him do it. I wasn't naive; I was simply dependent on a God who loved my children and employees more than I did.

People also asked me if I felt overwhelmed, and that became one of my least favorite questions. If I said "Yes," they inevitably followed up with "Then why don't you scale back?" And while I tried to answer nicely with my mouth, my brain said: "I'm raising a family and loving children with all my heart. I'm not running a business, so I can't just 'make some cuts.'" I'm sure everyone who suggested I lighten my load meant well, but I sometimes wonder what they would have said had I recommended that *they* simply discard one of *their* children.

Several people really did understand. My mother, who was nice to me when I was not nice in return and who did my laundry when I was too stressed out to thank her, understood. My roommate, who did my grocery shopping so I would have something to eat, understood. The May family, who invited me into their home, insisted I stay to eat dinner with their family and listened to me talk about my girls for hours on end, always promising to pray for us, understood. Gwen and Suzanne, who loved orphans and adoption and helped advocate for me and Amazima, understood. I knew that although lots of people didn't understand, I was enormously blessed because certain people did.

Nevertheless, the huge aloneness I felt continued to dog me. God was filling it slowly, but carefully, with people who cared. He sent me not only several families who understood but others who were happy to pay a water bill so my house in Uganda could continue to provide showers and clean drinking water for the village. He made sure that, just when I thought my heart would crumble with longing for my children, I received a phone call from a small chocolate-colored person who missed me and was eagerly awaiting my return. He provided for my every need and proved time and time again, in the most amazing ways, that He is in control.

One weekend, I especially needed to be reminded that God was in control. For a split second, my world was shattered. My best friend, who was studying to be an accountant, asked to take a look at Amazima's finances. As she and I saw it, this was a great opportunity for her to practice her accounting skills and I considered it a blessing to have someone who knew more than I did review our financial situation.

My friend was dumbfounded. She simply couldn't figure out how the ministry had stayed afloat. From an accounting perspective, and based on basic human logic, it simply didn't work. Out of 150 children who needed to go to school, only forty-four were sponsored. That meant the other 106 were going to school with fees paid by donations or from my personal savings account. At that time, in October, I still owed the schools in Uganda $8,000 to finish the term that would end in December. I also owed the next month's rent on my house.

My friend asked, carefully, how on earth I thought I could keep the ministry going and send the children to school in 2009 if I couldn't even finish paying for 2008, when I didn't have money for rent or other overhead expenses. My very unbusinesslike answer was, "So far we've made ends meet. The money just always shows up by the end of the month." I think she wanted to laugh at me, but I love her for not doing so.

She went on to explain to me, as others including my wise father had tried to do, that continuing to run the ministry as I had been doing was not possible. I would have to cut back; and only the forty-four children who had sponsors would be able to attend school in 2009. My friend suggested that whatever money came into the ministry for the remainder of 2008 go toward paying the remaining balances on the school fees and reasoned that we should build up some savings and then resume sending the other children to school.

The thought of telling 106 children I loved that they could no longer go to school—and also telling them I could no longer feed them or provide their medical care—was something I couldn't even imagine. I held my composure until my friend left and then broke down in tears.

That's when God grabbed my attention. The light came on and I remembered: I never chose these 150 children; God gave them to me. I never planned to send them all to school; He did. It wasn't Katie carrying out Katie's plan; it was the Lord, for whom all things, *all things*, are possible. I could envision Him chuckling at me, saying: "Oh, you of little faith! Ask anything in my name and it will be given to you!"

I had become so concerned about how I would continue to provide for the children that I forgot I wasn't even the one who was supposed to do it. I'd been so busy working to raise money that I forgot to ask God for it. I literally fell to my knees that day and said: "I am not cutting back. I am not going to tell 106 children that they won't be going to school next year."

All I had to do was look at what happened the previous year. Had God ever failed to provide exactly what was needed? No. Why, then, would I ever believe He would fail to provide now, even though I was living in America?

Still on my knees, I asked God to forgive me for wondering whether He would come through for us or not. Of course He would. In the days following, I fasted and prayed fervently for His continued provision. We needed a total of $70,000 to pay off the debt from 2008, send all the children to school in 2009, and have enough money left to feed them, pay rent, cover overhead, and provide for their medical needs. Within a matter of weeks, thirteen more children had been sponsored, three new fund-raising dinners were arranged, and friends began to rally around me and ask, without being prompted, what they could do to help. Gwen and Suzanne were some of the first to volunteer and were tireless in their efforts and enthusiasm. I did nothing but pray and believe God wanted to be involved in the life to which He called me. Nothing was impossible; no request was too big or too small.

After I prayed and surrendered this situation to the Lord, He began to do miracles. It was as though magical floodgates of provision were opened. Within a few months, we had the $70,000 we needed— and then some.

Maybe I wasn't comfortable in America; maybe I didn't fit in. But God hadn't left me there to fend for myself. He was with me and He was doing incredible things to keep the work going in Uganda while I was away.

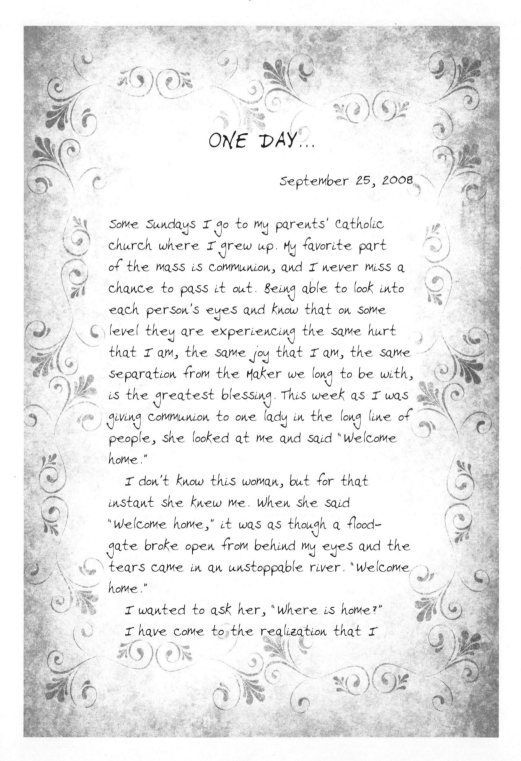

ONE DAY...

September 25, 2008

Some Sundays I go to my parents' Catholic church where I grew up. My favorite part of the mass is communion, and I never miss a chance to pass it out. Being able to look into each person's eyes and know that on some level they are experiencing the same hurt that I am, the same joy that I am, the same separation from the Maker we long to be with, is the greatest blessing. This week as I was giving communion to one lady in the long line of people, she looked at me and said "Welcome home."

I don't know this woman, but for that instant she knew me. When she said "Welcome home," it was as though a floodgate broke open from behind my eyes and the tears came in an unstoppable river. "Welcome home."

I wanted to ask her, "Where is home?" I have come to the realization that I

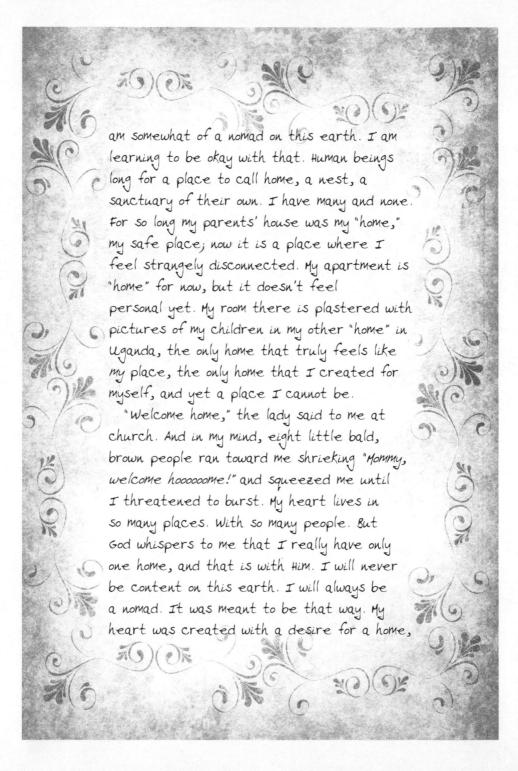

am somewhat of a nomad on this earth. I am
learning to be okay with that. Human beings
long for a place to call home, a nest, a
sanctuary of their own. I have many and none.
For so long my parents' house was my "home,"
my safe place; now it is a place where I
feel strangely disconnected. My apartment is
"home" for now, but it doesn't feel
personal yet. My room there is plastered with
pictures of my children in my other "home" in
Uganda, the only home that truly feels like
my place, the only home that I created for
myself, and yet a place I cannot be.

"Welcome home," the lady said to me at
church. And in my mind, eight little bald,
brown people ran toward me shrieking "Mommy,
welcome hooooome!" and squeezed me until
I threatened to burst. My heart lives in
so many places. With so many people. But
God whispers to me that I really have only
one home, and that is with Him. I will never
be content on this earth. I will always be
a nomad. It was meant to be that way. My
heart was created with a desire for a home,

a nest, a sanctuary, and that can be found only with Him in Heaven. And I will continue bouncing from one home to another, loving with everything I have in whatever location I currently reside, excitedly awaiting the day when I am called heavenward and He says to me, "Welcome home."

11

LIVING THE SECRET

I turned twenty one Sunday in early November and spent part of my birthday marveling at the last year of my life. Between nineteen and twenty, I learned to be a teacher, a nurse, a handyman (plumbing and electrical work included), a cook, an exterminator, a maid, a servant, a mentor, a mother, and, most important, a daughter of the King.

My gracious Father created for me a home with adoring children and began a rapidly growing ministry helping His people. While my hands had done some of the physical work involved in these endeavors, I actually accomplished none of it. People often asked me then as they do now, "How do you do it?" The answer has never changed and it is so simple: I don't. It's just a little bit of coffee and a whole lot of Jesus. This plan, these "accomplishments," they are *so* not my own.

I am *dependent*.

Powerless.

Weak.

Drowning.

While those adjectives may sound scary, they put me in a beautiful place, a place where I couldn't go one minute without crying out to my Father or I would sink. I remember being so grateful for that place, and I still am. Paul says in his letter to the Philippians that he "knows the secret." He has been well fed and he has been starving; he has lived in abundance and he has lived with nothing. His revelation? That he could do all things through Christ who strengthens (see Philippians 4:13).

I was learning that the powerless, broken, dependent place was actually the place where the Lord was closest to me.

At times, while I was attending college in the United States, I wished I were still living in the hungry, needy circumstances in which I lived in Uganda. Sometimes I felt it was easier to cling to Jesus in that state of having nothing than it was to cling to Him while surrounded by the abundance of America. Although I was not physically hungry or in need, my soul was thirstier than ever. And Paul's secret remained true: I couldn't do anything, but as I let the Lord strengthen me, I knew there was nothing He could not accomplish through me. I could hardly wait to see what would happen between twenty and twenty-one.

As Thanksgiving break approached, I stayed busy with school, work, and fund-raising for my growing ministry in Uganda. Plans for the ministry continued to unfold. Thanksgiving melted into Christmas, but while everyone around me was busy with lights, decorations, and gifts, I was desperately missing the other half of my family in Uganda and my mind was fixed on getting back to them. My semester in college, in my estimation, had been a disaster. I'm not saying God didn't use it; I made wonderful friends and raised lots of funds to continue doing what God had started in Uganda. I'm simply saying that college wasn't for me; Uganda was for me.

I'd tried college; one semester was enough. I simply couldn't live with my body in one country and my soul in another. And yet *I wanted to*. I wanted to figure out how to honor both my earthly father and my heavenly Father. The battle within me was agonizing.

A scripture I had memorized for years kept creeping into my heart and mind: "No servant can serve two masters" (Luke 16:13). In context, the verse pertains to serving God versus money, but I realized as I read that I could not serve God's eternal purpose and man's earthly desires. I couldn't fulfill both God's call on my life and my parents' desire for me to secure a "normal, successful future" with a college degree.

I didn't hate college or America; I just so desperately missed my new home and family. And as much as I reveled in my life, ministry, and motherhood in a village in Uganda, I also had moments when I wanted to live near my family and marry my high school boyfriend. I didn't want to give up everything I'd grown to love in Uganda; I wanted that—with a few American blessings added to it. But the reality is, no one can serve two masters. To follow Jesus, we have to make choices. Sometimes, making those choices is *anguish*.

Looking back, I now believe that during my time in the States, I was trying my best to live a life God did not intend me to live. I wanted to obey my earthly parents, but what they expected of me did not line up with what the heavenly Father asked me to do. While in the United States, I was not where God had asked me to be. I was not in the center of God's will, and that is a dark place.

This is not to say that my time in the States was not necessary or that God didn't bless it. He did, more than I could have ever asked or imagined. He put just the right people in just the right places. Some of them simply helped me get through every day on a practical level; some helped me fund-raise; and some, like my brother, Brad, my boyfriend, and my girlfriends, just helped me hold up my head, even though they didn't understand. God allowed me to do important and necessary fund- and awareness-raising during my time in the United States, and much of that work still helps fund the ministry today.

God taught me, over and over, that it did not matter what the world said, that it did not matter that almost none of the people closest to me believed in what I was doing or believed it would succeed, that it did not matter what they said was impossible, because God did this, and He was going to continue doing it.

I didn't realize then, but I strongly believe now that there is a common misconception that whatever happens to us is the will of God. It's as though we think: *Okay, I can do whatever I want and God will either do something or He won't and that will be His will. It will all work out. It will all happen just like it needs to.* I don't believe this anymore. I believe that God is in control, yes, but I also believe I have a choice: I can follow Him or I can turn my back on Him. I can say yes to Him, or I can say no. I can go to the hard places or I can remain comfortable. And if I remain comfortable, God who loves us unconditionally will continue to love me anyway. I may still see His glory revealed in my life and recognize His blessings, but not like I could have. I *can* miss the will of God. The rich young ruler certainly did. He didn't fall dead, as Ananias and Sapphira did; and maybe he went on to live a great life, but it wasn't the life he could have lived had he said yes to what Jesus was asking of him.

I don't ever want to miss God's will again. God grew me tremendously during my time in the States. He taught me many lessons and He never let go of my hand. But He also revealed to me more and more each day that this was *not* what He had for me. I don't want to miss what He has for me. Ever, ever again.

In Luke 14:26, Jesus says to His followers, "If anyone comes to me and does not hate his father and mother, his wife and children, his brothers and sisters—yes, even his own life—he cannot be my disciple." Obviously, this verse doesn't mean I was to literally detest my parents. But it means that I was to love God *so* much that my love for my parents and anyone else looked small, even like hatred. It means I was to so want to follow Him that I would leave all the things I loved, even if doing so made it appear that I hated these things. It means to me that I should have valued nothing even close to the degree to which I valued His plan for my life and His love for me. And that's where I landed.

I chose to value His plan, His calling, and His love over everything else. *Everything.* I *had* to be reunited with my heart and God's purpose; I had to get back to Uganda, not temporarily, but for the rest of my life.

With my parents' reluctant blessing, I didn't register for university courses after Christmas. Instead, I bought a one-way ticket back to Uganda.

ONE DAY...

December 29, 2008

"Remember, God will never give you more than you can handle."

People repeat this frequently; I heard it when I was growing up and I hear it now. It is meant to be a source of encouragement, and it would be if I believed it were true.

But I don't.

I believe that God totally, absolutely, intentionally gives us more than we can handle. Because this is when we surrender to Him and He takes over, proving Himself by doing the impossible in our lives.

This past year, God has given me eight more children than I can handle. He has given me an impossible number of dollars to raise to meet this need that He placed on my heart. He has asked me to do things I thought would surely break me.

God gave me a family and a home that I didn't expect; and once I had completely

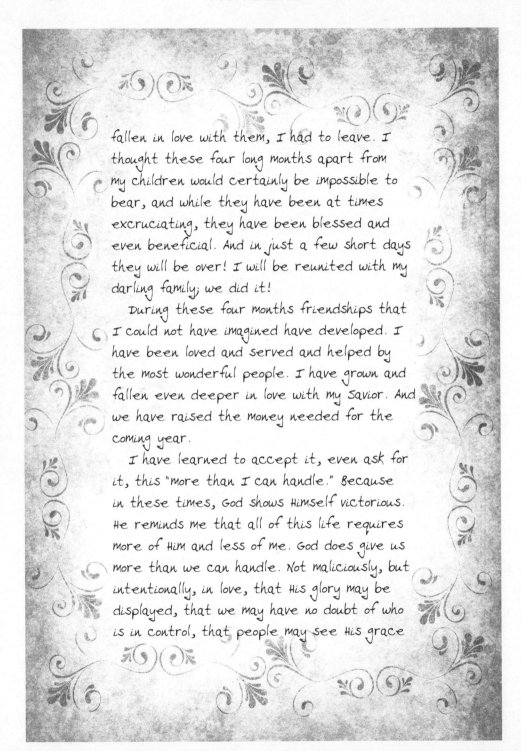

fallen in love with them, I had to leave. I thought these four long months apart from my children would certainly be impossible to bear, and while they have been at times excruciating, they have been blessed and even beneficial. And in just a few short days they will be over! I will be reunited with my darling family; we did it!

During these four months friendships that I could not have imagined have developed. I have been loved and served and helped by the most wonderful people. I have grown and fallen even deeper in love with my Savior. And we have raised the money needed for the coming year.

I have learned to accept it, even ask for it, this "more than I can handle." Because in these times, God shows Himself victorious. He reminds me that all of this life requires more of Him and less of me. God does give us more than we can handle. Not maliciously, but intentionally, in love, that His glory may be displayed, that we may have no doubt of who is in control, that people may see His grace

and faithfulness shining through our lives.

And as I surrender these situations to Him, watch Him take over and do the impossible, I am filled with joy and peace—so much more than I can handle.

12

A GLIMPSE OF HEAVEN

My taxi from Entebbe airport jostled its way down the bumpy road to my house. A short distance from home, I felt the jolt as people jumped on it from all sides. My children! I could hardly open the door of the taxi to climb out and greet them for all the excitement. Once I did, I couldn't keep my balance because my ecstatic girls were squeezing me, kissing me, and clamoring all over one another. We ran and skipped and jumped down the road, all the way home, with a most bewildered taxi driver following us.

I'd been away from Uganda for only four months, but it felt like a lifetime. I didn't have words to adequately express the deep joy I felt over being home. It was as if I could finally breathe again.

My family had grown again, about a week before I returned from the States. I received a call one day, letting me know that Prossy and Margaret had a biological sister named Hellen, who was eight years old and lived in an orphanage not far from our home. The three girls had never lived together and had seen each other only a few times, but I could not bear the thought of this young girl living so close to, yet isolated from, her sisters. Christine went to the orphanage and inquired about Hellen, then brought her to live at our house just before I came home.

Tall, bright-eyed, and easygoing, Hellen bounced into our lives a perfect fit, as if she had always been a part of the family. Hellen is naive and charming. She trusts quickly and loves deeply. Free-spirited, spunky, and outgoing, she is quick to make friends and to make people laugh with her expressiveness and animation. Hellen is stubborn and strong willed but almost always full of joy and was a delightful addition to our family.

On the night of my return, no one in our house could settle down. Everything about our home and all the people in it pulsed with excitement and happiness. After midnight, the girls all piled into my bed and sleep finally began to claim them, one by one. I was the last person awake and though completely exhausted, I lay under my mosquito net, smiling at the thought of their unbridled enthusiasm when they saw me.

"Mommy! Mommy! Mommy! Welcome home!" they shouted.

This must be a glimpse of heaven, I mused. *The angels shouting our names and Jesus saying "Welcome home."*

With that thought, I drifted off to sleep.

I couldn't have been happier to awaken in my own bed the next morning. The girls and I immediately fell back into our old routine, which, on that day, meant I made twenty-eight pieces of cinnamon toast for breakfast. I reveled in the chance to bathe nine little girls, rub lotion into their beautiful brown skin, change sheets, do laundry, mop floors, jump rope, dance, sing, and color, smiling my way through every activity of the day. By dinnertime all of us were still in our pajamas, and we ended the day by watching *Charlotte's Web.* The girls thought the idea of a talking pig was the most hysterical thing and we literally fell asleep laughing.

I spent the next few weeks walking around the six villages our program serves, visiting our children and even adding some. Visiting the villages is always pure joy for me. I relish being surrounded by the raw human need that seems to be on display everywhere, a true reminder of our immense need for a God and Savior. I stand in awe of the gratitude and happiness people express over their simple lives. Their neediness keeps them so dependent on God, and among them I always feel so very close to His heart. After four months in the "clean" culture of the United States, I was thrilled to be sweaty and dirty, with dozens of filthy hands pulling my arms in opposing directions. My heart thrived in the humble villages and huts of Uganda. "Welcome home, Katie," I said to myself.

While in the States I had raised enough money to add a few more children to our program (miraculously, we even had the $70,000 we needed to keep the program going for another year). We grew from sponsoring 156 children to sponsoring 202. Two hundred two precious young ones who have experienced more hurt and hardship than I can imagine; 202 children Jesus knows by name and delights to call "Mine." As the money came in, I sent word to Oliver to be looking for the children who most desperately needed the help we could provide. The school year in Uganda begins in February, so I wanted the assessments of the families done and the children signed up for the program as soon as possible.

When we assess a family to consider sponsorship for their children, we collect basic information such as the number of people in the family, how many of those people are children, and whether the primary caregiver is capable of holding a job or not (some caregivers are quite elderly or ill). We also determine whether they have electricity, access to clean water, and food to eat. Our goal at Amazima is to provide services to the neediest children, so part of our assessment includes verifying that the family genuinely needs our help.

Near the end of January, within the first two weeks I was back in Uganda, the time came to distribute school supplies to the children in our program. Eager children came to receive their supplies the way some people would receive gold or jewels. We gave out 1,740 books, 864 pencils, 54 rulers, protractors, and erasers, 100 boxes of colored pencils, 220 toothbrushes and tubes of toothpaste, 1,100 bars of soap, and 568 rolls of toilet paper.

I was amazed as I looked at those who had been in our program for the past year. They looked much healthier and happier. They were stronger, cleaner, and in most cases children who now knew Jesus. And I knew that the children joining us for the first time would, a year from now, look much different from the way they looked that day. The sight of beautiful children from extreme poverty, children filled with such potential who had made so much progress, gave me a renewed sense of purpose and energy.

One of my favorite mornings after I returned to Uganda began when my three oldest daughters, Margaret, Prossy, and Agnes, marched into my room, where I was still sleeping. "Mommy, there are children we need to help, please."

"Okay," I said groggily, "where?"

They took me to the abandoned house down the road. In the back room were seven children on the dirt floor. They were completely filthy and starving. The oldest was eleven and the youngest was two years old. I had never seen children so sick, and I have seen some *very* sick children. They all had severe ringworm, malaria, and scabies (my favorite), among other conditions. Two of them were the skinniest human beings I had ever seen. I would estimate that both were about four and a half feet tall and about thirty-five pounds.

Of course, the girls and I took them home. I have never been so proud of my family as I was when I watched their reaction. Prossy, Margaret, and Agnes went straight to the tub to give the children baths. Mary combed their hair while Hellen and Sumini rubbed lotion on them. (By this time, we weren't afraid of scabies anymore!) Scovia made tea. Sarah and Joyce went to their room, sifted through their clothes, and chose a new outfit for each of the children. In less than an hour, our seven neighbors were a new bunch of children— bathed, dressed, fed, and giggling.

Margaret looked at me with a twinkle in her eye and said, "Mommy, I love these children."

"Me too, Margaret," I said quietly.

This is what it looks like, I thought. *In so many places, we sit in church and talk about compassion, unimaginable love, revival. And then an hour later, we are* still sitting there *talking about it. But revival is happening.* Now. *Compassion is working; unimaginable, selfless love is real. It is right here. My five-year-old knows how to be Jesus' hands to others. I can stand and watch the children I have loved and cared for turn around and compassionately love and care for others.*

This was one of many, many times I have watched my children embrace and welcome into our home strangers and people in need. Every time, they amaze me with their care and compassion. Today, my family claims the unwanted and unloved for Him who loves us all. How beautiful it is to watch the unwanted feel loved and important, to watch strangers become family members.

By that time, I knew that God filled my heart in moments like those to prepare me for the next moment. Leaving my thoughts behind as I helped the smallest child, a little girl named Jane, my recently filled heart shattered and my mind went to work again: *She doesn't belong to anyone. No one will claim her. How can no one want this darling baby? But God does. She is a child of the King. She belongs to a wonderful Maker, and yesterday and today, as I lay her in my bed, she belongs to me.*

The next morning, I wrote in my journal the thoughts I struggled with after putting Jane to bed that night and about my great God, who spoke just the words I needed to hear.

Sunday, January 25, 2009

I don't sleep. Last night I put seven beautiful, sick little people from the abandoned house down the road to bed in my house and it hit me like a brick: They need a mom. My initial response was, of course, "Okay. I can do that."

And then I thought about it. Whoa. Uh-oh. Umm, God, please don't ask me to be their mom. I mean, really? If having nine children is crazy, what is having sixteen? Nope. I can't do it. Really. I even don't think I have the energy to bathe and feed them all every day, God. I won't be able to put them through school, not even in Uganda.

Ah, yes, I would like to proclaim that I always trust in God's perfect plan for my life and I always turn everything over to God, knowing that His peace surpasses all understanding, but here is the truth of it: I freaked out. I said, "God, if you ask me to be their mom, I won't do it. No." And then that didn't feel very appreciative of someone who died for me, so I said, "Okay, God, if you want me to be their mom, I want a dishwasher. Oh, and a bus." After about an hour of this conversation, which took place aloud as I lay on the floor next to my bed, I came to my senses and decided to get into the Word (duh).

And here is what God said to me:

It's okay to be human. I created you, I understand. Do not be afraid; do not be terrified. I am the LORD your God and I will go with you wherever you go. I will never leave nor forsake you (see Deuteronomy 31:6). Remember that my Word says you would be hard-pressed on every side, but never crushed; perplexed but not in despair, persecuted but never abandoned, discouraged but never destroyed (see 2 Corinthians 4:8-9). When you try to save your own life, your own desires, you will lose. But when you decide to put aside your desires, to lose your life for me, you will find it (see Matthew 16:25). Rest in my perfect peace. Trust me with all your heart and I will direct your path (see Proverbs 3:5-6). Sometimes I test your faith, daughter, because it develops perseverance in you, which you need to be mature and complete, not lacking in anything (see James 1:2-4). I know how much you hurt for these children; I hurt for them more. In the world you will have trouble, but take heart! *I have overcome the world* (see John 16:33). Never be lacking in zeal, but keep your spiritual fervor serving me, your Father. Be joyful in hope, patient in affliction, and faithful in prayer. Continue to offer my hospitality to people in need and let me take care of the rest (see Romans 12:11-13).

Of course. According to Suzanne, who called after a few very frantic text messages, it's okay to freak out every now and then.

Today the freaking out is over and though I still have no idea exactly what is going to happen, I do know what I am going to do. I am going to live day by day because today, this moment, is all I am promised. So I am going to bathe and feed and love these children,

nurse them back to health and wait in hope
as I watch God's perfect plan for their lives
unfold. I am going to pray over them every
night and I am going to pray for a mother, an
auntie, someone to love on the children. God
will not leave them as orphans.

After a few weeks of having the children stay with us, we were able to make contact with their parents, who had been away looking for work. The parents were desperate to be able to care for their children, but they could not find jobs in our area. Because their financial situation was grim, they certainly couldn't afford to pay someone to keep the children while they searched for work. When they returned, they were so thankful to find that their children had been looked after. They wanted to parent these boys and girls but still had very little money with which to provide for all the children's needs. I quickly agreed to put them in Amazima's sponsorship program so the parents could continue to love and care for their children without a huge financial burden. What a blessing it is to be able to tell parents that they *can* indeed continue to parent their children even if they lack the financial resources to do so.

Jane, the youngest child, was the only child of the seven who was not a biological child of these parents. She was the daughter of the wife's estranged brother and her parents had run away when she was just a few months old. The family wanted to find someone to care for her, as six children already felt overwhelming to them. I really wanted them to be able to parent their own children without feeling overwhelmed. Since they both worked in a factory during the day while their older children were in school, they had no one to care for two-year-old Jane, so I offered to keep her while we tried to locate her biological mother and father.

After about a month of searching, the police declared Jane abandoned and we decided to move forward with her adoption and make her part of our family. Jane was the most lovable two-and-a-half-year-old I had ever met, and she is still a cuddler today. She is a born leader, now protecting and looking out for her new younger sisters everywhere we go. Even at four years old, she is incredibly loyal and has a beautiful, compassionate heart. She is mommy's little helper, loving any task assigned to her that makes her feel "big." She is also my little songbird, singing and dancing through each day.

Children just kept coming. Not only did little Jane become a joyful member of our family, but more and more children joined our sponsorship program—248, to be exact. I finally reached the point where I would have said no to more children, but I found myself simply incapable of turning away children in need and God kept giving me the money to care for them, so I kept saying yes.

My girls have come to believe that taking in strangers, sick people, and outcasts is normal. In fact, it has always been abnormal for us *not* to have someone, or several people, who are not part of our immediate family living with us, some who need a place to stay while recovering from illness or injury, others who need a temporary home while we look for more ideal foster care situations for them. My children are always conscious of the fact that they themselves have not always had a home and they are eager to share what they have. I learn more and more about the generous and compassionate heart of the Father from them every time I watch them embrace someone new. We truly love welcoming into our overflowing house people of all ages, no matter what their needs may be.

Helping to care for people and then sending them on their way healthier and more loved is part of our family's DNA; it's what we do. I often thank God for the opportunity to teach my children the importance of loving His people by inviting them into our home. But as I watch them welcome the newcomers with open arms, without any hesitation, judgment, or condemnation, I realize that more often than not, they are the ones teaching me.

Not long after Jane came to live with us, the girls brought to our house four children who lived in our village and ranged in age from three years to ten years. All four of them were severely burned; I could hardly look at them without feeling sick. I kept waiting for someone to show up looking for the children, but no one did. The oldest assured me that they would not be missed. When they finally felt comfortable enough to start opening up to us, I gathered that the stepmother with whom they had been living was severely abusive. The children, who had not known how to cook while their mother was still alive, were being forced to cook for themselves over an open fire, hence the burns covering their arms and legs.

Of course, after several days of love and care, medicine and bandages, nutritious food and lots of prayer, the children began to look remarkably better and were soon laughing and playing with my own girls.

After the children had been living with us for about two weeks and their burns were healing nicely, we began looking for a place for them to go. With the stepmother's consent, we placed them in the home of our sweet, grandfatherly neighbor, Angello, and his twenty-five-year-old daughter. This kind father and daughter were more than happy to provide them with a loving family, since Amazima was providing them with education, food, and medical care. Time and time again, Christ and His body here on earth blew me away as we said yes to taking more short-term foster children into our home and local families agreed to take in these children as their own.

I marveled, not at the foster families or at my girls, who brought these children home so we could love them back to life and health, but at the God who is able to do immeasurably more than we could ever ask or imagine (see Ephesians 3:20).

"More" was the theme of my life. Every day I went to the school to register more children who had joined our program, and every day I went to town to buy more school supplies for them. And every day I had the financial provision needed to care for the "more" lives God sent my way.

Everything was growing at an astounding rate. Everything, that is, except our house. With the increase in the number of children in our sponsorship program, I simply could not continue to have the children spend the night on Fridays anymore. I had a four-bedroom house and ten children, plus Christine, myself, and our constant stream of guests. Trying to host 250 more people every weekend seemed impossible!

So Friday night sleepovers came to an end and our ministry began hosting instead an all-day get-together for the children every Saturday. Early on Saturday mornings, children began to arrive, eager to receive their breakfast of porridge and a hard-boiled egg, which the girls and I distributed from our front porch. They played and waited for Raoul, a local minister with a gift for teaching the Bible and leading children in worship, to come lead Bible study. After that, and a lunch of rice, beans, and chicken (a treat!), the children sang, played, ran, and laughed for the rest of the day before heading back to their homes.

During these days of such rapid growth and such busyness all around me, I was reminded of Paul's words to the Corinthians:

> People are watching us as we stay at our post, alertly, unswervingly . . . in hard times, tough times, bad times; when we're beaten up, jailed, and mobbed; working hard, working late, working without eating; with pure heart, clear head, steady hand; in gentleness, holiness, and honest love; when we're telling the truth, and when God's showing his power; when we're doing our best setting things right; when we're praised, and when we're blamed; slandered, and honored; true to our word, though distrusted; ignored by the world, but recognized by God; terrifically alive, though rumored to be dead; beaten within an inch of our lives, but refusing to die; immersed in tears, yet always filled with deep joy; living on handouts, yet enriching many; having nothing, having it all. Dear, dear Corinthians, I can't tell you how much I long

for you to enter this wide-open, spacious life. We didn't fence you in. The smallness you feel comes from within you. Your lives aren't small, but you're living them in a small way. I'm speaking as plainly as I can and with great affection. Open up your lives. Live openly and expansively! (2 Corinthians 6:10–13, The Message)

I want to give my life away for Christ. I want to exemplify Him in my every day. I want to live an open and expansive life, giving myself freely to all those around me for His glory. God answers this prayer every day of my life with new opportunities. I want to live openly and expansively, loving my neighbor as myself, until Jesus comes back.

ONE DAY...

Sunday, February 8, 2009
God of the Impossible.

This is my life. My real life. People say
to me sometimes, "There's no way that is
real, right? You do know how to tell a story,
though!" Let me tell you, as I fall onto my
bed at the end of the night, I look up at
the sky amazed and wonder, "No way is this
real, right?" Yes. It is.

Even those closest to me sometimes voice
their disbelief: "How is that *possible?!*" Most
of the time, I really don't believe it either.
Sometimes I pinch myself to make sure I am
awake. I am. Yes, it is happening. Ten
children, then seven who were abandoned.
Then four burn victims. In the last three
weeks we have added almost seventy-five
children to our program. When I get ready
to serve lunch, I have to take a new head
count every day, just to make sure I have
the number right. It's happening.

As I lay in bed in disbelief at the end of another beautifully exhausting day, I marveled with God at the "impossible" things that happen in my life. And I realized, when have you ever read a story of God's great work that made a lot of sense, a story that didn't seem a little over the top, a little impossible? Not often. Radical, extraordinary love just doesn't make sense in a fallen world; that doesn't mean it can't happen. But it is the very nature of God.

Moses parted the Red Sea, and I bet people thought, "No way this is happening!" Noah spent 120 years building an ark and I bet people thought he was crazy. When Joshua went to Jericho, God told him to march around the city once each day for six days and seven times on the seventh day with seven priests blowing trumpets made of rams' horns. I bet Joshua didn't think that made much sense. I bet Abraham didn't think it made a whole lot of sense when God asked him to kill the son through whom He had promised to send nations. Jesus told His

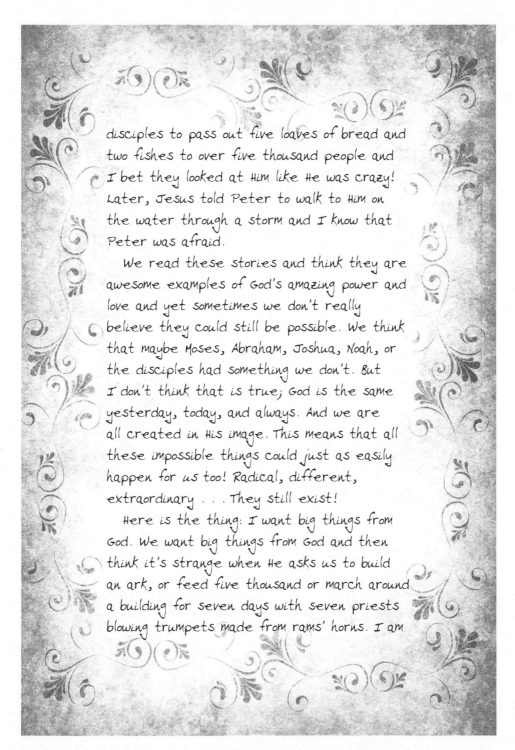

disciples to pass out five loaves of bread and two fishes to over five thousand people and I bet they looked at Him like He was crazy! Later, Jesus told Peter to walk to Him on the water through a storm and I know that Peter was afraid.

We read these stories and think they are awesome examples of God's amazing power and love and yet sometimes we don't really believe they could still be possible. We think that maybe Moses, Abraham, Joshua, Noah, or the disciples had something we don't. But I don't think that is true; God is the same yesterday, today, and always. And we are all created in His image. This means that all these impossible things could just as easily happen for us too! Radical, different, extraordinary . . . They still exist!

Here is the thing: I want big things from God. We want big things from God and then think it's strange when He asks us to build an ark, or feed five thousand or march around a building for seven days with seven priests blowing trumpets made from rams' horns. I am

asking for big things from God. Big things like a van I can take my whole family to church in and a house with ten showers. Bigger things like 147 million orphaned children in the world to each have a mommy who knows what they like for dinner. So really, I am not surprised at the craziness of my life. Every morning, as I wake up with some impossible task in front of me, I know that God will meet it with impossible strength and love. I serve the God who used Moses, a murderer, to part the Red Sea; a God who let Peter, who would deny Him, walk on water. A God who looks at me, in all my fallen weakness and says, "You can do the impossible."

13

AMAZING GRACE

The theme of my life seemed to be "more." God was expanding everything, including my family. Around February of 2009, about a year after Sumini had joined our family, her biological sister, Zuula, also came to live with us. The two sisters were delighted to be together again and stuck to each other's side for days. Sumini's prayer for months had been that she could live with her sister and I was once again blown away by God's faithfulness to answer even the prayers of a five-year-old.

Zuula is humble and gentle and gets along with everyone she meets. Her sweet spirit draws people to her instantly and enables her to form friendships effortlessly. She is a peacemaker in our home, floating between "groups" of sisters. Her eyes are patient and understanding. Because she is quiet, people often think she is timid, but she isn't. She is courageous. She is so strong and such a protector of her little sisters. She is wise and has a deep gratitude many people could learn from.

With Zuula's addition to the family, I had eleven children. In my mind, that was enough. I would like to say I prayed fervently and knew beyond a shadow of a doubt that God Himself had said,

"That's it, Katie. Eleven children for you and no more!" But He didn't.

I said it, to myself and to Him: "Enough, okay, God? No more kids. I am not taking any more kids!"

I knew I had to be firm with myself about limiting the size of my family. After all, I had taken in eleven girls in a relatively short period of time and my soft heart longed for every child to experience the warmth of home and family, but I had to stop.

My decision not to bring any more children into our home didn't stop people from asking me to do so. One elderly lady came to my house three or four times with her granddaughter tied to her back, having carried the child almost seven miles from her home to mine. This beautiful child was about two and a half years old and she could not walk, talk, or use her hands. Of course, I could easily see that the grandmother could barely care for herself. But I didn't think I could care for the child either. I already had eleven children of my own and almost three hundred to care for in various ways as part of our sponsorship program; my life was far too full for a child with such significant physical needs.

"I am maxed out," I told myself. "I would have to be *insane* to take on a special-needs child as my *twelfth* daughter!"

Every time the old grandmother came to visit and I declined to take the child from her, I gave her a bag of food and sent her on her way with the toddler on her back. But sometimes, after I sent them away, I couldn't get the child's little smile out of my head. Sometimes that little smile woke me up in the middle of the night.

A few weeks passed and in the busyness of my life, I forgot about the little girl and her grandmother. About a month later, I couldn't sleep. I knew God was trying to tell me something, but I couldn't figure out what. I felt strongly prompted to pray for something very specific. That night and for several nights afterward, I found myself reaching for my Bible. Morning after morning, I awoke and was unable to leave my bed without reading pages and pages of God's Word.

Multiple times, I woke up in the middle of the night to pray. I normally pray quite frequently and sometimes pretty intensely, but this was different.

Finally, on Sunday the Lord whispered through my spirit, much more clearly than I have ever felt Him speak in my life: "Your next child's name is Sarah."

I was a bit confused. Back in August, the Lord brought me a beautiful daughter named Sarah. "Lord, I already have her—?" But as He does, He whispered again, "Your next child is Sarah." Okay, Sarah. So, I began to pray for Sarah, wherever she was. I prayed and prayed. I dreamed of her; I longed for her; I missed her.

After a few days, Tibita, a little girl in our program, came to my house with one side of her face swollen to double its size. She had an abscessed tooth and had perhaps suffered with it for days. I took her to the dentist's office and made her some soup; she spent the rest of the day resting at our house. I sent one of our employees to Tibita's grandmother's house to tell her that she would spend the night with us so I could monitor her swollen cheek and help her rinse with salt water to prevent infection.

I fell into bed that night, exhausted but not too tired to say, "Lord, this is *Tibita*. You said *Sarah*. Where is Sarah? Did I hear you wrong? Lord, you know what my heart can handle. Please know that my heart *cannot* handle knowing that there is a child out there who needs me to be her mom and not being able to help her. I believe you spoke, Father. If you need me to be Sarah's mom, I need you to bring Sarah to my front door. *Please.*"

I slept hard for the first time in days.

At eight o'clock the next morning, I heard a knock at our gate. It was Tibita's *jja ja* (grandmother), carrying Tibita's little sister—the same grandmother and little girl I had been turning away from the gate. This time I took the little girl from her and smiled as she snuggled her head into my chest.

She pleaded one more time for me to take her baby, insisting that the Lord kept prompting her to come here. I wondered. *Could it be?* I asked the grandmother, "What is her name?"

"Sarah," she replied.

The grandmother struggled to kneel on the ground in front of me. "Please help me," she begged. "I would never ask for this, but the Lord told me to get up and come here. He said you can help this child. She is two and a half years old and she has never walked. I don't know what is wrong with her, but there is no money to visit the hospital. God keeps telling me to come here for help. You have done so much for Tibita and I do not want to ask for more, but please, *help Sarah.*"

Right then and there, Sarah's little hand grabbed hold of mine and she looked up at me and, in a soft, high-pitched voice, called me "Mama." The grandmother looked as though she had seen a ghost. She was astonished because the child had hardly spoken before.

I looked at her with wide eyes as we both began to laugh and cry, looking heavenward.

I realized we were still standing in the driveway and asked the grandmother to please come inside, make herself at home, and stay for lunch. I needed to wait for my kids to come home because I never brought a new child into our home without first having a family meeting, where we prayed and talked about it. My precious children have never said no. They wanted this little Sarah, and of course Tibita too!

Having recently experienced bringing Zuula into our family to join her biological sister, Sumini, I decided that yes, it was best to take both of them. After all, their grandmother was elderly, in poor health, and had been experiencing some chest pain. I remembered thinking when we went for their last home evaluation that soon we would need to look for a foster home for these sweet girls.

It is an extraordinary feeling to pick up a precious child, bathe her in warm water for the first time, wash her little feet, wrap her in a snuggly towel, dress her, feed her, and cuddle her in your arms as you tell her, "You are *mine*. I am your Mommy. *Forever.*" I was reminded of

1 Samuel 1:26–28: "Yes, I am the woman who stood here praying to the Lord. I prayed for this child and the Lord has granted me what I asked. So now I will give (her) to the Lord, let Him be the Lord of (her) life."

As I carried my new little girl into the bedroom and put her in a new dress for the first time, fear overwhelmed me. What does one do with a child who may never walk? How would I keep a semblance of normal life for my other girls? Would I have time to continue loving them enough while caring for a special-needs little girl? Oh, what were people going to say?

God simply whispered that His grace was going to allow me to raise this little girl, even after I had turned her away from my gate several times.

Each time God brings a new daughter into my family, I am in awe that He would entrust me with such a blessing. Each time, I fall to my knees with tears of thankfulness. I cannot thank Him enough for my beautiful children.

After such a remarkable experience with God and feeling Him speak Sarah's name to me, we ended up needing to change it. When the girls and I had our family meeting about bringing Sarah and Tibita into the family, their only concern was that they already had a sister named Sarah, and Sarah herself was feeling a bit tentative about sharing her name. I told them at that time that once this new little sister was settled in our family, we would give her a new name. She soon became Grace, which fits her perfectly. The name seemed only fitting because of the grace God had shown me in bringing this wonderful little person into a home that I had declared full. His grace to overlook my silliness in thinking that I knew what to do and bless me with what He knew was best anyway. He promised that His grace was sufficient, that His grace would be enough to allow me to parent this child and my other children too.

Her need for God's gracious touch overwhelmed me at first but soon became something I simply accepted and learned to manage. I knew God was going to take care of the situation somehow. I didn't know what He was going to do, but He had promised me that His grace would be sufficient and, day by day, I found that to be true.

Tibita and Grace both brought new life and energy to our family. Tibita is tall and gangly with a huge grin and a huge, outgoing personality to match. She is very much her own person, sassy and hilarious, always having a great time and entertaining those around her but also helpful, outspoken, and both strong *and* strong-willed!

Grace has a sly, infectious little smile that captures people's hearts immediately. She is the most hilarious, imaginative child I have ever met. She loves deeply, never meets a stranger, and is quick to give hugs and the most perfect wonderful kisses (in abundance) to even her newest friends. She absolutely sparkles and is full of strength and grace and favor. She has a resilient quality that will not be defeated.

The day Tibita and Grace came to live with us, I immediately began praying for Grace's legs. I wasn't worried about them because my God is a healer and a protector, and I know how much He loves His children. My plan for Grace's health and physical well-being was simply to pray for her first.

I believe in miracles and mostly I believe in love, God's love—big, extravagant, unconditional. His love moves mountains and changes the world, love that is freely given, that we may also freely give it to others. I wrote to friends and family all over the world and many believers joined our family in asking God to heal Grace.

As much as I wanted God to simply reach down from heaven and do an instant miracle in Grace's body, I knew I needed to start by using common sense and taking advantage of the medical resources available to us, even though they were somewhat limited. I took Grace to several doctors, all of whom said she had cerebral palsy, resulting from a lack of oxygen at birth. All agreed that while she could begin to speak at some point (she had continued to utter only one word, "Mommy"), she would never walk. One doctor told me with absolute confidence that she would one day be completely paralyzed and that process had already started in her legs.

Having heard the doctors' conclusions, I often felt overwhelmed with fear. Some days I felt such sorrow for Grace's poor little body, other days I felt anger. I wondered what life would look like from that moment on. But God kept repeating: "My grace is sufficient."

I did everything I knew to do to help Grace, but perhaps the most important person who helped her was her new sister Jane. Grace and Jane were about the same age, so we referred to them as "twins." Before Grace came to live with us, Jane was the only one of my girls who didn't attend school during the day, and she was desperate for a friend. Jane quickly embraced Grace not only as a sister and a friend but also as someone she wanted to help. Jane wanted Grace to walk, and Jane wasn't one to take no for an answer, so every day as they played, in a way that was both very sweet and fairly bossy at the same time, Jane commanded Grace: "Come!" When Grace didn't move, Jane marched over to her, wrapped her small, chubby arms around Grace, and tried to pull her to her feet. This sometimes-humorous, always-sweet scene replayed itself over and over again, as Jane was determined for her "twin" to walk.

I worked with Grace; Jane worked with her in her unique three-year-old way; and many people continued to pray. Soon I got to send them happy news, one of the most joyful messages I've ever sent.

March 9, 2009

Grace can walk.

She can't walk very well, just a few steps with bent legs, but she can walk. Two weeks ago Grace came to our family and her grandmother explained to me that she was "lame."

At two and a half years old she could not stand, walk, hold her spoon, or complete a sentence. I took her to a doctor who said she had "ascending paralysis," meaning her legs were paralyzed and the rest of her would slowly become that way. Something didn't resonate in my spirit, and being that these doctors have been wrong before, I (with all my medical knowledge) decided not to believe them. Where was the fun in that anyway?

We began stretching little Grace's legs, helping her eat, cuddling her constantly, and covering her in prayer. Grace began pulling herself up on the furniture. She began to take a few steps holding on to my hands. Today she walked about ten steps alone before she had to sit down. Grace can hold her spoon, and although she makes quite a mess, she can feed herself. Grace laughs about thirteen out of the fourteen hours we are awake each day. And Grace can say a full sentence without stuttering: "I lub lou, Mommy."

Grace's sisters love her to pieces. When I was worried that she was pretty delayed, because she had some "special needs," her sisters never saw anything different about her. They knew her only special need was love.

They stretch her little withered legs as she sits on their laps and help her not spill her juice everywhere. Jane, my only other child who does not go to school during the day, so desperately longs for Grace to play with her that she can often be found holding

Grace's hand and walking/dragging her everywhere she goes.

When Grace took her first steps, Jane was the one who pushed her to do more, prodded her to take one more step, and pulled her back to her feet when she fell. Those two are inseparable! They are "partners in crime" at times, but more than that, they are loving and devoted sisters, and Jane, even at her young age, is an amazing encourager for Grace. What a gift.

In a very short time, I have been able to watch God give back to Grace everything that was taken from her during the first two and a half years of her life. I have watched Him not only begin to restore her physically but to restore her spirit, her little heart that He so loves and desires intimacy with. He has reminded me how deeply He longs for each one of His children to know His intimate love. He has reminded me how He longs to restore our brokenness. He has reminded my girls what His love can do through their little hands. What's most incredible is that I know He is not done yet but only getting started.

Lord, we give you our brokenness, that you may fully restore us. Remind us of the intimacy that you long for with each of us, your deep, passionate love for your children. Father, you have given so freely, you have loved so extravagantly. Let us give. Let us love.

I went from having children who were fairly independent to having one who could not go anywhere or do anything herself. I thought I had made huge adjustments before—just the task of preparing meals for and keeping up with homework of one more person sometimes seemed daunting in the past. Just the emotional adjustment of one more child, even a self-sufficient one, could be exhausting. This was something different altogether. It was a time of learning to rely even more completely on God, begging Him for even more strength, and watching Him do miracles in Grace's body. Today, Grace can run. Her gait is still a bit awkward, but it's adorable to see her moving quickly across the grass with her bright, determined smile. She can feed herself and use both hands; she can speak in complete sentences with her soft little voice; and like a typical preschooler, she does *not* like to take a bath! His grace is sufficient.

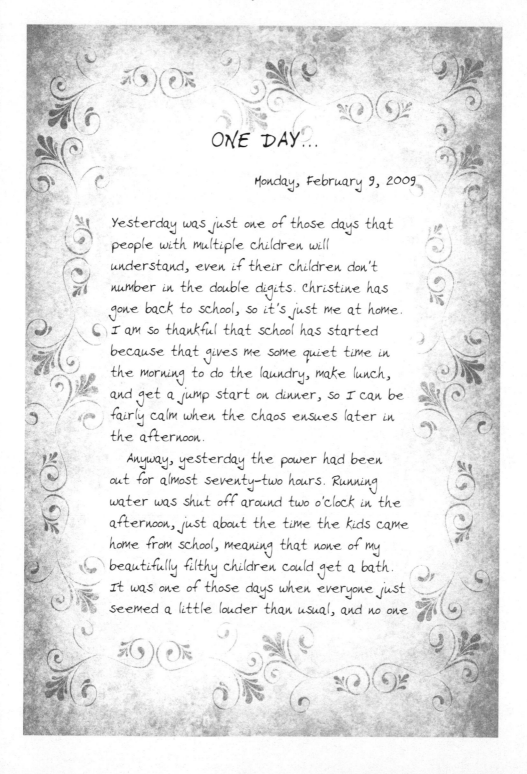

ONE DAY...

Monday, February 9, 2009

Yesterday was just one of those days that people with multiple children will understand, even if their children don't number in the double digits. Christine has gone back to school, so it's just me at home. I am so thankful that school has started because that gives me some quiet time in the morning to do the laundry, make lunch, and get a jump start on dinner, so I can be fairly calm when the chaos ensues later in the afternoon.

Anyway, yesterday the power had been out for almost seventy-two hours. Running water was shut off around two o'clock in the afternoon, just about the time the kids came home from school, meaning that none of my beautifully filthy children could get a bath. It was one of those days when everyone just seemed a little louder than usual, and no one

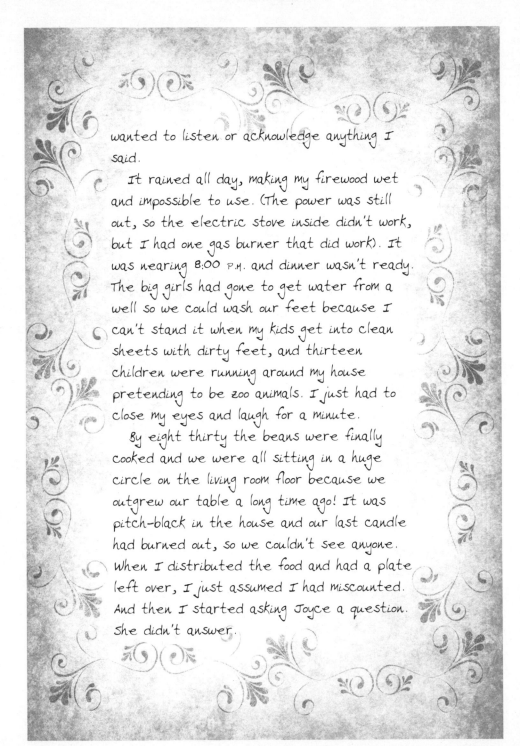

wanted to listen or acknowledge anything I said.

It rained all day, making my firewood wet and impossible to use. (The power was still out, so the electric stove inside didn't work, but I had one gas burner that did work). It was nearing 8:00 P.M. and dinner wasn't ready. The big girls had gone to get water from a well so we could wash our feet because I can't stand it when my kids get into clean sheets with dirty feet, and thirteen children were running around my house pretending to be zoo animals. I just had to close my eyes and laugh for a minute.

By eight thirty the beans were finally cooked and we were all sitting in a huge circle on the living room floor because we outgrew our table a long time ago! It was pitch-black in the house and our last candle had burned out, so we couldn't see anyone. When I distributed the food and had a plate left over, I just assumed I had miscounted. And then I started asking Joyce a question. She didn't answer.

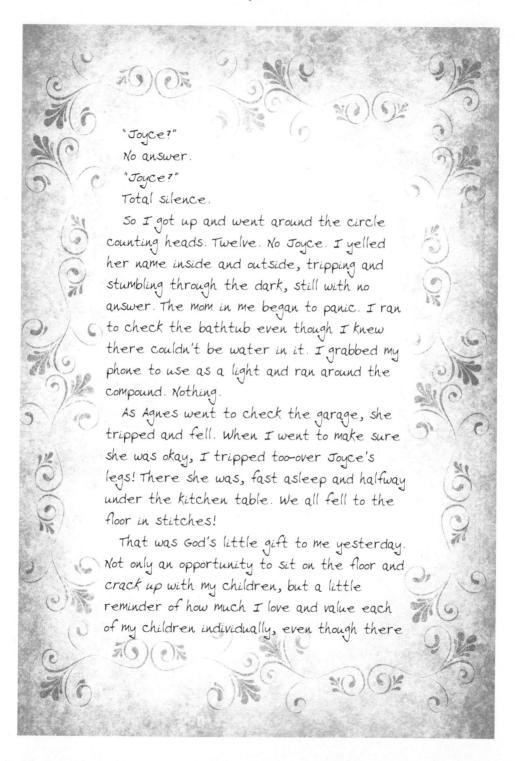

"Joyce?"

No answer.

"Joyce?"

Total silence.

So I got up and went around the circle counting heads. Twelve. No Joyce. I yelled her name inside and outside, tripping and stumbling through the dark, still with no answer. The mom in me began to panic. I ran to check the bathtub even though I knew there couldn't be water in it. I grabbed my phone to use as a light and ran around the compound. Nothing.

As Agnes went to check the garage, she tripped and fell. When I went to make sure she was okay, I tripped too–over Joyce's legs! There she was, fast asleep and halfway under the kitchen table. We all fell to the floor in stitches!

That was God's little gift to me yesterday. Not only an opportunity to sit on the floor and crack up with my children, but a little reminder of how much I love and value each of my children individually, even though there

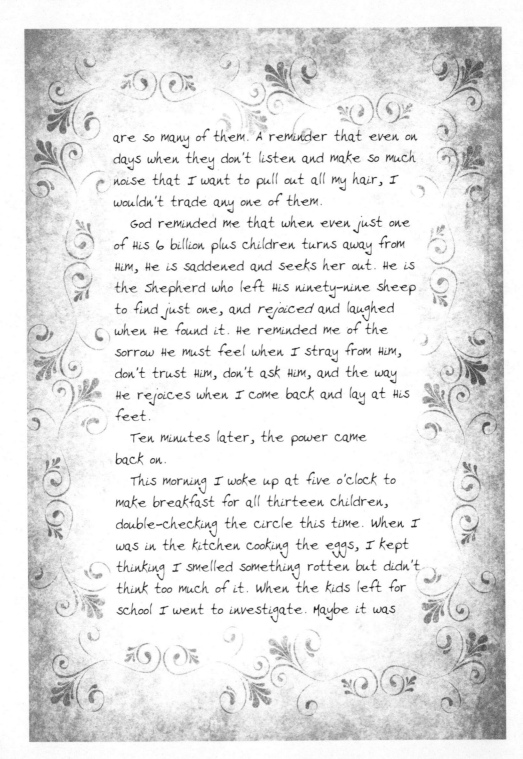

are so many of them. A reminder that even on days when they don't listen and make so much noise that I want to pull out all my hair, I wouldn't trade any one of them.

God reminded me that when even just one of His 6 billion plus children turns away from Him, He is saddened and seeks her out. He is the Shepherd who left His ninety-nine sheep to find just one, and rejoiced and laughed when He found it. He reminded me of the sorrow He must feel when I stray from Him, don't trust Him, don't ask Him, and the way He rejoices when I come back and lay at His feet.

Ten minutes later, the power came back on.

This morning I woke up at five o'clock to make breakfast for all thirteen children, double-checking the circle this time. When I was in the kitchen cooking the eggs, I kept thinking I smelled something rotten but didn't think too much of it. When the kids left for school I went to investigate. Maybe it was

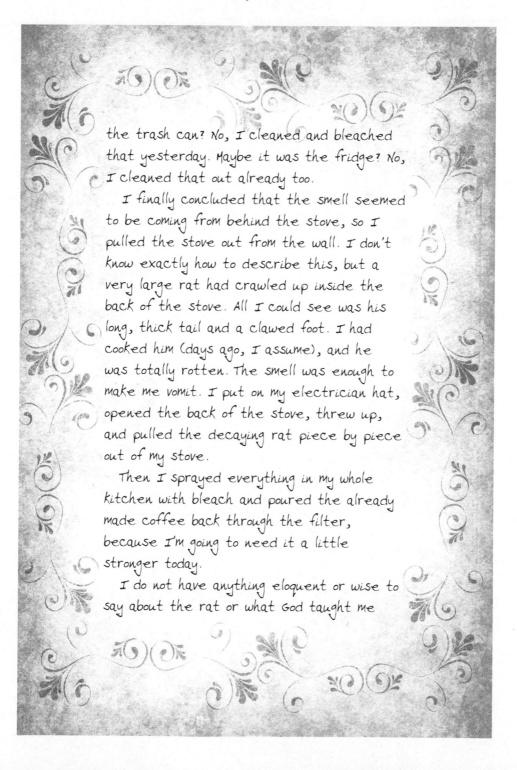

the trash can? No, I cleaned and bleached that yesterday. Maybe it was the fridge? No, I cleaned that out already too.

I finally concluded that the smell seemed to be coming from behind the stove, so I pulled the stove out from the wall. I don't know exactly how to describe this, but a very large rat had crawled up inside the back of the stove. All I could see was his long, thick tail and a clawed foot. I had cooked him (days ago, I assume), and he was totally rotten. The smell was enough to make me vomit. I put on my electrician hat, opened the back of the stove, threw up, and pulled the decaying rat piece by piece out of my stove.

Then I sprayed everything in my whole kitchen with bleach and poured the already made coffee back through the filter, because I'm going to need it a little stronger today.

I do not have anything eloquent or wise to say about the rat or what God taught me

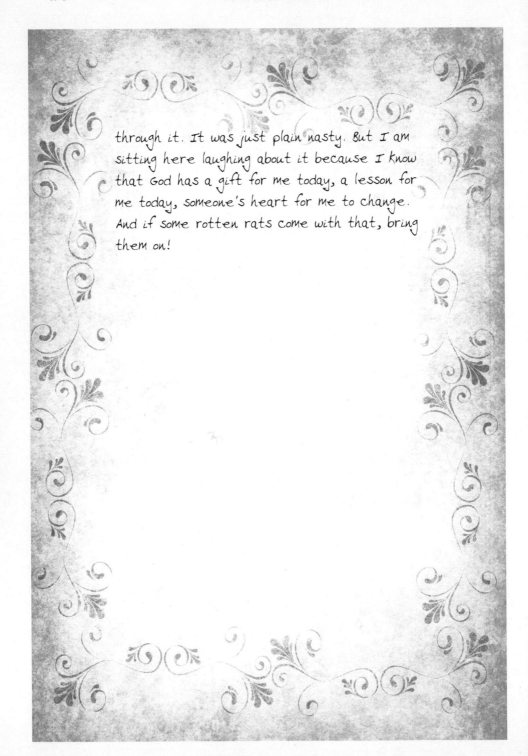

through it. It was just plain nasty. But I am sitting here laughing about it because I know that God has a gift for me today, a lesson for me today, someone's heart for me to change. And if some rotten rats come with that, bring them on!

Mom and me with the children at the orphanage on our very first trip (Christmas 2006)

Fatuma, Ato, and Maria taking a break from learning (2007)

My first kindergarten class, hard at work! (2007)

Hellen and Mommy (2008)

Photograph by Renee Bach

Sisters walking home arm in arm: Sumini, Mary, Scovia (2008)

Our big pot of beans that we cook for Saturday Bible studies (2008)

One of the sponsored-children packages (2008)

With some of the children in our sponsorship program (2009)

Serving up food with Christine (2009)

The market (2009)

The children of Masese (2009)

Dancing with a friend in Masese
(2009)

Napongo and Alapea,
our Karimojong friends

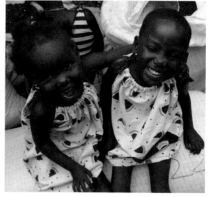

Hungry children waiting for their
food, even in the rain (2009)

Jane and Grace (March 2009)

Agnes and Auntie Christine
(August 2009)

Photograph by Kristin Laughlin

Dad, Jane, and Agnes
(August 2009)

Photograph by Kristin Laughlin

Suzanne on her first trip to adopt
Josephine, and me with Patricia
(September 2009)

With my not-so-little brother,
Brad, and Gracie (August 2009)

Removing jiggers and bandaging feet
(2009)

Photograph by Kristin Laughlin

My sweet friend Betty, one of our sponsored children (2009)

Uncle Raoul leading worship (2009)

Photograph by kristin Laughlin

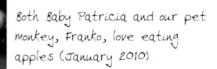

Both Baby Patricia and our pet monkey, Franko, love eating apples (January 2010)

The beads made by the women of Masese are sold to provide them with a sustainable income for their families (2010)

Driving through Masese with my van full of girls (2010)

Photograph by karen Logan

Visiting with Jja Ja Grace

Zuula and Sarah giving a hand to their friends (2010)

New Amazima playground (2010)

Photograph by Kim Nunn

Margaret, Jja Ja, Patricia, Zuula, and Prossy

The children at our Saturday Bible Study (2010)

Photograph by Kim Nunn

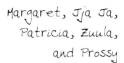

Sumini (2009)

Photograph by katie Lentile

Michael, all better! (2010)

Sarah, Mommy, and Tibita
(2010)

Photograph by kim Nunn

Baby Agnes, one of many
children we have had the
privilege of loving back
to health

Margaret and Prossy (2010)

Joyce (2010) *Photograph by Karen Logan*

Mary (2010)
Photograph by Karen Logan

Baby Katie, My sweet friend in Masese
(2010) *Photograph by Karen Logan*

Zuula and Scovia (2010)

carrying food bags home after
Bible study. THe bags are heavy,
but the kids are all smiles! (2010)

Photograph by Kim Nunn

The gate of our home is always
open *Photograph by Kristin Laughlin*

14

A DIFFERENT KIND OF EDUCATION

When I decided not to complete my college degree, some people said I wasn't going to "finish my education." They were terribly mistaken. Maybe I didn't sit in lecture halls and listen to people with lots of initials after their names talk about their areas of expertise, but one thing I learned quickly was that following God is an education of its own.

What I was learning was that there is a lesson in everything, big or small.

One of the first things I learned is that God cares about my feelings, even the ones that don't seem particularly spiritual. We had been experiencing extremely hot weather during January and February. Even though that time of year is supposedly the "rainy season," the rain simply didn't fall, and that made for extra-sticky, sweaty days. On one of these days when I was feeling especially nasty I pulled into a gas station. The attendant looked at me and exclaimed, "Wow! You are so beautiful; your skin is glowing!"

"Ha! It's sweat," was my unconvinced reply.

"You have some really beautiful sweat," she said as we pulled away.

When you live in Africa, or maybe when you are the mom of thirteen children, moments when you actually *feel* beautiful are in short supply. I feel on many days that I am radiating God's love, but there are few days that I actually think I *look* radiant. Not that God cares what I look like, but as a human and as a woman, sometimes I do wish to look nice.

Lesson: God cares about my feelings, even the petty ones like wanting to look pretty, so He has someone tell me that my sweat is beautiful. Really, God has created and clothed the lilies of the fields, how much more will He take care of me? Through this dear woman at the gas station God reminded me how beautiful we all are to Him, after all, we were created in His own image. And He looks at me, at you, in all our sweat and dirt and brokenness, and says, "I choose you. You are beautiful."

Later that week, my sweet daughter Margaret, one of the gentlest and humblest of all my children, beat up our neighbor, who happens to be one of her best friends. I was making lunch when Olivia, the little girl, and her mother came to the gate.

The woman started shouting "Your daughter punched my daughter!" and then she turned and went home, leaving Olivia in our yard. I called Margaret, Agnes, and Hellen (all were accused of being involved) into the yard. As we spoke with Olivia, the whole story came out.

Olivia had been making fun of Agnes and Hellen for having a white mother. Her exact words were, "Your mom is white so you eat fish. You are going to get fat!" (At this point I walked away from our circle, pretending to be seriously upset, but actually resisting the urge to laugh at this nonsensical comment.)

After I composed myself I came back and explained to Olivia that since these girls were her friends, and since Jesus wants us to love our friends and even our enemies, she needs to be careful to choose kind words. I explained to my children that no matter what people say to them, as long as they are not being physically hurt, they must not hit their friends. We had a group hug and invited Olivia in for lunch. Ironically, we were having fish.

After Olivia left, our whole family had a talk about how we are all going to have to endure some teasing because of our family. Children often make mean comments to my daughters about having a white mother. I explained to them that in America, and in Uganda, people often say ignorant and rude things to me because I have many children from many different tribes and cultures. We talked about how we have a choice: We can live together as a family and sometimes hear rude remarks that we ignore, or we cannot live together as a family and then we won't have to hear the mean words. Of course, this really is no choice at all; we choose our family, our family from many different tribes and cultures and countries and colors. Sometimes it's tough, but we wouldn't trade it.

Lesson: Jesus knows that we are a family, a *real* family. And He doesn't see the colors of our skin. Besides, in heaven I am going to be black; I have already asked God for it.

Another lesson: Parenting is sometimes tough. Parenting is almost always hilarious.

My daughter Sumini once invited a woman most people consider our local lunatic to her birthday party. The woman's name is Jja Ja Nakibuuka and she had something to teach me. She is the village leper. Her fingers and toes are missing. Everyone in the village thinks she is crazy because she burned down her house in order to live in the bush. She has no possessions but lives completely on the land, by faith. My children often take her food and small gifts. Every time she sees us, she has one thing to say: "God is good and He is coming back." She says it over and over: "God is good and He is coming back." She believes it, and she lives it. She has nothing on this earth, she is fully prepared for Jesus to come and take her home. And they call her crazy.

If this woman is crazy, I think perhaps we could all benefit from being a little crazier. As I pray for Jja Ja Nakibuuka, I ask God often why He doesn't heal her wounds; I know He can. Today it hit me. My faulty, shaky faith has to sometimes see it. I need to see the lame walk. Jja Ja Nakibuuka doesn't need a miracle, because she already knows. God loves me enough and desires my heart enough to help me see; Jja Ja Nakibuuka already sees. Her body may be broken, but her heart is full. Jesus says, "Because you have seen me, you have believed; blessed are those who have not seen and yet have believed" (John 20:19).

Lesson: Open your eyes. God is good and He is coming back.

One of the simplest lessons I was learning was that almost anything, or anyone, can be a teacher on some level. I even learned from Céline Dion.

I was missing my boyfriend terribly and, undoubtedly, this was Céline Dion's fault. Thanks to our wonderful friends and donors, Amazima Ministries purchased a van, which was such a blessing to us. When we got it, we were able to distribute more than eighteen hundred pounds of food to more than fifteen hundred children every week. It became a great teaching tool when learning the story of the loaves and fishes. The van also enabled our family to all go to church together, which was truly wonderful.

Céline Dion is extremely popular in Africa. In the town of Jinja, she can always be heard coming from one market stand's radio or another. In the van, Céline was constantly on one of the only two radio stations we received, and we often came upon a Céline Dion marathon, when they played what seemed to be every song she ever recorded.

Don't get me wrong; I appreciate and enjoy some good Céline. I love to crank it up loud and sing it all the way to town with Grace and Jane dancing in the back. I guess when I first started hearing Céline Dion songs when I was about eight years old, though, I did not realize that she is *always* singing about someone she is so desperately in love with. She has such longing, such agony as she is away from her lover. When I heard these songs in Uganda, they did usually make me miss having a boyfriend to cuddle.

But once again, even in this little thing I tried to see the lesson. I think the way Céline Dion feels about her lover is the way God must feel about the church, which seems in some ways to have strayed so far from Him. I think He allowed me to really miss my boyfriend so I could catch a tiny glimpse of what His heart must feel as the church strays into religion and away from the things that are so important to Him, like the impoverished, unwanted people of the world. How He longs and desires for my heart, each and every minute of each and every day.

Lesson: Everything can teach you something. God so deeply, passionately, desperately loves us. He so intensely longs for His lover, the church, to come back to His teachings of giving everything we have to serve the poor, of living in community. He wants to woo us, each one of us, as we are the body who make up the church. I am still trying to get there, and it makes me feel special to know that He sings over me even more passionately than Céline Dion. That is pretty wonderful.

During this same time, I was also becoming more keenly aware than ever of the spiritual battle that raged around me. I went to visit some friends in a nearby village. One of them was weeping when I arrived. When I asked what was wrong, she told me a horrific story of how her neighbor had killed his stepson, cut off his head, and sold it to the witch doctor for a little more than $100. We cried together. This woman, who was not a Christian a few months earlier, pulled out her Bible and told me how thankful she was that God had moved her children so that they did not have to witness this.

Lesson: Satan is not a fan of Christ's winning this beautiful nation. Christ will win anyway. In fact, He's winning every single day—and *that* is the best lesson of all.

As much as I was learning about God and other people, I was also learning some things about myself, and some of the lessons were painful. As many people do, I dreamed of bigger and better things at times; sometimes I dreamed about them too much. I justified my dreaming by saying all these things would be used for the children.

For example, our house became way too small for Friday night sleepovers, so I dreamed of a bigger and better house—a large house with separate rooms for my big girls and my small girls and a big wraparound porch. Christine and I often talked about the new, bigger house, where a table big enough for all of my family would fit comfortably and we would not have to sit on the floor to eat, a house in which our kitchen would be more than ten feet by fifteen feet, big enough for more than two people to stand in and help cook.

One day, in the midst of my wanting more, I dropped in to visit the home of eleven children in our program. They are siblings and cousins who live with their aunt. They all live, eat, and sleep together in one room a little bigger than my little girls' bedroom. The degree of my selfishness hit me like a rock. How in the world could I dream of a *bigger* house when people around me live in such need? How could I possibly feel that my kitchen was crowded when twelve people lived in this tiny house? My house is even made of cement while these precious children live in a home made of dirt. I was embarrassed about my desires, but the truth is that everyone has "flesh" moments.

I sometimes got caught up in "I deserve this" moments; I still do. I have moments when I compare myself to other people and trick myself into believing that I am doing pretty well. There are still moments when I believe I should be able to relax and do nothing some afternoons, instead of taking care of one more sick person. There are moments when I think that because I have worked hard all day, I deserve to be able to sit down and eat my food instead of answering the door for one more person who needs help.

The truth is that these thoughts are not at all scriptural. Nowhere in the Bible does it say that I deserve a reward here on earth. Colossians 3:23 says, "Whatever you do work at it with all your heart." It does not end in, "and after this hard work you deserve a long hot bath and some 'me time.'" It does end with, "since you know that you will receive an inheritance from the Lord as a reward."

Matthew 19:21, Mark 10:21, and Luke 18:22 all make exactly the same point: "Go, sell everything you have and give it to the poor, and you will have treasure in heaven." I live in a world that tells me that if I sell what I have and give it to the poor, if I leave my rich American life to live in a cockroach-infested, cement house in a Third World country, I am doing a wonderful and radical thing. The truth is, I am only doing what I love doing, and what God who gave His life for me asks me to do.

By most people's standards, my little family does not have much, but we have *more* than enough. And we know in our hearts that, really, Christ is *all* we need. He said, "Do not lay up for yourselves treasures on earth, where moth and rust destroy and where thieves break in and steal; but lay up for yourselves treasures in heaven, where neither moth nor rust destroys and where thieves do not break in and steal. For where your treasure is, there your heart will be also" (Matthew 6:19–21, NKJV).

Serving Jesus and my family with all of me, that is my treasure.

ONE DAY...

July 3, 2009

"Mommmyyyy!" I heard a yell as I bounced quickly along the pitted road that leads to our program in my sixteen-passenger van. I stopped quickly, turning the van around to go back for Prossy, who had been walking home to get something.

"How did you see her?" asked my dad, who was visiting.

"I didn't! I heard her yell, 'Mommy,'" I replied.

"But everyone calls you Mommy. Even people we don't know call you that around here," Dad questioned.

"Yeah, but I know when it's mine," I explained matter-of-factly.

And then I thought about what I had said and tears began to well. How incredible, what God has done for me. For us. It is true, hundreds of people in this area call me Mommy. Even people whom I have not met before recognize me as the woman who cares for the children in this area and call me Mommy before even having made my acquaintance. On any given day, I can drive down the road between my home and Buziika and, if it is the right time, when kids are heading home from school, I will hear "Mommy! Mommy!" being shouted about every two seconds as I pass all the children on the road. I smile as I hear them yell "Mommy!"

But for fourteen "Mommy"s, I stop. I can hear the difference. I know. My family is all things unconventional. But it is real. Real because God has knit our hearts together in a way that only He can and real because no matter what anyone says or thinks, I am their Mommy, and they are mine.

I was reading today in Genesis, chapter 33. Esau and Jacob meet for the first time in a long time. As Jacob approaches Esau, with his many children following close behind, Esau asks, "And who are these with you?"

Jacob replies: "These are the children that the Lord saw fit to bless me with."

My family and I get all the questions:

"Why do you do it?"
"Why so many children?"
"How in the world..."
"Why these specific girls?"
"Do you think it's okay to adopt as a single mother? Don't they need a father too?"
"Do you think they will have issues since you are not the same race as they are?"

We also get the compliments:

"I don't know how you do it!"
"Good job!"
"You must be so responsible!"
"Your girls must be so well behaved."

We get crazy stares and huge smiles and every look in between.
This is our perfectly God-orchestrated family.
I don't mean to give the impression that this all happened naturally or easily; there

were definite struggles involved. I believe
that adoption is absolutely God ordained, but
it is also about the most unnatural way to
grow a family. And it comes with huge
heartache and huge God-wrestling.

How do I tell a child I love her when she
doesn't know love? How do I expect her to
trust me when all she has ever known is
broken trust? I prove it. I earn it. I remind
them over and over again with words, actions,
hugs, and kisses. I remind myself over and
over again that Christ incarnated in the
parent is the only hope of incarnating Christ
in a child. When a child bites me, hits me,
or looks into my eyes and tries to shove me
away so she can hurt me before I hurt her,
when a child overeats to the point of vomiting
because she was once so hungry and is afraid
of that hunger or she hides food under her
covers "just in case," when my child cries
out for a birth mother or birth father who
was abusive, what then?

I love anyway. I get on my knees and
I cry to God about the hurt they have

experienced and I ask Him why. And then I remember that a good God who wants good for His children can give only good. I remember that all of this, even this hard part, is working for the good in their lives, for the good of God and His kingdom. I remember that these hardships are gifts that He is using to strengthen us as a family and in Him so that He may transform us into His likeness.

We cherish the grace that is this unique family. And to the questions and the comments and the compliments, this is my reply: "These are the children that the Lord saw fit to bless me with."

15

THREE THOUSAND FRIENDS

Just fifteen minutes outside of Jinja is a hill. On one side of the hill is the city's landfill. On the other side of the hill, I have three thousand friends who make their home in a slum community called Masese.

The majority of the men, women, and children who live in Masese are known as Karimojong, a seminomadic tribal people whose homeland is in northern Uganda, near the Sudanese border. Many governments advise their citizens to avoid this region when traveling, as it is known for being unstable. Karimojong culture is primitive, aggressive, and according to the state departments of the world, dangerous. Throughout Uganda, the Karimojong are marginalized, despised, and feared—simply because people do not understand them.

Many years ago, Karimojong families from the north fled to this hillside plot of government-owned land in the Jinja area to escape the horrors of war and famine ravishing their homeland. They imagined that the prospering town of Jinja would offer them a better life. But unthinkable poverty, hunger, and disease, coupled with lack of infrastructure, unemployment, landlessness, inadequate medical care, and rampant alcohol addiction, make Masese a deadly combination of the worst of village and city life. Because the land on which they live belongs to the government and cannot be purchased or owned, the people cannot farm to feed their families. For their livelihood and sustenance, they turn to brewing alcohol, prostitution, and picking trash from the landfill or rubbish bins in town, hoping to find things to use for themselves or to sell for a small sum of money.

The fact that the Karimojong cannot farm not only creates the immense problem of not being able to grow food, it also *prohibits them from being who they are as a people*. As a tribe, Karimojong are cattle herders. In fact, cattle are the currency of their culture; cows equal wealth. Every aspect of Karimojong life as a community—their social, religious and political activities, and of course, their economy—revolves around cows. The number of cattle a person owns determines his social status, and those who do not have cattle are considered "sick."

Traditionally, Karimojong farm and grow crops in order to feed cattle. The cattle, in turn, feed the people, as the Karimojong diet consists predominantly of milk mixed with cow's blood. Without agriculture and livestock, they feel helpless and purposeless, estranged from their own culture yet not welcomed into any other Ugandan culture either.

The Karimojong people are even more ostracized by the local government's push to move them back to their native land in the north. They don't want to go; the sandy desert that characterizes Karamoja and only one rainy season that is becoming increasingly unpredictable justifies their fears of another famine. Many of them remember or have heard horror stories of the 1980 famine in Karamoja, which wiped out 21 percent of the population, including 60 percent of their infants.[1] Now estimates say that approximately 250 of every 1,000 Karimojong babies die before their fifth birthday[2] and that 82 percent of the Karimojong people live below the poverty line.[3] Life is difficult for these people.

To say that I am in love with the people of this community would be a huge understatement. I do not really even have words to describe the way I cherish these beautiful people. They challenge me; they love me unconditionally; and they allow me to see Jesus in their faces.

I visit Masese several times a week. As I drive into the community, bright yellow flowers line the narrow dirt road and the cool breeze and beautiful view of Lake Victoria allow me to forget for a moment where I am headed. The simple, beautiful scenery fills me with the joy of creation and life as I head into a dark pit of unimaginable poverty and death. Despite their horrendous living conditions, though, the people greet me with gorgeous white smiles on ebony faces, waving their hands and shouting "Auntie Kate!" along with traditional Karimojong greetings.

The people in Masese have not always been glad to see me. The first year I lived in Jinja, I made many friends among the young Karimojong children who lined the streets of Jinja, begging or picking through the trash for something to eat. Their wounded feet, scarred and dirty, and their beautiful faces caught my attention, as did the primitive, exotic sound of the language in which they attempted to speak to me. As I had seen often, though, the language barrier did not discourage us from forming fast friendships. On many occasions, I took these friends home with me for a meal and a hot shower before returning them to the streets, where their parents had sent them to spend the day begging, so they could make their trek home, wherever home was.

One day my friend Abra, a girl of about ten years old, stepped on a bottle cap and cut her foot badly. I took her and her younger sister to my house to clean and bandage the wound, but I was worried that if I took her back to Main Street, she could not possibly hobble her way back to wherever she slept. I insisted on driving her home.

She was hesitant at first; she didn't know what her village mates would say if she showed up with a *mzungu* (white person), as the Karimojong are traditionally very distrusting of outsiders, especially those whose skin color differs from theirs. But she finally relented. Because Abra knew only back routes through bushy trails and over railroad tracks my large van could not cross, our journey took us quite some time. Eventually, I put the van in "park" and we all climbed out and walked into the bush.

After walking only a few minutes, we came to a clearing jam-packed with little shanty houses and bustling with people of a totally different culture from that of the Baganda and Basoga people who fill the town of Jinja. The harsh accents and tribal jewelry of these new people intrigued me, but what grabbed my attention most was the sheer poverty of this place. I had experienced squalor before, but this was unlike anything I had ever seen. Some appeared to be starving to death, literally. Children were covered with deep infected wounds, fungus, and other sores, with their bellies round and distended because of worms and their skin pale and peeling because of severe malnutrition.

Tentatively, nervously, but also with a bit of excitement, Abra took me to her house, where I was offered chicken feet, which lay on a smoky pile of charcoal roasting, without a pan or a rack. Abra's family of twelve would share these five feet, all their aunt could find as she picked through the trash that morning, as their only meal of the day. When Abra and I showed up, she was immediately scolded for not bringing home enough charcoal from the rubbish bin and I apologized profusely, explaining that I had taken her from her work early to bandage her foot.

"These people are sick," I told myself. "They are hungry." I could not imagine pulling myself away without at least trying to do something for them.

I soon remembered that Amazima had been given a feeding grant that provided for more food than was currently needed to feed our sponsored children. In what I now recognize as stunning naïveté, I thought, *Well, I can bring the extra food here. These people are hungry. We will share.* It seemed a reasonable, fairly easy solution to a basic human need.

The next day was Sunday and I woke up early to prepare to take food to Masese. "Today we are going to have a different kind of church," I told my children. We cooked a huge pot of beans, another pot of rice, and loaded the van with Bibles and two hundred pounds of food. Into the bush we drove, excited to help the people with whom I'd become acquainted.

The villagers were *not* glad to see me or my children or our large van in the midst of their community. I don't know why I believed that taking food to them would be similar to feeding the children in our sponsorship program. We had taught our children to form an orderly line in which to wait patiently for their food, to say thank you, and to move along quickly so others could be served.

Perhaps I had some skewed picture of a modern-day "loaves and fishes" moment, all of us sitting around, eating together happily. This is *not* what happened. Chaos ensued. These people had absolutely no idea why I was there, what I was doing, or what I was saying. They were simply hungry, and they saw food. People were pushing and shoving and shouting; and one drunken old man stood beside me as I served, hitting my head with a plastic plate. I promptly locked all of my children in the van and firmly told them not to get out.

I could hardly keep my balance for all the crowding, but I continued serving my food as best I knew how and tried to avoid falling into the huge, hot pot of beans. Rain began to fall. I began to sing.

And then I whispered, "This is not what I had in mind, God. I just wanted to feed the hungry, like you said, you know?"

I estimate that maybe half the people in Masese ate that day. *Disastrous* would be a good word to describe the whole experience. I drove away drenched, exhausted, and covered in mud and bean juice, but not discouraged. Somehow, God was going to reach these people. Not through my hauling our extra food and trying to throw them a picnic, but somehow.

On one of my first visits to Masese, I noticed that a school sits at the top of the hill. After a bit of research and a few weeks of meetings and organizing, I was able to negotiate a deal with the school's headmaster. He agreed to let me use the school's kitchen (which hadn't been used in years) to prepare meals for the children in Masese if I would also feed all the students in the school. As a bonus, if I would also provide the lunch for teachers, he would allow some of the older children from Masese to attend school without paying fees!

This arrangement was an answer to prayer. It would keep the children of Masese from having to beg for food on the streets and provide, at the same time, a way for some of them to be educated, offering them a previously unthinkable chance to someday leave behind the life of begging and foraging that was all they and their families knew. I was blown away, once again, by the way God was orchestrating His plan for these people all around me in ways I never would have imagined.

We started slowly, during a school holiday, feeding the students, the teachers, and the village children twice a week at the school. Raoul and I led a Bible study and time of worship in the big open field behind the kitchen for those who chose to come early. As people from the States found out about my new endeavors in the community of Masese, money poured in and soon allowed us to provide the children with food five days a week, Monday through Friday. As financial support increased, we were able to feed the children once at the school and also send them home with a plate of food that they could share with their families for an evening meal. Later, we were also able to provide free medical care once or twice a week, which included deworming all the children once every six months.

These children became my doorway into Masese. I often walked them home and spent hours sitting and talking or doing sign language with their parents or adult relatives. And then something happened, something that is incredibly rare in this broken, slum community: We became friends.

I began to know these people on a deeply personal level and that only drove my desire to help them more.

Beatrice was a prostitute, sneaking quietly away from her home after her children had fallen asleep and selling her body in the dark so she could put some food on the table for them in the morning.

Fatuma was brewing alcohol as a quick way to make money to support her children, one of whom was literally dying of starvation. On days when alcohol didn't sell, she took the mash from which it is made home to her family and they would swallow it until they fell asleep. She was making her children drunk so they were unable to feel the pains of hunger.

Elizabeth, whose husband left after her third child was born, had recently taken in her sister's five children after her sudden death. "What was my choice?" she asked when explaining the situation to me. "God says I look after the orphans, I look after the orphans." Elizabeth and the eight children sleep together on the floor in a home smaller than my tiny kitchen.

Jja Ja Sofia cares for her three grandchildren, though she is elderly and can barely walk due to severe back pain.

Brenda has use of only one arm as a result of polio when she was younger but uses it to pick through the trash, hoping to find some food for her six children.

Each of my new friends had a story that broke my heart.

I wanted to do something for these women. I couldn't imagine having to work so hard and still not be able to provide for the basic needs of my family. There had to be a way out. In the local mud-and-stick church, I gathered twenty of the women I had gotten to know—women all from different tribes, of all different ages, with all kinds of different hardships. But they had one thing in common: They were all trying to support their families and feed their children and they were not succeeding. Well, that and the fact that they all had stolen my heart.

After some friends taught me how to make necklaces out of long, thin, triangular-shaped pieces of colorful, recycled paper rolled into beads, we began teaching the women how to make them. We spent the first few months simply getting to know one another as we learned to make necklaces, crying together when someone announced that her HIV test had come back positive, and laughing with one another when someone made an awfully misshapen bead. We formed bonds that transcend all racial and social differences and, most important, we began to teach each other about Jesus.

One of the many things I love about these women is that they are happy to have honorable work. Those who are part of the bead group are not allowed to engage in prostitution, brew alcohol, or pick through trash; those are the rules. They must make a certain number of necklaces each week and bring them to our group meeting. There I purchase the necklaces from them and then send them to the States to be sold.

When our weekly meetings conclude, the women climb into my van and I take them into Jinja to deposit half of their earnings in their savings accounts. The other half of their earnings covers living expenses for them and their families until the next week. The fact that the women in the group are prospering is not only amazing, it also benefits the entire village and inspires others to try to raise themselves above their current levels of poverty.

Even with the amazing things happening in the women's group, there are still days when I walk through Masese and feel completely powerless and totally overwhelmed. The illnesses are more than I can treat even if I sit in the makeshift clinic in the back of my van for fifteen hours a day. Sometimes the sadness seems almost unbearable, the problems unsolvable, the wounds unhealable. This has taught me one of the greatest lessons: the tension between inefficiency and faithfulness. The assurance that I must obey and be faithful only to what He has asked of me, even when tangible, earthly results or successes are not seen. I want to help them all, fix all their problems, and successfully find a solution to their horrendous living conditions. But often in an unideal situation, there is not an ideal solution this side of heaven. The projects Amazima has started in this community are wonderful, but they meet the needs of only *some* people; they only scratch the surface of the problems. God assures me this is okay. If I continue to preach the gospel, and more important, *live* the gospel, here—even if outward conditions never change or change very slowly—and these people can live eternally with Jesus in heaven someday, a few years of suffering will pale in comparison. In the meantime, He allows me to see Him in their faces and to love Him by bandaging their wounds and letting their charcoal-and-mud-covered children curl up in my lap.

One day, as I drove into Masese with a friend in the passenger seat of my van and with Prossy, Jane, and Grace in the back, we came upon a roadblock. It was an odd place for a roadblock, because government agencies responsible for road repair wouldn't normally pay any attention to the deep holes and large crevices that punctuate the road into a place like Masese. Nevertheless, I stopped the van and spoke with the man doing the work, a man wearing a hard hat that did *not* look official.

The man had placed a piece of lumber, a two-inch by two-inch board across the road, then tied a rope to stretch across the road, between two trees. To move the rope and the board so I could pass through, he wanted money. I am well acquainted with this kind of scheme, and our conversation went something like this:

Katie: "What are you doing?"

Man in hard hat: (Looks at me, mumbles and gestures toward the road as if to say, "Can't you see? I'm fixing the road. Now pay me to let you continue.")

After a spirited exchange in Luganda, I finally said in English: "I will pay you when I come back. If you fix the road and you are working hard when I return, I will pay you. Now let me go."

He did.

We continued into Masese and went to bead group. By the time we left the village, we had a van full of industrious, necklace-making women on their way to the bank. When we reached the roadblock, I stopped and the man in the hard hat approached me, expecting his money. All he got was an observation: "Nothing about this road is different and you aren't working very hard. I am not going to pay you."

Soon a chorus of Karimojong voices from the seats of the van affirmed my decision, saying, "Doooo *not* pay theeeess mahn!"

Some men, when trying to swindle a woman, would give up at the sight of seventeen resolute females. Not this one.

He tried to convince me he had been working hard, but hard work is its own evidence, and the proof simply wasn't there. I inched the van closer to the rope, almost touching it. The man stood and watched, asking again for money. And round two of the chorus urged me not to pay him.

Finally, I said: "If I drive through your rope, it will break. You will not have a rope anymore." Still, he stood there, waiting to be paid.

I'd had enough. I turned off the van's ignition, climbed out, picked up the two-by-two, and tossed it aside. I then proceeded to untie the rope from one of the trees, placed it on the ground, and climbed back into the van. My friend in the passenger seat was speechless.

"Two years ago I wouldn't have done that," I told her. "I would have been terrified of what that man would do to me. But now, in that village behind us, I have three thousand friends who may literally kill him if he hurt me."

God has given us this friendship in the most unlikely place, in this most unlikely condition. He has made us feel like family, even though we come from completely different worlds. Because of this beautifully God-orchestrated, unexpected friendship, hope courses through my veins even on the most difficult days.

God teaches me, and Masese teaches me, this: Resurrection is real. Life is more powerful than death. Light can pierce darkness. I may never see the end of horrendous situations on this earth, so instead of trying to fix the situations here and now, I will focus on helping these people come to heaven with me, so we may say together: "Death and sadness have been swallowed up in a victory. Oh, death, where is your victory? Death, where is your sting?" (see 1 Corinthians 15:54). Christ has overcome the mess that is this world and I am humbled to get to witness His salvation on a daily basis.

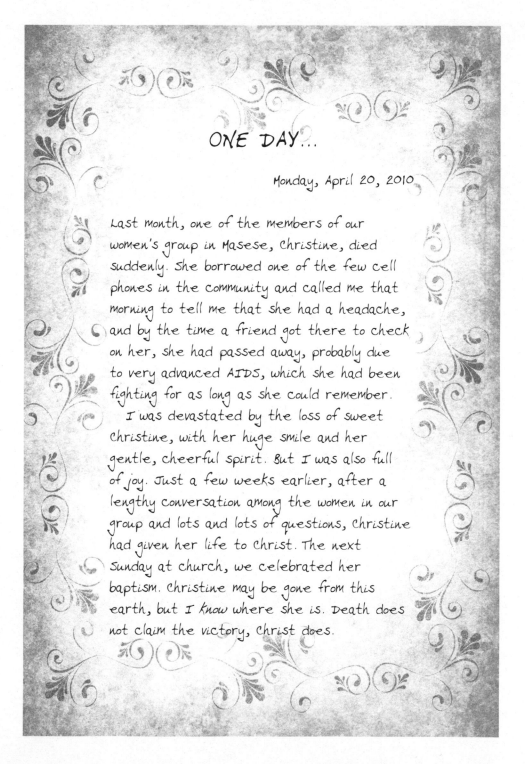

ONE DAY...

Monday, April 20, 2010

Last month, one of the members of our women's group in Masese, Christine, died suddenly. She borrowed one of the few cell phones in the community and called me that morning to tell me that she had a headache, and by the time a friend got there to check on her, she had passed away, probably due to very advanced AIDS, which she had been fighting for as long as she could remember.

I was devastated by the loss of sweet Christine, with her huge smile and her gentle, cheerful spirit. But I was also full of joy. Just a few weeks earlier, after a lengthy conversation among the women in our group and lots and lots of questions, Christine had given her life to Christ. The next Sunday at church, we celebrated her baptism. Christine may be gone from this earth, but I know where she is. Death does not claim the victory, Christ does.

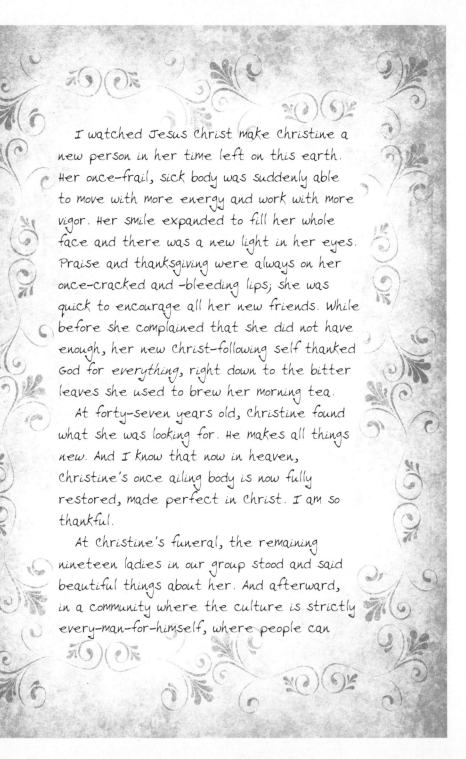

I watched Jesus Christ make Christine a
new person in her time left on this earth.
Her once-frail, sick body was suddenly able
to move with more energy and work with more
vigor. Her smile expanded to fill her whole
face and there was a new light in her eyes.
Praise and thanksgiving were always on her
once-cracked and -bleeding lips; she was
quick to encourage all her new friends. While
before she complained that she did not have
enough, her new Christ-following self thanked
God for everything, right down to the bitter
leaves she used to brew her morning tea.

At forty-seven years old, Christine found
what she was looking for. He makes all things
new. And I know that now in heaven,
Christine's once ailing body is now fully
restored, made perfect in Christ. I am so
thankful.

At Christine's funeral, the remaining
nineteen ladies in our group stood and said
beautiful things about her. And afterward,
in a community where the culture is strictly
every-man-for-himself, where people can

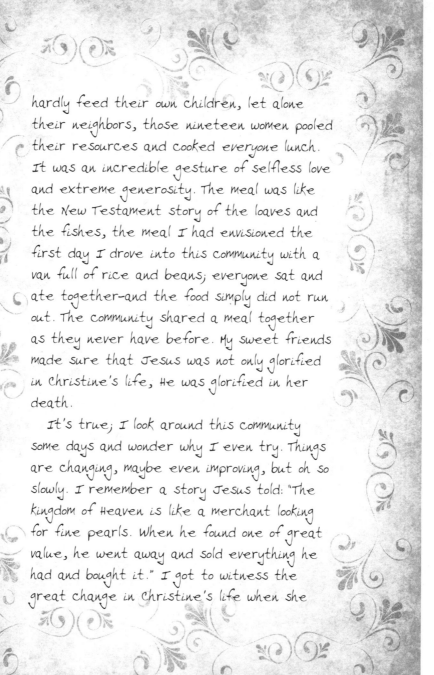

hardly feed their own children, let alone
their neighbors, those nineteen women pooled
their resources and cooked everyone lunch.
It was an incredible gesture of selfless love
and extreme generosity. The meal was like
the New Testament story of the loaves and
the fishes, the meal I had envisioned the
first day I drove into this community with a
van full of rice and beans; everyone sat and
ate together—and the food simply did not run
out. The community shared a meal together
as they never have before. My sweet friends
made sure that Jesus was not only glorified
in Christine's life, He was glorified in her
death.

It's true; I look around this community
some days and wonder why I even try. Things
are changing, maybe even improving, but oh so
slowly. I remember a story Jesus told: "The
kingdom of Heaven is like a merchant looking
for fine pearls. When he found one of great
value, he went away and sold everything he
had and bought it." I got to witness the
great change in Christine's life when she

learned of Jesus' great love for her. One
day, I believe I will get to laugh with her
again in heaven. This is why. The gospel of
Jesus Christ changes people's lives and
their eternity. And that is worth spending
my life for.

16

JUST ONE MORE

W here is that hungry little boy?" I asked a friend who accompanied me one morning to the school where Amazima runs our feeding program.

He looked at me like I was absurd. "Katie, they're *all* hungry," he replied, with obvious question in his voice.

There was one, though, who was hungrier than all the others.

I stood in the schoolyard, literally surrounded by hungry children, but one in particular caught my eye that day. As I scanned the sea of faces, I couldn't locate him. Then I saw him, a tiny boy who looked to be about three years old (but was actually six), with white hair and swollen cheeks, sitting alone beside a small tree.

I took him a plate of food and a cup of water. He registered absolutely no emotion when he looked at them. When he finally decided to reach for the food, I saw that his body was covered with open sores and his arms were dotted with small burn marks. His feet were so cracked and blistered I couldn't believe he had walked up the hill from Masese to the school that day. He was terribly malnourished; I could tell because his splotchy yellow skin was peeling off him, and his short hair, which should have been black as coal, looked like a blanket of snow on his head.

I knew this little boy needed help, so I asked some of the nearby children to find his parents so I could speak with them. His father came up to the school to see what was going on. I asked this man if I could take the child home with me to clean and bandage his wounds. He agreed.

Then I asked, "What is his name?"

To my great shock and sadness, the father replied, "I don't know."

One of the children around me said, "His name is Michael."

I don't know if Michael had ever been in a car before; he certainly hadn't been in a van as large as mine, and he rode home with my friend and me without saying a word or making a sound.

When we got home I fed him my lunch and gave him a big glass of milk, which he drank quickly but still without making a sound. I wanted to get Michael clean as soon as possible, so I hurriedly helped him undress. More burn marks covered his back and legs, probably as a result of being punished with hot sticks, fresh from the fire—on purpose. As we began to bathe his filthy body for probably the first time in a long time, he finally spoke, saying: "I want to go home."

But I couldn't take Michael home, not yet. He needed so much care! I wrapped him in a towel and, as my friend held him tightly, I began to cut away the dead skin that hung from his heels and the insides of his feet. Then I went to work extracting the jiggers and removing the egg sacs and the caked mud and rocks embedded in the holes the jiggers had eaten in his feet. My friend watched in horror and Michael didn't say anything. He didn't scream or cry; he simply sat there in what must have been excruciating pain as tears rolled down his beautiful, little, expressionless face.

I, on the other hand, ran out of the room and threw up.

I quickly returned to put clean clothes, a fresh pair of socks, and a new pair of shoes on Michael in preparation to take him back to his family. As we drove along in the van, my friend searched for some kind of little treat to give to Michael and finally found a lollipop with a whistle on the end of its plastic stick. He demonstrated for Michael the *wheee* sound it made, then handed it to Michael to try for himself. *Wheeee.* We watched in awe as, for the first time, Michael displayed some emotion. His big brown eyes lit up and a wide, happy grin overtook his face. It was as though he had held joy inside for all of his brief life—and could at last express it. The fifteen-minute drive back to Masese was so unlike our silent journey to my house earlier that day. Michael was happy, and I watched in the rearview mirror as he blew his whistle all the way home.

Michael's mother saw us coming and greeted us with one comment: "He looks smart," meaning he looked nice. I wondered about this woman. Was she his biological mother or was she his stepmother? I didn't know. I tried to show her how to care for him and explained that feeding him protein-rich foods would improve his health, because he was otherwise healthy. I left him with some powdered milk and multivitamins, prayed with their family, and promised to check back again soon.

A few weeks later, I went to check on Michael and noticed that his condition had deteriorated significantly in the weeks since I had seen him. He was dirty and hungry, obviously in need of immediate attention.

I knew I could help Michael, but had one problem: I had promised myself over and over again that I would not take any children from Masese into my home for more than a bath, a meal, or some kind of basic medical care, such as bandaging a cut or removing jiggers. I warned myself against getting involved in this way.

"Katie," I said to myself, in my firmest tone of voice, "these children are *all* sick. And they are always sick. If you start caring for them in your home, *it will never end.*"

After all, we fed these children lunch and dinner every day and twice a week, I drove my van, stocked like a minipharmacy, into their village to provide whatever simple medical care I could offer them. I told myself that these twice-weekly visits were all I could handle. I could *not* take children to my house for several days or weeks to help them recover from their various illnesses or injuries. I really, really wanted to keep this promise to myself, but as I looked at Michael that day, I saw no alternative, or at least no alternative that would keep him alive. He needed to be bathed in warm water every day. He needed to eat milk and eggs, fresh fruits and vegetables. He needed multivitamins and fluids high in electrolytes if he was going to live.

For me to get all these things to him every day in Masese would have been impossible. Even if I could have done so, there was no guarantee his parents would not sell these valuable commodities and continue to feed him *posho*. No matter how malnourished he was and how much care he needed, Michael was also fearfully and wonderfully made, created in the image of my Savior. I owed it to him, and to the Lord, to give him a chance to live, so with his parents' permission, I put him in the van and took him home.

I started Michael's "rehab" process with some basic medical tests, and thankfully he tested negative for HIV, TB, and typhoid. We began a rigid deworming routine and I fed him a high-calorie, protein-packed diet. During the first five days he lived with us, he gained two and a half pounds, which was great because he only weighed twenty pounds when he arrived. Over the course of that first week in our home, Michael began a remarkable transformation. He went from being an unresponsive, lethargic, expressionless child who slept all day to being an extremely cheerful, sometimes ornery, delightful little boy who rarely stopped smiling and loved playing games with other children.

During the time Michael was staying with us, a desperate woman in Masese put her infant niece—a very sick, very tiny, very hungry baby girl—into my arms. She was beautiful but so fragile, and I didn't think she could survive much longer without medical intervention. With the woman's permission, I did the only thing I knew to do: scooped up the baby, put her in the van, and drove as fast as I safely could to the best hospital in town. After having the baby admitted to the hospital, I drove back to Masese to explain to the woman that the baby would need to stay there for a while.

The family's house was made of cardboard and was smaller than the bed I sleep in at night. On the floor lay filthy old rags on which they slept and a pile of charcoal on which they cooked (when they had food, I guess). I almost dropped to my knees right there when I saw the conditions in which these people were living. No wonder the baby was so sick.

The baby's family knew she was sick, but they had no means to help her. They were afraid she would die, so they never gave her a name. Instead, God gave me the privilege of naming her, and I could think of no one better to name her after than my precious mother, whose middle name is Patricia.

During our one-night hospital stay, doctors diagnosed sweet baby Patricia with pneumonia and severe malnutrition. Her HIV test came back negative and I praised Jesus for that. In the hospital, I fed her high-energy formula and then took her home to continue to care for her until she was well. For the first twenty-four hours, I could hardly stand to look at her. The hurt and the hunger in her lifeless little eyes were simply unbearable. Every time I changed her diaper, it was filled with large worms—big, fat earthworm-sized worms. To add to her misery, she could hardly sleep at night because of the cough that as-sailed her weak little body.

As I cared for Patricia, I cried for the things this child had been forced to endure for so long. And I cried because I knew I could de-worm her while she was in my care, but the minute I took her back to Masese, the worms would return. But over the next few weeks, through a series of undeniable impressions and events, I knew God was asking me to bring Patricia into our family as my fourteenth daughter and my girls' beloved baby sister, so we began the adoption process once again.

This child, whose eyes were once empty with hunger and dark with sadness, now shines and radiates life and vitality. She is simply indescribable, with a personality that is all her own. She is spunky, confident, curious, happy—and sassy like her mother. She laughs and dances her way through every day, enjoys the affection of her sisters, and spreads joy everywhere she goes. Her simple trust and dependence on me is a constant reminder of my dependence on the Father and her total confidence in the goodness of people is a reminder to me of the way Jesus desires us to see others.

While I was delighted to have Patricia in our home as a new member of the family, I was sad at the same time, knowing I would soon have to take Michael back to Masese. His family had the means to provide for him, they simply needed to know how to do it. He stayed in our home for about a month and, as his condition improved, I began talking with his parents to help them prepare for his return. By this time, I understood his family dynamics, unfortunately. Michael's "mother" was actually his stepmother, his father's second wife. Quite frequently in Ugandan culture, second wives do not want to care for the children their husbands have from previous marriages or relationships. Sometimes, women view their stepchildren as "cursed" in some way or as unworthy of food or basic provisions. I didn't know any details about Michael's specific situation with his stepmother: I simply knew someone was not taking care of him. So, before sending Michael back to live in conditions that were not beneficial for him, I decided to try to counsel his father and stepmother and let them know which foods would be most nutritious for him, how often he needed to eat, how frequently he should bathe, and other simple-but-important information. As I spoke with them, I knew my heart would break to take him back when the time came, yet I also believed they were going to make a sincere effort to provide better care. I knew that going home was best for him and his family.

I decided to take him back to his father and stepmother one Sunday afternoon, after taking him to church with our family. That morning, I packed his clothes, plenty of powdered milk, and a supply of multivitamins.

I cried all the way through the church service as I thought about having to take Michael home. I could hardly bear to think of this precious child, whom I had so fallen in love with, going back to a place where there was no guarantee that his stepmother would not simply sell the milk we sent with him.

And God spoke so plainly to me. He did not apologize for my heartache; even better, He shared it. He *knew*. The pain in my heart over having to give up a little boy I had loved for a month did not even come close to the pain He felt when He gave His only Son. And He did that for me. The pain I felt was so unbearable, but it was just a fraction of what He felt when He sent His one and only child to save me, to allow me to spend eternity with Him. He *knew*. And while it still hurt to put Michael back in a situation where I could not guarantee his care, I knew God was going with him.

My heart was being broken. The situations with Michael and Patricia and so many other children were breaking it every day. While I never lost my love or compassion for the children, I did sometimes lose my patience with the circumstances in which they were living.

I remember at times, when I was not overwhelmed with sadness for the children, feeling so angry. I was angry that the culture in Uganda lies to women like Michael's stepmother, causing her to believe she does not have to care for a child who is not biologically hers, even when she has ample means to do so. I was angry that in the "Pearl of Africa" and, in fact, the most fertile area of this region, an auntie had no food to feed her baby niece or herself. I was angry that these things resulted in such tremendous suffering for these innocent children.

I was angry because I believed, and still believe, that the God who created the universe did *not* create too many children in His image and not enough love to go around. And I wanted to do more. I wanted to help them *all*.

God whispered that one is enough. He assured me that He would hold the others while they wait for someone to come along and give them their milk and their medicine. He doesn't ask me to take them all but to stop for *just one*, because, as I do it for *one* of "the least of these" I do it for Him (see Matthew 25:40). I felt deep in my spirit that He was teaching me to care for the one person in front of me. Stop for the little boy with white hair and scabs covering his body; stop for the baby girl with feces covering her dress, so weak that she can't hold up her head. Stop and love the ones right in front of me and trust Him with the rest. He whispered that it would be okay and that I didn't have to be angry, I could smile because one less baby was hungry, and that was good enough for that day.

This is a lesson He has continued to teach me. And it is sometimes hard and ugly. Because every time I stop for that one sick child, that one hungry old man, that one new baby girl, my mind races with the statistics of how many more I am not touching, not feeding, not saving. God whispers every time, though, that this one is enough. It is enough that this one is feeling His love and that love is eternal. *Eternal.*

Today, that anger is gone, though sometimes I still have to sit with the Father in my sadness and brokenness over all the hurt in this world. Sometimes I still have to cry to Him and ask Him why innocent children must suffer and beg Him to move people to action. Still, we as a family just love the ones with whom God has entrusted us as best we can. We let Him hold us as we hold the little ones He has given us to look after. We do what we can do, and we trust Him with the rest.

When I have a rough day, or several rough days in a row, as I did around the time Patricia joined our family, I can easily forget why I do what I do. I used to repeat to myself, "Do not forget in the darkness what you have been promised in the light." When my days are dark and difficult, I am tempted to look around and think, *Why? Why do I do this? Why would I take one more child? Why would we live with less so we can give to others more? Why did I leave family and friends to go to a land of strangers? What am I doing here?*

I do not usually forget the answer to all these questions: "For

Jesus. Because He called me to this and because He gave His life for me." This means that it has been granted to me, it is my *privilege*, not only to believe in Him but also to suffer for Him (see Philippians 1:29). That suffering is not alone, but is with Him, and oh, what a privilege it is just to be able to be in His presence, to share that with my sweet Savior.

This is what it means when I say I do it for Jesus. He loved me first; I love Him back. And sometimes it hurts. But even then it is pure joy to even be considered worthy to share in His suffering. That is the promise: not that He is sorry that it hurts, but that He sees; that He knows; that He is here with us.

I think of various "ones" with which I have been blessed.

I think of Michael, who is back at home with his stepmom, healthy now, but maybe still mistreated. God knows that, in Uganda, as a single woman I cannot legally adopt a little boy, so how could my heart be so knit to his?

I think of a girl named Gloria, whose brain was so damaged from her high fever she may always be in a vegetable-like state. God in His infinite wisdom knew that had I been there a few days sooner, this potentially lifelong damage could have been prevented.

But then I think of fourteen little girls who have a home and food and a mommy, and who know Jesus. I think of sixteen hundred Karimojong children, modern-day lepers in Uganda, singing about God's love for them and leaving the school with their bellies full. I think of four hundred sponsored children who sometimes show up on Saturday in new clothes because their parents can finally afford to buy them a new dress or shirt, now that Amazima provides for all their basic needs (food, education, medical care).

I see thousands of deep brown eyes and feel thousands of little brown hands and I know that even on the hardest day, stopping is worth it. A life changed is worth it, even if only one. God's love made known is worth it, even if only to one. I will not save them all. But I will keep trying. I will say "Yes." I will stop for one.

ONE DAY...

Tuesday, March 9, 2010

Praise the Lord, O my soul; all my inmost being, praise His holy name. Praise the Lord, O my soul, and forget not all His benefits—who forgives all your sins and heals all your diseases, who redeems your life from the pit and crowns you with love and compassion... (Psalm 103:1-4).

I met Michael in August of last year and felt fairly certain he was on death's doorstep, or if not, pretty close. His hair was white and fuzzy, his face swollen, his growth stunted, and his skin just about peeling off, all from severe malnutrition. After doing everything I could for him while keeping him in his home and seeing very little improvement, our family decided to move him in with us as we nursed him back to health. What a blessing it was to watch this sweet

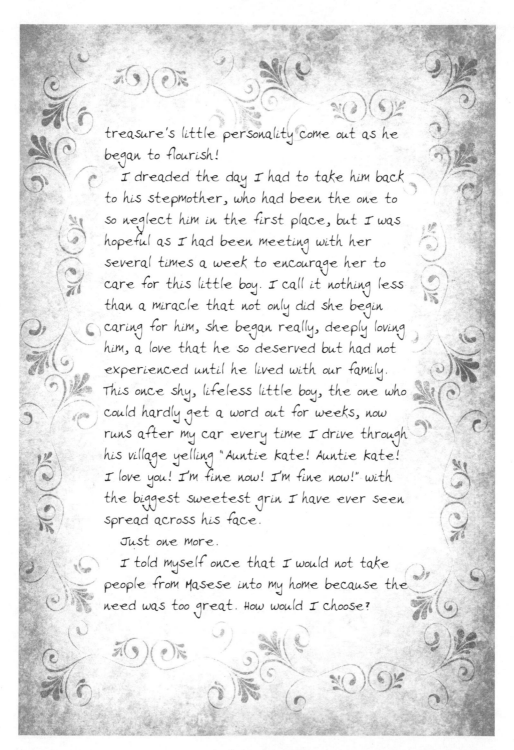

treasure's little personality come out as he began to flourish!

I dreaded the day I had to take him back to his stepmother, who had been the one to so neglect him in the first place, but I was hopeful as I had been meeting with her several times a week to encourage her to care for this little boy. I call it nothing less than a miracle that not only did she begin caring for him, she began really, deeply loving him, a love that he so deserved but had not experienced until he lived with our family. This once shy, lifeless little boy, the one who could hardly get a word out for weeks, now runs after my car every time I drive through his village yelling "Auntie Kate! Auntie Kate! I love you! I'm fine now! I'm fine now!" with the biggest sweetest grin I have ever seen spread across his face.

Just one more.

I told myself once that I would not take people from Masese into my home because the need was too great. How would I choose?

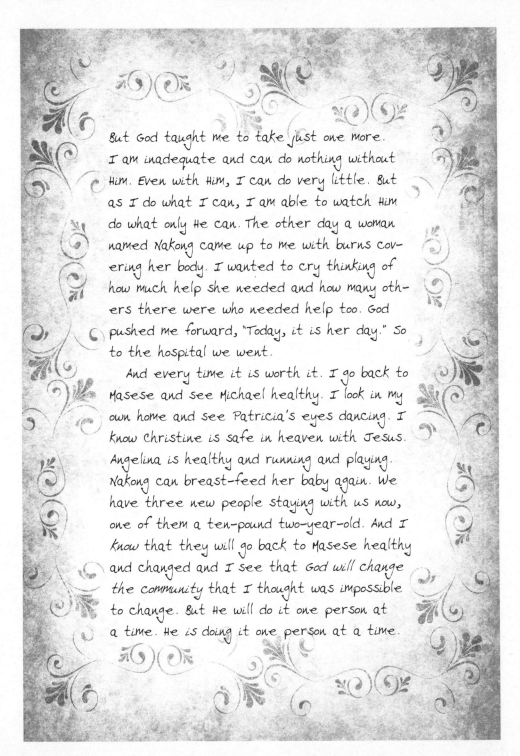

But God taught me to take just one more.
I am inadequate and can do nothing without
Him. Even with Him, I can do very little. But
as I do what I can, I am able to watch Him
do what only He can. The other day a woman
named Nakong came up to me with burns covering her body. I wanted to cry thinking of
how much help she needed and how many others there were who needed help too. God
pushed me forward, "Today, it is her day." So
to the hospital we went.

And every time it is worth it. I go back to
Masese and see Michael healthy. I look in my
own home and see Patricia's eyes dancing. I
know Christine is safe in heaven with Jesus.
Angelina is healthy and running and playing.
Nakong can breast-feed her baby again. We
have three new people staying with us now,
one of them a ten-pound two-year-old. And I
know that they will go back to Masese healthy
and changed and I see that God will change
the community that I thought was impossible
to change. But He will do it one person at
a time. He is doing it one person at a time.

And that He would use me just blows me away again and again and again.

I could try to find words enough to praise my loving Father. They would not be sufficient.

He lifted me out of the slimy pit, out of the mud and mire; he set my feet on a rock and gave me a firm place to stand. He put a new song in my mouth, a hymn of praise to our God. Many will see and fear and put their trust in the Lord (Psalm 40:2, 3).

17

HE SETS THE SOLITARY IN FAMILIES

One day I counted the number of people and animals living at my house. I had fourteen children, ten dogs (because one of our dogs had eight puppies), two goats, one monkey, sweet Christine, and me. That's a *lot* of life.

At that point I didn't think I could handle one more person, or animal, or urgent situation. I didn't think our everyday existence or my immediate surroundings could get any more hectic. *I really didn't.*

I was wrong.

God could have brought me a crying mother holding her four-pound, four-month-old baby girl who could hardly breathe.

And He did.

A dear friend and Amazima employee brought her sister, Susan, to our house with her infant daughter, named Happy. At first glance anyone would have thought this little girl was dead, but upon closer inspection I could see her chest, barely moving in and out.

We rushed her to the nearest hospital, where they put her on IV fluids and oxygen. The next morning we made the two-hour drive from my house to Kampala to take Happy to International Hospital there. This hospital is the biggest and most modern in

Uganda, though still inferior to many western medical facilities.

After much testing, doctors concluded that Happy had a nine-millimeter hole in the wall between the ventricles of her heart. This meant that her heart could not oxygenate blood properly, causing its left ventricle to fail. This resulted in extreme pulmonary distress, which led to a very rapid heartbeat, decreased appetite, and poor weight gain.

The doctors in Kampala inserted a small feeding tube into Happy's tiny body, put her on oxygen, and pumped intravenous fluids into her. Their plan was to continue this treatment for a few weeks in an attempt to increase her weight so she might be able to withstand the surgery needed to repair the hole in her heart. They didn't know whether the operation could be performed in Kampala and told us she might have to go to Nairobi, Johannesburg, or even the United States to undergo it. While that would have been expensive, I was eager to try to raise the money because there was a strong possibility her life could be saved.

I tried not to be frustrated by the lack of necessary equipment and medical care in Uganda or by the fact that a simple checkup when she was a few weeks old could have identified Happy's problem and prevented her suffering. Her situation, really, was no different from anyone else's, no matter what country they live in. All over the world, God is the Healer. He is the one whose mighty touch strengthens and restores people. He is the one who makes sick people well. He is the one who calms and sets free those who are fearful and in pain. I knew that if Happy survived, it would be because God chose to work a miracle in her life. And I prayed with all my heart that He would do so and be glorified through it.

But He didn't. He chose a different kind of healing for her.

The Lord gave, and the Lord has taken away;
blessed be the name of the Lord!

—Job 1:21 NKJV

Lots of emotions; there are too many words to really even write. Above all else, I am resting in knowing Happy is whole and rejoicing with Jesus. Oh, thank you, sweet Lord.

Yesterday I was sad and frustrated. I wasn't sad that Happy was with our Creator or frustrated that she had passed away; I know that was His plan. But seriously, she was four months old; she weighed four pounds; and she had a nine-millimeter hole in her heart. The doctors at the government hospital where treatment is supposed to be free for everyone, looked at her, looked at her mother, saw they had no money, and sent her away. They looked at her sweet face and sent her away. At that hospital, they have a heart surgeon who might have been able to fix the hole! Happy didn't have to struggle so much. In this country, there is medication that would have helped her.

Yesterday I was tired; not sleepy, just plain worn out. I knew Happy for about seventy-two hours. Sure, for those seventy-two hours I was able to help her, to comfort her mom, to rock her to sleep. I fell in love with this baby girl who barely had the strength to breathe but clutched my finger with all her might. But why? Why am I constantly falling in love with people I cannot help, people who are taken out of my life so quickly?

As I read my Bible last night after falling into bed, the Lord continued to take me to the miracles of Jesus. And something I have never noticed before really stood out. The Bible tells us of Jesus magnificently raising Lazarus from the dead, healing numerous deathly ill people, and feeding thousands.

What the Bible does not mention, but what must be true is that, years later, Lazarus still died. The people Jesus healed were inevitably sick again at some point in their lives. The people Jesus fed miraculously were hungry again a few days later. More important than the very obvious might and power shown by Jesus' miracles is His love. He loved these people enough to do everything in His power to "make it better." He entered into their suffering and loved them right there.

We aren't really called to save the world, not even to save one person; Jesus does that. We are just called to love with aban- don. We are called to enter into our neigh- bors' sufferings and love them right there. Maybe I did nothing but allow Happy to strug- gle a few days longer. But I did love her, and she now has a spot in my heart, a heart that is forever changed.

Today I am rejoicing in my few days with Happy. I am rejoicing that one day I will see her again and be able to tell her how she changed my heart and taught me about love. In the past few days, I have received countless e-mails and phone calls from doctors, nurses, friends, and strangers *offering help and encouragement. What a beautiful example of the body of Christ.*

I received several e-mails last night and this morning from different doctors in the States who had been helping me, all telling me a bit about how Happy had changed their hearts and given them a stronger desire to provide better medical care in Uganda.

Sweet Happy, you are paving the way for greatness. In four months you have brought about change, you have taught people, you have broken people's hearts. We love you, sweet baby girl.

The Bible says that God sets the solitary in families (see Psalm 68:6 NKJV). This is what He did for Happy when He brought her into our lives. This is what He's done for many others, some who have stayed with us for weeks or a few months, some who have been our guests for only a few days, and those like Happy, who capture our hearts as we care for them in the hospital or in their own homes. The number of days or weeks we are together isn't important; what really matters is the way God knits our hearts together during the time He chooses for us to be in one another's lives.

This is also what God did for me while I was in the States attending college. He connected me with two families from my hometown of Brentwood, Tennessee, Gwen and Scott Oatsvall and Suzanne and Mike Mayernick. These two couples, and their children, opened their hearts and their homes to me, and we bonded almost instantly. To my delight, I discovered that they felt as passionately about orphaned children as I do and believe, as I do, that God's people are the solution to the world's problem of fatherless, motherless boys and girls. I fell in love with the Oatsvall and Mayernick children and spent hours playing with them. In addition, in Gwen and Scott and in Suzanne and Mike I found wonderful Amazima supporters. I don't think the ministry would have really gotten off the ground without them! Both these families have been to Uganda multiple times and have adopted children from my new home country.

The Mayernicks brought their children, their nephew, and a couple of their friends all the way to Uganda in early 2009 for the first of several visits. Every time they come, they bring such joy to my girls and such love and encouragement to me. Their children play happily with my children; Suzanne makes my coffee in the mornings; and Mike reads Bible stories and dances around the living room with my girls. All of us adore one another, and even though our homes are half a world apart, we are family.

Not only are the Mayernicks family to my girls and to me, they also became family to a little girl I met when I first arrived in Uganda in 2007 to volunteer at the babies' home. The minute I walked into that place, my mom and I fell in love with the sickest baby girl I had ever seen (I had no idea what lay ahead of me!).

Her name is Josephine, and at one year old she could not hold up her head or roll over. She had no teeth and was about the size of a baby two months old. My mother and I took turns holding her and carrying her all over Jinja. When she was sick, we took her to the hospital and spent evenings holding her while nurses poked and prodded. I sang her to sleep. I cried when she cried. I begged the Lord, "*Please don't let her die!*" I went home to America with Josephine still in my heart and spent countless hours thinking and praying about her.

While in the United States, I watched Josephine grow through photographs posted on the Facebook pages of various people who volunteered at the babies' home, and when I returned to Uganda to teach kindergarten, the first thing I did was scoop sweet Josephine into my arms. When I wasn't teaching, I spent many hours holding Josephine, bathing her, and giving her bananas. And I prayed that her forever family would come soon to take her home.

In December 2008, I sat in Mike and Suzanne Mayernick's home and listened as Suzanne said that if she ever had another baby girl, she would name her Josie Love.

My heart leaped. *Josephine!*

I went straight to Suzanne's computer and showed her every picture I could find of Josephine, talking about how wonderful it would be if Suzanne and Mike could adopt her. Suzanne looked at me as though I was certifiably crazy and laughed.

Three months later, when the Mayernicks and their friends came to visit for the first time, I quickly took them to meet Josephine. By this time they had been praying about making her part of their family, but were unsure what her special needs would entail.

But little Josephine did it again; she stole their hearts immediately, just as she had stolen mine. Not long after they returned to the States, I received the phone call I'd been waiting for: They were going to adopt her.

I continued to visit Josie at the babies' home whenever I could. I was so excited to visit her and whisper to her, "They are coming. Your mommy and daddy are coming to get you."

Several months later, Mike and Suzanne arrived in Jinja to take Josie home with them. The routine medical tests performed on children who are going to the United States revealed that Josie had tuberculosis and was HIV-positive (she had tested negative previously, but sometimes the disease takes awhile to show up). The Mayernicks then had to return to the States to complete some paperwork, so I offered to keep her until they could get back to Uganda. She ended up living with us for a few months. The girls and I were delighted to have this adorable child in our home; she has an infectious personality and is like family to us.

In the wake of Josie's diagnosis, my devastated friends demonstrated wholehearted trust in God. I was truly challenged and encouraged as I watched them process Josie's health information and decide to take her home regardless of her condition.

I marvel at God's goodness, His plans that are greater than anything I could have ever imagined. The sweet baby girl I fell in love with years ago went home to live with two of my favorite people in the world. Because Mike and Suzanne are neighbors of my parents, Josie is growing up down the street from my mom, who loves her to pieces. In addition, this little girl with special medical needs now lives near one of the best children's hospitals in the world. Her tuberculosis has been cured and the HIV viral loads in her blood are so low that they are virtually undetectable. She can run now, though she could hardly walk when Mike and Suzanne took her home. She goes to preschool, fights with her brothers, laughs hysterically, and inspires everyone she meets.

I can't even convey how beautiful and how amazing it is, that God would knit our hearts together as He has and that He would weave our stories together in such a powerful way.

He really does set the solitary in families.

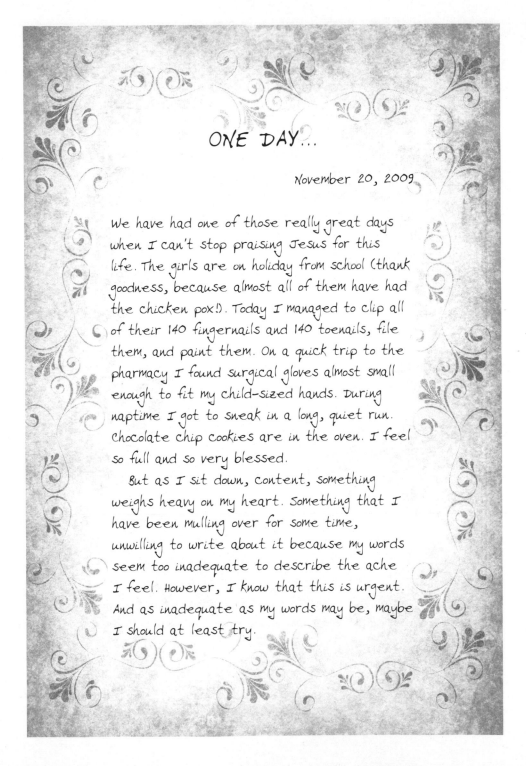

ONE DAY...

November 20, 2009

We have had one of those really great days when I can't stop praising Jesus for this life. The girls are on holiday from school (thank goodness, because almost all of them have had the chicken pox!). Today I managed to clip all of their 140 fingernails and 140 toenails, file them, and paint them. On a quick trip to the pharmacy I found surgical gloves almost small enough to fit my child-sized hands. During naptime I got to sneak in a long, quiet run. Chocolate chip cookies are in the oven. I feel so full and so very blessed.

But as I sit down, content, something weighs heavy on my heart. Something that I have been mulling over for some time, unwilling to write about it because my words seem too inadequate to describe the ache I feel. However, I know that this is urgent. And as inadequate as my words may be, maybe I should at least try.

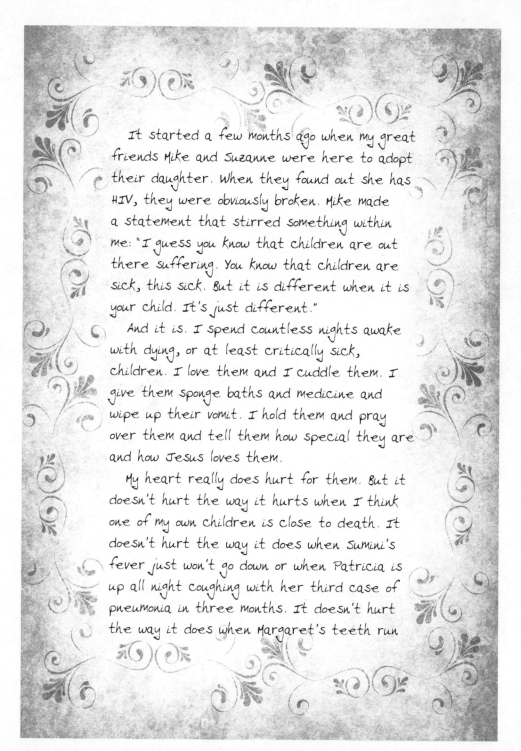

It started a few months ago when my great friends Mike and Suzanne were here to adopt their daughter. When they found out she has HIV, they were obviously broken. Mike made a statement that stirred something within me: "I guess you know that children are out there suffering. You know that children are sick, this sick. But it is different when it is your child. It's just different."

And it is. I spend countless nights awake with dying, or at least critically sick, children. I love them and I cuddle them. I give them sponge baths and medicine and wipe up their vomit. I hold them and pray over them and tell them how special they are and how Jesus loves them.

My heart really does hurt for them. But it doesn't hurt the way it hurts when I think one of my own children is close to death. It doesn't hurt the way it does when Sumini's fever just won't go down or when Patricia is up all night coughing with her third case of pneumonia in three months. It doesn't hurt the way it does when Margaret's teeth run

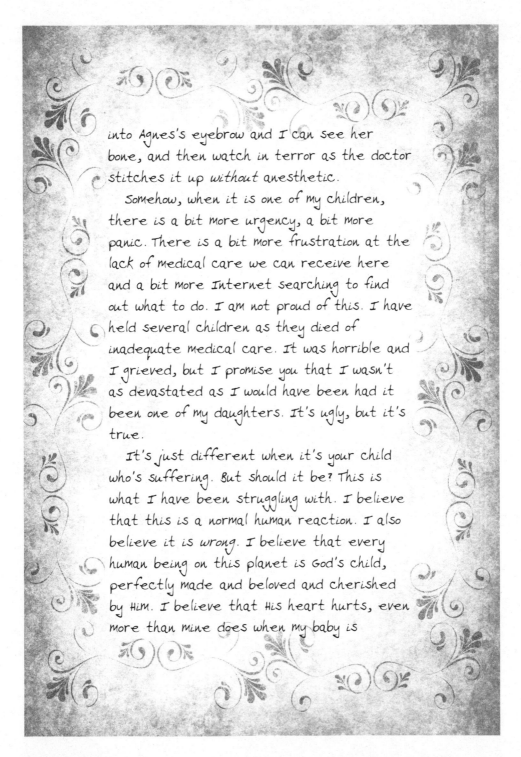

into Agnes's eyebrow and I can see her bone, and then watch in terror as the doctor stitches it up *without* anesthetic.

Somehow, when it is one of my children, there is a bit more urgency, a bit more panic. There is a bit more frustration at the lack of medical care we can receive here and a bit more Internet searching to find out what to do. I am not proud of this. I have held several children as they died of inadequate medical care. It was horrible and I grieved, but I promise you that I wasn't as devastated as I would have been had it been one of my daughters. It's ugly, but it's true.

It's just different when it's your child who's suffering. But should it be? This is what I have been struggling with. I believe that this is a normal human reaction. I also believe it is *wrong*. I believe that every human being on this planet is God's child, perfectly made and beloved and cherished by Him. I believe that His heart hurts, even more than mine does when my baby is hurting, for each and every one of the hurting, dying, starving, crying children in our world. So I have to believe that if my heart was truly seeking to be aligned with the heart of God, that I would hurt for each of these children as well. But sometimes, I forget. Sometimes I'm busy. Sometimes hurting for my very own children just feels like enough. I believe the world says this is okay. I believe it is wrong. And this keeps me up at night.

Angelina is seven years old and barely weighs fifteen pounds. Her mother has not had any food to give her in more than four months. When Angelina musters enough energy to let out a cry of hunger (she is far too weak to walk or even hold her head up), her mother gives her some locally brewed alcohol to keep her quiet. For four months, keeping Angelina slightly drunk has actually probably been what is keeping her alive. The dirt floor where she has been lying for her whole life, accumulating bedsores, is covered in waste, animal and human. Jiggers burrow deep into

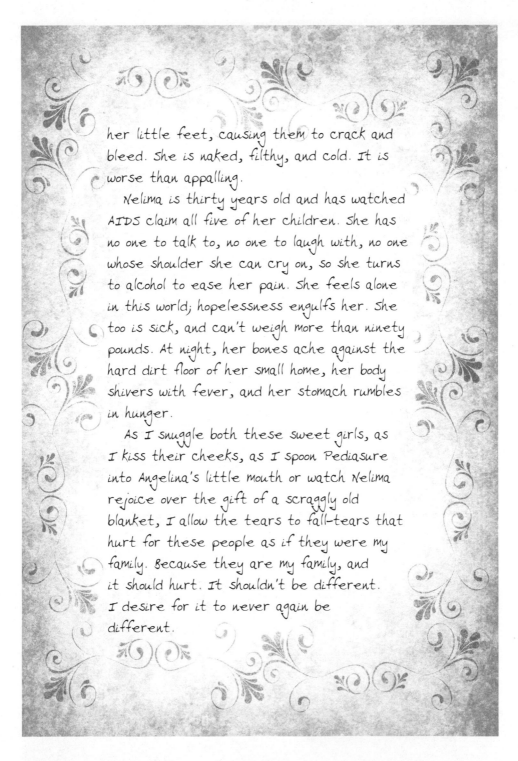

her little feet, causing them to crack and
bleed. She is naked, filthy, and cold. It is
worse than appalling.

Nelima is thirty years old and has watched
AIDS claim all five of her children. She has
no one to talk to, no one to laugh with, no one
whose shoulder she can cry on, so she turns
to alcohol to ease her pain. She feels alone
in this world; hopelessness engulfs her. She
too is sick, and can't weigh more than ninety
pounds. At night, her bones ache against the
hard dirt floor of her small home, her body
shivers with fever, and her stomach rumbles
in hunger.

As I snuggle both these sweet girls, as
I kiss their cheeks, as I spoon Pediasure
into Angelina's little mouth or watch Nelima
rejoice over the gift of a scraggly old
blanket, I allow the tears to fall-tears that
hurt for these people as if they were my
family. Because they are my family, and
it should hurt. It shouldn't be different.
I desire for it to never again be
different.

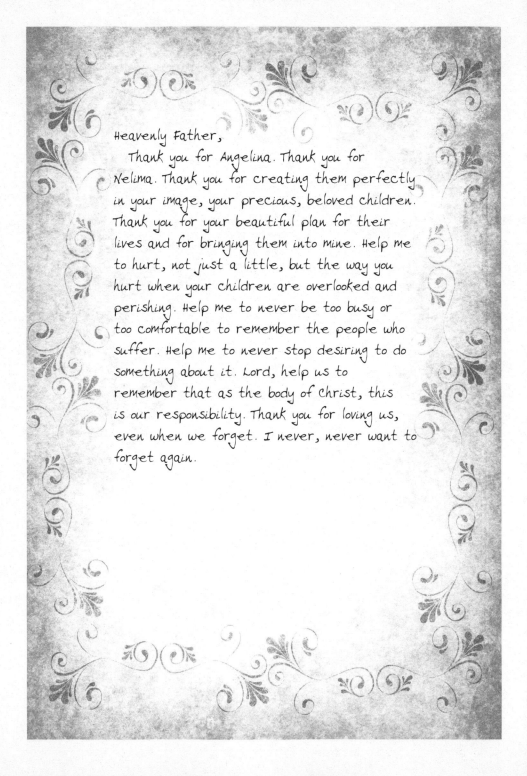

Heavenly Father,

   Thank you for Angelina. Thank you for
Nelima. Thank you for creating them perfectly
in your image, your precious, beloved children.
Thank you for your beautiful plan for their
lives and for bringing them into mine. Help me
to hurt, not just a little, but the way you
hurt when your children are overlooked and
perishing. Help me to never be too busy or
too comfortable to remember the people who
suffer. Help me to never stop desiring to do
something about it. Lord, help us to
remember that as the body of Christ, this
is our responsibility. Thank you for loving us,
even when we forget. I never, never want to
forget again.

18

COUNTING THE COST

For eight months, Grace loved to take a bath. Then she turned three. Whoever named the "terrible twos" obviously had not experienced three yet.

I don't exactly remember when it started. One day, she simply would *not* get into the bathtub. So I didn't make her. I let her get in bed dirty that night. The fight just wasn't worth interrupting everyone else's bedtime. But on the second night, I couldn't ignore her again. She really needed that bath. So we began the struggle, and it continues to this day.

Night after night, we go through the same motions. The scene unfolds like this: I ask Grace to get into the bathtub, to which she quietly replies, "I don't want."

I, in my kindest, sweetest Mommy voice, explain to her that she is three years old, that she does not always know what is best for her, and that she does not always get what she wants. I tell her that this is about her health and well-being; everyone has to take a bath! She simply looks at me, not understanding *at all* what I am trying to say.

Not to be deterred, I try a different approach, saying excitedly, "Come on, Gracie! Let's go play in the bathtub!"

At this point she blinks her eyes very fast, and big crocodile tears begin to run down her cheeks, another plea for sympathy. When she sees that her tears are not getting her anywhere, she begins to shriek "No bath, no bath, *no bath!*" as if the water would melt her.

I say it more sternly the next time. "Grace. Bath time."

I then lift her to her feet and practically drag her down the hall to the bathroom. Her sorrow turns to anger. She makes her best "I don't like you, Mom" face, folds her arms, and plops to her bottom. *"I don't want!"* she shouts.

So I pick her up. She kicks and screams, and eventually I get her into the bathtub. She flails around in there for a bit, letting me know with her wails that I am ruining her life and she may never be happy again.

And then, a funny thing happens. As she splashes water on herself, she remembers: She likes the bath! The bath is fun. Not to mention a really great way to get clean.

By the end of the scenario, Grace usually enjoys her bath so much she doesn't want to get out of the tub.

The bath time struggle never is about the bath at all. It is about obedience. Grace is three years old and she simply does not want to obey. She thinks *she* should be the one to decide whether she gets in the tub or not. She is three years old, and she is trying to figure out just how much control she has in her little life. At this point, not much.

Maybe I am a bad mother for not disciplining Grace more severely for her disobedience, but the reality is, little disobedient Grace reminds me so much of myself.

I shudder to think what I could have missed in life because of my disobedience. I am so thankful that God in His grace does not allow me to win. Because usually, the fight is not really about what He is asking me to do. It is not about the bathtub. It is about me, trying to figure out just how much control I have over my little life. At this point, not much.

I would like to be able to say that I always do exactly what the Lord asks of me. I would like to say that I always seek Him first when a difficult situation presents itself. While I am getting better at it, sometimes I don't. Sometimes I still think what I do with my life should be my decision. God asks, and reasons, and encourages. He gently explains that I do not know what is best for me and that I do not always get what I want. And I just look at Him, not understanding at all what He's trying to say. Sometimes, I even whine and sob and shriek, just like a tired, angry three-year-old.

So God picks me up, exhausted from struggling, and plops me in the center of His will for my life. And then a funny thing happens. As I kick and scream and struggle, I remember: I like being in the center of God's will for my life. God's plan is usually pretty great. It is a whole lot better than mine anyway. I am so glad that He does not allow me to win.

The more I strive to live in the center of God's will, the more He asks me to give up, the more uncomfortable I become. He teaches me, over and over again, that He does know best. The "bathtub," the uncomfortable places, they get only more difficult. But I am learning to remember, before I even get there, that eventually this will be what is best for me, and more important, what is best for His glory.

I remember the first time it hit me really hard, the magnitude of what He wanted me to give up, how much He desired me to be completely His and His alone. I'd done "difficult" since I first arrived in Uganda. But nothing was more difficult, more grueling, more heartbreaking than the moment He asked me to give up one of the most important things in my life. I thought I had given it all for Him. I thought I had made sacrifices. He wanted more.

Thursday, February 11, 2010

She was eighteen years old and she had
never been in love with anyone she could

touch before. I mean, she had been in love with Jesus since she was little, but this was different, touchable love.

In her eyes, he was perfect. He loved the Lord, not to mention he was pretty darn cute. He went to church with her and joined her on silly errands and at family dinners. He made her giggle by saying things that only she found funny. He made her heart flutter when he swept that one always-stray piece of hair out of her eyes.

They were the "perfect couple." They were desperately in love; one lit up as the other entered the room. They could see their beautiful future together. After high school, they would go together to college, get married, work a bit, settle down, and have children with his eyes and her big smile. They would grow old together, laughing at secrets and kissing each other good night.

Then God asked her to move to Uganda. At first it was going to be for only one year. They could do a year. She would come back and they could still go to college together and all their dreams would still come true.

When the Lord asked her to adopt her first children, it became a bit more complicated. She rationalized, at that time, that her youngest was five, so in thirteen years she could move back home and be with him. But her children kept getting younger and His call kept getting stronger. She would go back in fifteen years, in seventeen

years, in twenty years. Finally she came to
terms with the fact that God was just
asking her to stay. And that when He said He
wanted all of her, He meant all.

Okay, then. She would live in Uganda. But
she held on to her love because remaining
comfortable was so much easier than dealing
with the hurt and the emptiness would be.

Even though he fully supported her work in
Uganda and visited when he could, he never
seemed quite able to envision himself living
the life she embraced. She wanted to live
in both worlds, but it was becoming impossible. Her eyes were opened and her life
was changed. She couldn't pretend to be the
same person. She couldn't sit still in his world
anymore; it made her head spin and her heart
ache. And still she held on because she didn't
love him any less. She knew God could move
mountains and she prayed God would change his
heart. After all, such a love must have been
God orchestrated.

He made her feel beautiful as she walked
through life as a single mom covered in dust
and spit-up. He appreciated her even when
everyone else forgot to say "Thank you." He
believed in her when the rest of the world
said raising $80,000 or adopting ten children
was silly. Even from the other side of the
world, he cheered her on and he picked her
up when she just didn't feel strong enough.
His voice on the other end of the phone
turned a rough day right around.

They were moving in opposite directions. They both knew it, but they both refused to let go.

So she asked God for a very specific sign, for something she thought very unlikely, if not absolutely impossible. And then something devastating happened. God gave her the sign that she asked for. So she kissed him good-bye and drove away and cried so hard that she doubted she would ever breathe again. She tried not to wonder if anyone would ever love her like that again or how she would do her life all alone.

And that's when He reminded her that she wasn't alone at all, that He would make her feel beautiful as a single mom covered in dust and spit-up. He let her know that He appreciated her even when everyone else forgot to say "Thank you," that He believed in her when the rest of the world thought everything she did was crazy, that He would cheer her on and pick her up when she just didn't feel strong enough. He told her that His voice whispering in her ear would turn those rough days right around, that He would always be faithful, that His love would be un-conditional. He reminded her that He, her one true love, would never leave or forsake her and would give her the desires of her heart. That He would make all things new, even her shattered heart.

I still cry when I read these words I wrote so long ago. I still feel the sharp pain of that loss. The thought of spending eternity with Jesus, however, makes the pain seem trivial and momentary. That thought reminds me quickly that I *want* to forsake everything to remain in the center of God's will for my life, that I *want* to give up everything for the sake of the Gospel. I believe with all of my heart that *nothing* is a sacrifice in light of the promise that one day I will get to live with Him forever. I want to obey. I want to give my life away.

The life that I live is full and joyful and wonderful, but it is *not* easy. It certainly is not glamorous. I do not expect it to be. In my NIV Bible, the header above Luke 9:57–62 reads: "The Cost of Following Jesus." Here it is, plain and simple, laid out for me by the Lord.

As they were walking along the road, a man said to Jesus, "I will follow you wherever you go." Jesus replied, "Foxes have holes and birds of the air have nests, but the Son of Man has no place to lay his head." He said to another man, "Follow me." But the man replied, "Lord, first let me go and bury my father." Jesus said to him, "Let the dead bury their own dead, but you *go and proclaim the kingdom of God*." Still another said, "I will follow you, Lord; but first let me go back and say good-bye to my family." Jesus replied, *"No one who puts His hand to the plow and looks back is fit for service in the kingdom of God"* (italics mine).

Sometimes, I am so tempted to look back, but I do not want to. I want to only look forward to what He is going to do.

A little later, at Luke 14:25–33, Jesus tells the crowds gathered around Him,

If anyone comes to me and does not hate his father and mother, his wife and children, his brothers and sisters—yes, even his own life—he cannot be my disciple. And anyone who does not carry his cross and follow me cannot be my disciple. Suppose one of you wants to build a tower. Will he not first sit down and estimate the cost to see if he has enough money to complete it? For if he lays the foundation and is not able to finish it, everyone who sees it will ridicule him saying, "This fellow began to build and was not able to finish." Or suppose a king is about to go to war against another king. Will he not first sit down and consider whether he is able with ten thousand men to oppose the one coming against him with twenty thousand? If he is not able, he will send a delegation while the other is still a long way off and ask for terms of peace. In the same way, any of you who does not give up everything he has cannot be my disciple.

In the days of Jesus, He expected *everything* of His disciples. Do I believe He requires the same today?

I do. And I want to live like I believe it.

I do not claim to have the answers. I do not claim to be "doing it right." I do claim to believe that the words of Jesus are absolutely true and apply to me, right now today. I want to give *everything,* no matter the cost. *No matter the cost.* Because I believe that nothing is a sacrifice in light of eternity with Christ.

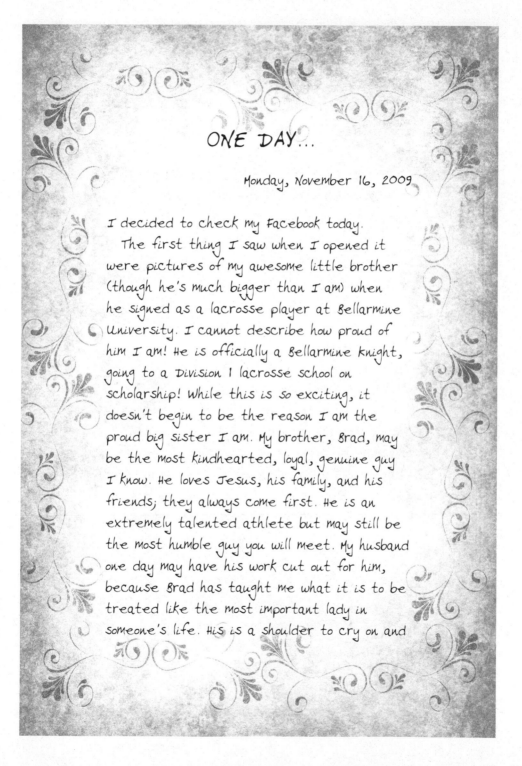

ONE DAY...

Monday, November 16, 2009

I decided to check my Facebook today.

The first thing I saw when I opened it were pictures of my awesome little brother (though he's much bigger than I am) when he signed as a lacrosse player at Bellarmine University. I cannot describe how proud of him I am! He is officially a Bellarmine knight, going to a Division 1 lacrosse school on scholarship! While this is so exciting, it doesn't begin to be the reason I am the proud big sister I am. My brother, Brad, may be the most kindhearted, loyal, genuine guy I know. He loves Jesus, his family, and his friends; they always come first. He is an extremely talented athlete but may still be the most humble guy you will meet. My husband one day may have his work cut out for him, because Brad has taught me what it is to be treated like the most important lady in someone's life. His is a shoulder to cry on and a friend to laugh at everything with. I miss him more every day.

As I looked at the beautiful pictures, I could not hold back the tears, because you see, these pictures are missing something. It's me. The part of my heart that will always stay in Brentwood, Tennessee, with my sweet family throbbed and ached. I longed to be there with them.

Every day of my life is filled with immense joy—more joy than anyone ever deserves. I know the joy that comes from knowing Christ died for me and longing to give my whole life to serving Him. The joy that comes from standing in the center of His will and just watching Him orchestrate everything perfectly. The joy that comes from being able to look into a little brown face that seems hopeless and tell her that Jesus loves her. The joy that comes from being called "Mommy." But that does not mean it doesn't hurt to be so far away from the ones I love so much—hurt deep in the pit of my stomach, where Paul's words "I want to know the power of His

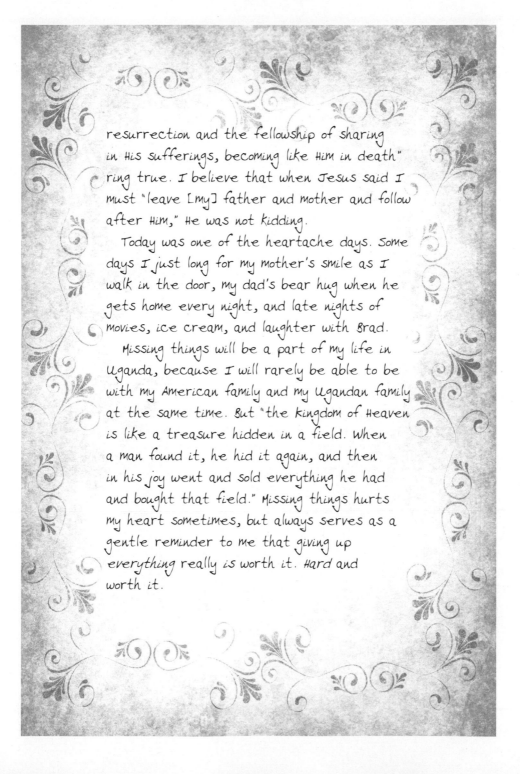

resurrection and the fellowship of sharing
in His sufferings, becoming like Him in death"
ring true. I believe that when Jesus said I
must "leave [my] father and mother and follow
after Him," He was not kidding.

Today was one of the heartache days. Some
days I just long for my mother's smile as I
walk in the door, my dad's bear hug when he
gets home every night, and late nights of
movies, ice cream, and laughter with Brad.

Missing things will be a part of my life in
Uganda, because I will rarely be able to be
with my American family and my Ugandan family
at the same time. But "the kingdom of Heaven
is like a treasure hidden in a field. When
a man found it, he hid it again, and then
in his joy went and sold everything he had
and bought that field." Missing things hurts
my heart sometimes, but always serves as a
gentle reminder to me that giving up
everything really is worth it. Hard and
worth it.

19

A *JJA JA* FOR US

In Masese, it was dark. It was quiet. The cold rain dripped through her thatched roof into her house of about four feet by four feet, soaking through the thin sheet she wrapped around her skeletal, frail body. Her bones ached against the hard dirt floor and her feeble body shivered with cold. Her stomach rumbled with hunger, making sleep impossible.

Grace was sixty-five years old, though when I met her I thought she must have been eighty because of the way poverty, illness, and other hardships had aged her. She was totally blind and all alone. Her HIV had progressed into full-blown AIDS, making it impossible for her tiny body to fight off any type of infection. A merciless cough, caused by tuberculosis, racked her body. In despair she cried out to God, a God she has not spoken to in twenty years, believing He had forsaken her when AIDS took her precious husband and four children from this earth, and when her other two children, who later died of AIDS, abandoned her in search of a better life. She wailed to Him and asked if He could hear her. She knew her life was nearing its end. She desperately wanted to believe in something, anything, before she departed this world. She begged the Lord, if He was indeed real, to send her a friend, a visitor, some kind of sign that someone cared. She fell asleep shivering, with a plastic trash bag over her head to keep the rain off her face.

Completely unaware of an old woman's passionate prayer, I made the familiar trek into Masese the next day. As usual, I bandaged wounds, administered malaria tests, and kissed foreheads with Patricia strapped to my back. A woman from our beading group said she had heard of an elderly blind woman who might need some assistance. So I grabbed my dear friend Tamara and headed deep into the village in the direction in which we had been pointed.

I was not prepared for the sight that met my eyes.

Grace was indeed old and blind, but those realities only scratched the surface of her troubles. Frankly, I stood there looking at her for a few minutes, marveling at the fact that she was still alive. Her body was hardly strong enough to sit upright, certainly not able to stand or walk. She had not eaten in three days, and she hadn't been able to see for the past five years.

She can't weigh more than eighty-five pounds, I thought.

What most caught my attention was the eerie silence that surrounded her house, in the very back of the village near a trash pile. All of her neighbors had gone to work their menial jobs or do whatever they did to pass their time. Even the wind seemed quiet that day.

I thought for a moment that Grace's tiny mud house was exceptionally dark inside, and then I remembered that for her, it was already dark anyway. I embraced this sweet woman, patted her back, and kissed her cheeks; and I told her that Jesus loves her and I love her.

"He does!" she exclaimed. "He has sent me visitors as I asked!"

Her excitement turned to a whisper. "I wanted to stop believing. I did not think God cared for me. Lord, I believe in You."

Tears streamed down both of our faces and together we began to pray to our Father, who sees and hears and answers even the smallest of our requests.

That day was just the beginning of lots of time spent with Grace.

I immediately began to take her food a few times a week, and her neighbor helped her cook it every day. We went to many, many doctors' appointments getting treatment for her TB, blood transfusions, and lots of vitamins. When I took the girls to meet her, they instantly fell in love and immediately adopted her as their *jja ja*.

Before long, the girls and I had developed a habit of packing a picnic lunch and heading over to Jja Ja Grace's house to share a meal with her, read the Bible, sing, and dance. The girls loved it and Grace loved having her tiny home filled with noise and laughter.

Of course, she could hear the girls' happy chatter and giggles and she could feel their soft, loving touches as they patted her on the arm or gave her gentle hugs. And soon, she was able to see them too! When she began eating nutritious food and taking multivitamins, her sight improved dramatically. She certainly didn't have twenty-twenty vision, but she could see. She was thrilled and we were thrilled for her.

On Christmas Day 2009, we ate lunch at her house and God gave all of us the most beautiful Christmas gift (second only to His Son, of course!): Jja Ja Grace, who just months ago had been too weak to stand, began to walk. She walked around the outside of her entire house, praising the Lord the whole time. As neighbors came to watch and ask what had happened, many asked us to pray with them as they accepted Jesus. Grace's testimony was changing lives right before our eyes.

About three months later, the girls and I went to visit Jja Ja Grace and were surprised to see that the food we had sent her for the week remained uncooked and uneaten. She said the neighbor who had been helping her cook the food had moved away three days ago, and she had not eaten since. I asked her how she had been taking her medicine, and she said she simply felt around for each of her five packets of medicine and swallowed one pill from each. This presented a problem, as her pills were all different, some to be taken three times a day, some to be taken two at a time, some to be taken with food, and some without. This arrangement clearly was not going to work.

After talking to more of Grace's neighbors and finding no one who was willing or even able to help, the thought struck me: *We are going to have to move Jja Ja Grace in with us.* To say that this idea overwhelmed me is an extreme understatement.

For the remainder of our visit to Grace that day, the thought of moving Jja Ja Grace into our home ran around and around in my mind as the girls helped me cook her lunch and wash some clothes for her. When we finished, we headed home so I could think and pray about what to do next.

I rolled around in my bed, unable to sleep that night. "God, are you truly asking me to do this?" I kept asking Him.

And God said, "I think you know the answer. You don't actually wonder if I am asking you to do this. You are just afraid of the inconvenience it may cause you to have a blind old woman in your care." He was right; this was true. Somehow, adopting a grandmother seemed much more daunting than adopting a child.

But, for me, the whole situation could be reduced to one question: Did I believe that Jesus was serious? Did I believe what He said was true? The answer was yes. I believe He was serious when He said to love my neighbor as myself, and I believe He meant this even when my neighbor was not tiny and cute and cuddly. I believe when He said to love my neighbor as myself, He really meant to care for others as I would care for my family or myself, and I would never let my family or myself live in such conditions.

As I thought of all the different life changes that would need to take place for us to accommodate Jja Ja Grace, I was completely overwhelmed. But the only reasons I could think of *not* to move her in with us were completely selfish. We had enough space; we had enough food; we had enough love. We had enough.

I kept going back to Matthew 25, where Jesus said,

When the Son of Man comes in his glory, and all the angels with him, he will sit on his throne in heavenly glory. All the nations will be gathered before him, and he will separate the people from one another as a shepherd separates the sheep from the goats. He will put the sheep on his right and the goats on his left.

Then the King will say to those on his right, "Come, you who are blessed by my Father; take your inheritance, the kingdom prepared for you since the creation of the world. For I was hungry and you gave me something to eat, I was thirsty and you gave me something to drink, I was a stranger and you invited me in, I needed clothes and you clothed me, I was sick and you looked after me, I was in prison and you came to visit me."

Then the righteous will answer him, "Lord, when did we see you hungry and feed you, or thirsty and give you something to drink? When did we see you a stranger and invite you in, or needing clothes and clothe you? When did we see you sick or in prison and go to visit you?"

The King will reply, "I tell you the truth, whatever you did for the one of the least of these brothers of mine, you did for me."

Then he will say to those on his left, "Depart from me, you who are cursed, into the eternal fire prepared for the devil and his angels. For I was hungry and you gave me nothing to eat, I was thirsty and you gave me nothing to drink, I was a stranger and you did not invite me in, I needed clothes and you did not clothe me, I was sick and in prison and you did not look after me."

They also will answer, "Lord, when did we see you hungry or thirsty or a stranger or needing clothes or sick or in prison, and did not help you?"

He will reply, "I tell you the truth, whatever you did not do for the least of these, you did not do for me."

Then they will go away to eternal punishment, but the righteous to eternal life.

I read this passage again and again. Sometimes I can hear Jesus whispering, "I'm sick. Will you look after me? Will you invite me in?"

Yes.

The next morning, I sat the girls down for a family meeting. I knew before I even began talking that they would be willing, excited even, to have Jja Ja Grace come to live with us. They loved this joyful woman and they are so much better than I am at giving without holding anything back. The vote was unanimous, they jumped up and down and squealed and told me, "Thank you for having such a good idea!"

I laughed to myself and thought: *This was* so *not my idea.*

That afternoon, we went back to Masese for our women's meeting. When we finished, the girls and I walked to Jja Ja Grace's house to invite her to move into our home. Tears welled in her eyes and a grin crossed her face. "God has given me a family!" she cried. "All these years with no one, and He has given me a new family!"

What happened next shocked me, though; she said no! I looked up and wondered: *All that thinking and processing and not sleeping I have done, and she said no?* She said she was too old to start a new life and would be too much of a burden on us. She said that Jesus would be the one to take care of her and we could just continue to do whatever we could at her house. The girls begged and pleaded, but she had made up her mind. I will not pretend that my selfish human heart didn't feel some relief.

As we left, all feeling encouraged by the love God had sown into our relationships with Grace, I wondered if He just wanted to grow me, if He just wanted to see if I would say yes. I wondered if, in some small way, I was like Abraham and He just wanted to make sure I was willing to sacrifice it all for Him, only to tell me that I didn't really have to.

Jja Ja Grace did not move in with us at that time. God wanted to do something else to help Jja Ja Grace, and He had a plan that blessed her and several of the women in her community—and thrilled me. Several days after Jja Ja Grace declined to move in with us, I asked the women in our beading group if seven of them would volunteer to take one day of the week and spend a few hours with Jja Ja Grace, cooking a bit of food and making sure she took her medicine. To my wonderful surprise, not seven, but *all nineteen* of them agreed to do so.

On Mondays, I went to her house, taking enough food and charcoal for the week and the envelopes of pills. Each day, two or three ladies would go to Grace's house and wash her clothes, cook some of the food, make sure she swallowed all her pills, and just visit. They loved it, and so did she.

While the girls and I were willing to have Jja Ja Grace move in with us and thereby "love our neighbor," I discovered that there is only one thing that feels better: empowering people to help their own neighbors.

The women did a remarkable job taking care of Jja Ja Grace, but after five or six months I saw clearly that she needed more care than even her nineteen new friends could provide for her. The once- or twice-a-day visits helped her greatly, but her illnesses progressed to where she needed around-the-clock attention. The time had come to move her in with us, and this time, I felt no hesitation about doing it.

When I realized Jja Ja Grace was suffering with active, contagious tuberculosis, I knew I couldn't actually move her into our house, under the same roof with my children. So I asked Christine to look for a place as close as possible to our house. Thankfully, she found the perfect spot for Jja Ja Grace, a small, one-room house two doors down from us was available for rent. Jja Ja Grace had no furniture or anything else that required much effort to move; she didn't even have a stove to cook on or a plastic basin with which to bathe or wash her clothes. We packed all her earthly possessions—her clothes and some blankets—and moved her to our village. I knew she was dying, but she was going to die with dignity, surrounded by love.

Many times over the course of each day, my children put on dental masks and walked over to check on our new neighbor, their beloved grandmother. Whether they took her food, bathed her, or simply sat with her in silence, they treasured their opportunities to minister to her and did so with tremendous affection.

But no matter how hard we loved her, we couldn't change the fact that our *jja ja* was near the end of her life. For quite some time, I had planned to return to the States for a few weeks. As the day for my departure drew near, Jja Ja Grace grew sicker, weaker, and ever closer to her final hours. She needed the services only a hospital could provide, and I was thankful to be able to arrange for a place that would care for her in my absence. The girls and I visited her often in the hospital, carrying with us each time we left sadness over her suffering and the loss we would face, but also joy that she would soon see Jesus. I didn't know whether she would be alive when I returned to Uganda or not, so before I left, I said to her the things I wanted to say.

In God's plan, Jja Ja Grace was still alive when I arrived home from the States, and she lived several days after my return. I remember holding her hand into the wee hours of the morning just before she passed away. She had reached the point where she simply could not fight anymore. She had, once again and for the last time, deteriorated to being unable to hold up her head. She could barely speak but rather just groaned to let me know she could hear me, that she was still here.

As I grasped her frail hand gently in those last hours, I whispered to her, telling her not to be afraid. I reminded her that even though she was in immense pain, Jesus had not forgotten her; He was preparing her place and soon she would be with Him forever. As I spoke the words into her ear, my heart said a silent prayer, "Soon, Lord. Quickly, Lord. Please. Please, please."

Just hours later, she went to be with Jesus.

When Jja Ja Grace died, the hospital called me. Selfishly, I was devastated by her death. Selfishly, I hated having to tell my girls that their beloved grandmother was no longer here with us. After I broke the news to them, the girls climbed into the van, and we headed to the hospital. All of us went to Jja Ja Grace's room, where the body of this woman we so loved was lying on her bed, just as it had been when I left her the previous evening. But now, though a sheet covered her head, she was alive and vibrant again, in the place prepared for her. We removed the sheet just enough to see her face and when we did, though we all wept, I felt great relief for her.

That night, as I lay in bed, I was sad. I missed Jja Ja Grace's sweet personality and her kisses and her whispers in my ear. More than I was sad, though, I was so thankful for our time with her; and I remain full of love and deeply thankful for her. I am thankful for what we learned from her and what she learned from us, thankful that God sets the lonely in families, and brought her into ours. And I am beyond thankful that she is now safe with Him.

ONE DAY...

July 20, 2010

I am twenty years old and have fourteen children and four hundred more who all depend on me for their care. Who are all learning to love Jesus and be responsible adults and looking up to me. The reality of it all can be a bit overwhelming at times. However, it is always pure joy. There is a common misconception that I am courageous. I will be the first to tell you that this is not actually true. Most of the time, I am not brave. I just believe in a God who will use me even though I am not. Most mornings, before I even get out of bed, I am overwhelmed with His goodness, with His plan for my life; I stand in awe of the fact that He could entrust me with so much. Most days, I don't have much of a plan. I might have to take a friend to the hospital or I might have a meeting with the principal at school. One of my children could wake up with a fever and I might be in my pajamas all day cleaning up vomit. My dog might have puppies in the bathtub or I might have to perform minor surgery on a neighbor. We could have some extra people in our home or maybe just a monkey that my children insist on nursing back to health.

I don't always know where this life is going. I can't see the end of the road, but here is the great part: Courage is not about knowing the path. It is about taking the first step. It is about Peter getting out of the boat, stepping out onto the water with complete faith that Jesus will not let him drown.

I do not know my five-year plan; even tomorrow will probably not go as I have planned. I am thrilled and I am terrified, in a good way. Some call it courage; some call it foolish; I call it faith. I choose to get out of the boat. Sometimes I walk straight into His arms. More often, I get scared and look down and stumble. Sometimes I almost completely drown. And through it all, He never lets go of my hand.

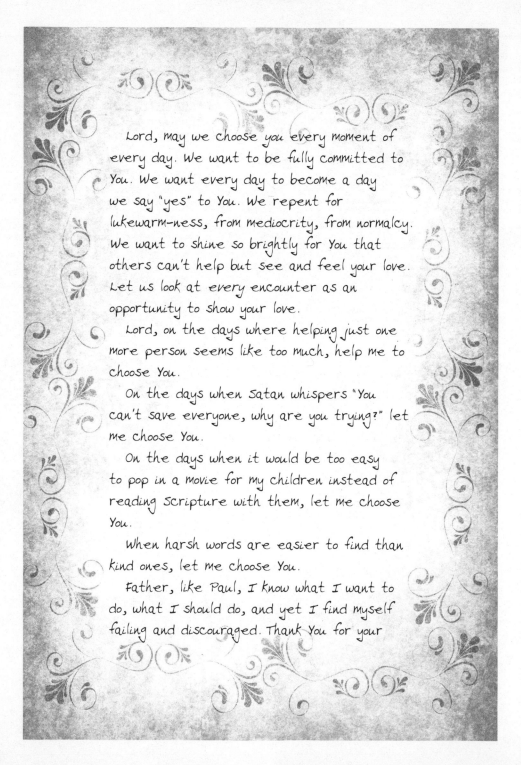

Lord, may we choose you every moment of every day. We want to be fully committed to You. We want every day to become a day we say "yes" to You. We repent for lukewarm-ness, from mediocrity, from normalcy. We want to shine so brightly for You that others can't help but see and feel your love. Let us look at every encounter as an opportunity to show your love.

Lord, on the days where helping just one more person seems like too much, help me to choose You.

On the days when Satan whispers "You can't save everyone, why are you trying?" let me choose You.

On the days when it would be too easy to pop in a movie for my children instead of reading Scripture with them, let me choose You.

When harsh words are easier to find than kind ones, let me choose You.

Father, like Paul, I know what I want to do, what I should do, and yet I find myself failing and discouraged. Thank You for your

grace. Thank You that You who sit so high
would look low upon people like me and use us
as a vessel for you. How blessed we are to
even be called servants, to be able to share
in your kingdom and share your love with
others. Thank you for the cross, where you
have given us peace and holiness. Father, we
long to say Yes to You.

20

ALWAYS ENOUGH

I believe there is only one truly courageous thing we can do with our lives: to love unconditionally. Absolutely, with all of ourselves, so much that it hurts and then more.

I am so thankful for my children's example of loving their neighbors and welcoming them into our home without blinking an eye. They see a baby who needs love and carry him off to feed, bathe, and dote on him as if doing so is the most normal thing in the world. They see a stranger who needs a home and beg me to let her stay. While I am starting to feel overwhelmed, they are feeling overjoyed at the prospect of helping someone else. We face urgent situations frequently; we see devastation sometimes multiple times a day, but my children continue to love, to hope, to believe we can help make someone's life better. Oh, what I learn from their beautiful hearts.

I would like to say that as I become more and more surrounded with sorrow and destitution, it gets easier or less painful. But it doesn't. The brokenness of this world does not become any less sad. Each and every time, it is overwhelmingly devastating that people have to live, and die, like this—like my girls and I see happening around us. While it does not get easier, I have found that I am able to face each situation with a little more hope. I always hope my friends will live here on earth with me, but I tell them with a new sense of urgency about Jesus because mostly I want them to live with Him, experience His profound, unconditional love, whether here or in heaven. I see the sadness, but I also see the redemption.

I have learned along my journey that if I really want to follow Jesus, I will go to the hard places. Being a Christ follower means being acquainted with sorrow. We must know sorrow to be able to fully appreciate joy. Joy costs pain, but the pain is worth it. After all, the murder had to take place before the resurrection.

I'll be honest: The hard places can seem unbearable. It's dark and it's scary, and even though I know God said He will never leave or forsake me, sometimes it's so dark that I just can't see Him. But then the most incredible thing happens: God takes me by the hand and walks me straight out of the hard place and into the beauty on the other side. He whispers to me to be thankful, that even *this* will be for His good.

It takes awhile sometimes, coming out of the dark place. Sometimes God and I come out into a desert and he has to carry me through that too. Sometimes I slip a lot on the way out and He has to keep coming back to get me. *Always*, on the other side is something beautiful, because He has used the hard place to increase my sense of urgency and to align my desires with His. I realize that it was there that He was closest to me, even in the times when I didn't see Him. I realize that the hard places are good because it is there that I gained more wisdom, and though with wisdom comes sorrow, on the other side of sorrow is joy. And a funny thing happens when I realize this: I want to go to the hard place again. Again and again and again.

So we go. This is where our family is today and where I hope to stay—loving, because He first loved us. Going into the hard places, entering into the sorrow because He entered for us first and because by His grace, redemption and beauty are on the other side.

I really did want to go to the hard place again and again. But I had no idea that, as God taught me about suffering and joy and wisdom, He was actually preparing me for my hardest place yet.

October 29, 2010, will stand in my mind forever. This day when all hope seemed lost, when even faith in the One who created me seemed shaky. It was the day when the world seemed to fall apart, never to be put back together again.

Most of the girls and I were involved in homeschool. I was helping four of the girls with math problems at the kitchen table; Prossy was reading quietly near us; and the little girls were playing happily in the backyard. Thankfully, my mother was visiting from the States and was busy doing our laundry. A woman I had never seen showed up at my house with a man I recognized as the government social worker who handles all the adoption papers for my girls. His face was grave as he explained to me that this woman was Jane's biological mother. Years ago I had searched for her, wondered about her, prayed for her to come for her daughter, and she had never answered our advertisements or our prayers. She had abandoned her baby girl when she was only three months old and never returned. Now she wanted Jane back, for some reason she seemed unable to explain.

I don't remember much of what the social worker said to me, except the shocking news that Jane's birth mother wanted Jane back. He went on to explain that, even though we had done everything correctly and legally to determine that Jane was abandoned, there was not much we could do to stop the birth mom from taking her. He reminded me that as a foster parent, I have very few rights in this country, and most courts would probably rule in favor of the biological mother. He said he had to take Jane into police custody until we could go to court. As I listened, unable to believe that this was really happening, he instructed me to go get Jane, pack a bag for her, and take her to the waiting police car.

As the other girls watched silently, I went to the backyard and held Jane so tight; I wept and called out to Jesus to please, please help us. I carried her inside and told her she was going on a little trip and to pick out some clothes; she carefully chose her favorites. I ran and got Jane's toothbrush out of the cup where it sits with mine and Grace's and Patricia's, and put that in her bag, along with some snacks.

Jane's sisters, who didn't know exactly what was happening, continued to watch quietly; some began to weep and in their own unique ways, they kind of said good-bye. Grace was hysterical, and I was so thankful that my mom was there to hold her.

A policewoman took Jane from me and put her in the car that would take her to the police station in her biological mother's home village, six hours away.

I sat down in our gravel driveway and wept.

After a few minutes, I went inside and gathered the girls and my mom. I explained as best I could what was happening and promised that I would do everything in my power to get their sister back. We sat in a circle on the floor, and we prayed and wept and prayed some more.

All I knew about a possible next step was that I needed to appear in court in Jane's birth mother's village on Monday. But Jane was taken on a Friday, and I couldn't sit idly by and do nothing for the entire weekend. So, on Saturday I gathered the girls together and we sat in a circle on the floor again and prayed. A family friend was going to stay with them while I went and got their sister back. I hugged and kissed each one good-bye, then began the long drive to the village with my mom and Patricia in tow.

The weekend in the village felt like hell—full of lawyers and arguing and maneuvering in court. Monday morning, November 1, 2010, the matter was settled. Custody was granted to the birth mother. For more than a year, I had been a mother to fourteen wonderful girls and for the past two years, I had been the only mother Jane knew. And now she would live with a different mother, in a different home, so far away.

The whole day is a blur when I think about it. But little sharp moments are forever etched in my mind. When I finally saw Jane that day, I squeezed my little girl as tightly as I could, and I put a pink dress on her—one that matched the one Patricia was wearing. Her soft hair was matted and filthy after a weekend in police custody, but she stuck a flower in it anyway, hopeful even in this terrible situation. As lawyers argued, she entertained her baby sister and shared her ice cream with anyone who wanted a taste. She held her head high and tried to smile. She told me not to cry, that it would be okay. She is only *four* years old. And there she was, so brave, so big, so beautiful. I was—I *am*—so proud of her.

I was watching Jane and Patricia play together under an orange tree when my lawyer told me that custody of Jane had been granted to her birth mother; she would not be going home with me. I nearly collapsed, unable to catch my breath and unable to look at my daughters, who had no idea what was in store for us.

Once the custody decision was made, Jane's birth mother took Jane and left, telling me on her way that she would call me if she needed anything. Brokenhearted and devastated, my mom, Patricia, and I began the long drive back to Jinja and I tried to wrap my mind around how in the world I would tell Grace her "twin" sister was not coming home.

I didn't think I would ever be able to breathe again. Not that day; not *ever*.

We arrived home late Monday night, and Tuesday morning, my twenty-second birthday, I didn't think my legs would be able to carry my body as I willed myself to get out of bed, overwhelmed with pain and heartache. I looked around and I did not want to be this person; I did not want to be this woman who had to grieve the loss of her daughter. I did not want to be a woman who had to walk her children through the grief and trauma of losing a sister. I did not know how. And I am still learning. Sometimes, I still do not want to be this person. But I am learning how to be this person with grace, because *this* is the path God intended for me. It came as no surprise to Him. Even this, for my *good*.

I marvel when I think about the timing of my mom's visit and the fact that she—the one person I needed most in the whole world—was with me when I had to say good-bye to Jane. I'm not sure I would have been able to deal with it without her. She was the glue that held my family together for those first few days after we returned home without Jane. She was the one who kept the family going when I could hardly get out of bed.

I think about that moment when Jane walked away from the police station with her birth mother. In my unspeakable anguish, God spoke to my shattered heart. He whispered to me that we had loved Jane back to life. He promised that she knows His love and that He will go with her where I cannot. We gave Jane a family when no one else could. We spoke up for her when she could not speak for herself. I fought as hard as I knew how for my little girl. And God, who sees and knows what is very best for her and for the rest of my family, allowed her to go live with someone else. For the good of me, for the good of her and the rest of my children, for the good of His Kingdom and the glory that is His. So I trust Him. I cling to His promises. I believe in His goodness.

Still, I think of Jane and I grieve. I see her little fingers, chipped pink polish, and dirt under her fingernails, which I should have clipped yesterday. I see the gap between her two front teeth and the dimples that pit her cheeks as she giggles that high-pitched, uncontrollable, contagious laugh of hers. And for a brief moment I wonder how God can be good when babies starve and people die cold and alone and children are ripped from their mothers. But only for a moment. Because then I look around and I know that I am *nothing* without Him. That none of this, none of this life I have, would exist without Him. "Surely just as I have intended so it has happened and just as I have planned so it will stand," He says in Isaiah 14:24. My good God gives only good things; He planned this and He will use this. In Him, even sorrow is Joy.

Just a few days after Jane left, I opened my Bible to 1 Kings 17. I hear the desperation in the widow's rough scratchy voice, and I see the bags under her eyes as she wearily replies to the prophet, "I don't have any bread—only a handful of flour in a jar and a little oil in a jug. I am gathering a few sticks to take home and make a meal for myself and my son, that we may eat it—and die" (1 Kings 17:12). She has nothing left to give. *I know this kind of desperation.*

But the prophet knows more. And he says to her, "Don't be afraid. Go home and do as you have said. But first make a small cake of bread for me from what you have and bring it to me, and then make something for yourself and your son. For this is what the Lord, the God of Israel, says: 'The jar of flour will not be used up and the jug of oil will not run dry until the day the Lord sends rain on the land'" (1 Kings 17:13, 14).

So she went. And she did exactly what he said. *I want to know this kind of trust.*

First Kings 17:16 continues with the story of the widow: "So there was food every day for Elijah and for the woman and her family. For the jar of flour was not used up and the jug of oil did not run dry, in keeping with the word of the Lord spoken by Elijah." He is always enough. Like manna that fell for the Israelites, His grace falls, enough for today and then enough again for tomorrow.

I am learning. I am learning to hope when nothing makes sense and to know that God knows best, even when what He is asking of us seems so impossible. I am waiting and God is teaching me this: I beg Him to bring me close to His heart, to even transform my heart that it might be more like His. I think orphan care gets us close, because He sees us as orphans. I think adoption gets us close, because this is how He brings us into His family. The poor, the beggar, the widow, the prisoner, they get us close to His heart because these people are so dear to Him.

But nothing gets us much closer than injustice.

The way Jane was taken was horribly unfair and totally unjust.

When babies starve and people die cold and alone and children are ripped from their parents—these are some of the injustices of a broken world. And I think of a Savior who spent His whole life doing nothing but good, saving and healing and feeding and helping even the most undeserving of people, dying on a cross like a thief or a murderer. I think of Father, a Father who desires good things for His children even more than I desire good things for mine, a Father who could have stopped His Son's torture at any time but instead watched it happen. For me. For you. And I weep at the injustice of it. I think that while *no* part of me wants to be in this place of losing Jane, not at all, this is where I asked to be: closer and closer to His heart. He knows this pain. He knows what it is to lose a child to the injustice of a fallen world. And so while I still cry and beat my fists on the floor, I find comfort in that, and I ask to *be closer still.*

Suffering. Rejoicing. Squalor. Beauty. Love. Pain. These are the things that surround me, and all of them are from Him. This life is beautiful and terrible and simple and difficult, and He is using it for His glory.

My knees are dusty orange, stained by the soil into which they press for hours as I beg God for the mercy and strength to continue. My tears flow in puddles that do not soak into the red, parched earth of Uganda. The puddles and the color of my knees remind me that I was not to leave this life unstained or unscarred. Even Jesus kept His scars after the resurrection. My stains are beautiful to Him and as I become dirtier and more beat up, I am becoming perfect, transformed into the image of the One who made me. And I am thankful.

We recently put up the Christmas tree that has watched our family grow, year after year. We still hung fourteen angels, one for each of my daughters, on our tree; we still had fourteen stockings. Only thirteen sets of hands helped our tree glitter, but fourteen places are forever notched in my heart.

We lovingly displayed our nativity set and I thought of Mary, young, tired, and alone. Completely unable to understand why this would be His plan for her. Chosen. Carrying our Savior into a dark world.

Jesus is here with us and He is coming back. And I am young and sometimes tired and completely unable to understand why He has graced me with this plan for my life. But I am chosen. Instructed to carry the story of our Savior, to shine His light in a dark and broken world. You are chosen too. His life and His strength and His grace, they will not run dry until He gets here, fresh rain on a parched land.

December 25, 2010

It is Christmas, a day of joy and light and hope coming into a fallen world. Friends have all left and the girls are all asleep. There is nothing I enjoy more than a house full of noise and laughter and chaos, except these quiet moments with my Savior just after the noise and laughter and chaos.

I hold sweet baby Winnie, a two-week-old we are keeping for the first month of life while her mom recovers from illness; and I marvel at the miracle of new life. There is a gaping hole in my heart, but there is a love that is even bigger.

All day long we have celebrated Jesus' birth and now, as I gaze into this newborn baby's eyes, I whisper my gratitude for His death. Love that conquers all. Love that is always enough.

We wait in hope for Him.

ONE DAY...

Monday, October 5, 2009

John is a sweet fifteen-year-old karimojong boy with the most beautiful servant's heart. He lives in Masese with a very old grandmother. She is not his own grandmother, just a woman he cares for because she is unable to walk well or find food for herself. And they live with a baby who came from I don't know where. I am constantly humbled by John's sweet disposition, his desire to help this vulnerable grandmother and child even though they are unrelated. How many fifteen-year-old boys spend their lives serving "the least of these" in their own community? He is precious.

On Sunday John was waiting for us when we pulled up to the restaurant where we normally eat after church. He greeted us sweetly but then turned to show me a quarter-sized hole in the back of his foot. Through the language barrier, all I could

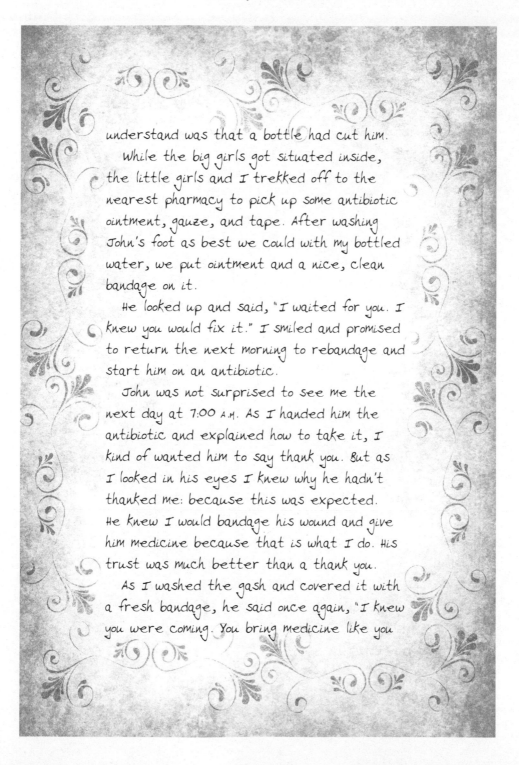

understand was that a bottle had cut him.

While the big girls got situated inside, the little girls and I trekked off to the nearest pharmacy to pick up some antibiotic ointment, gauze, and tape. After washing John's foot as best we could with my bottled water, we put ointment and a nice, clean bandage on it.

He looked up and said, "I waited for you. I knew you would fix it." I smiled and promised to return the next morning to rebandage and start him on an antibiotic.

John was not surprised to see me the next day at 7:00 A.M. As I handed him the antibiotic and explained how to take it, I kind of wanted him to say thank you. But as I looked in his eyes I knew why he hadn't thanked me: because this was expected. He knew I would bandage his wound and give him medicine because that is what I do. His trust was much better than a thank you.

As I washed the gash and covered it with a fresh bandage, he said once again, "I knew you were coming. You bring medicine like you

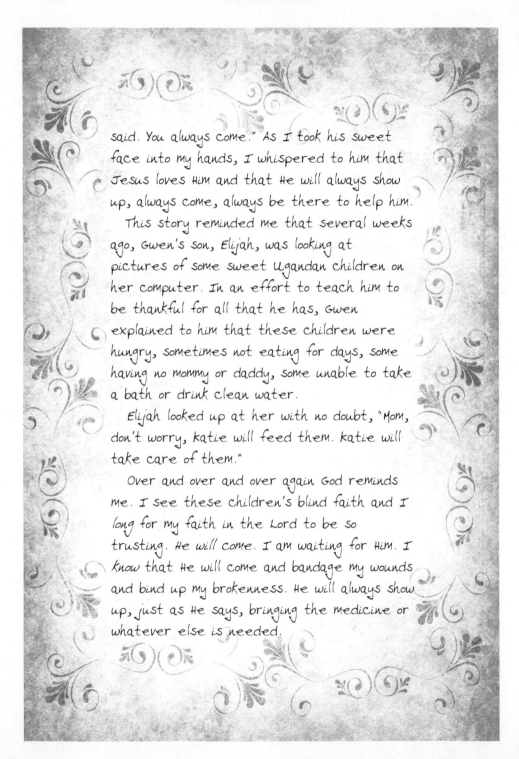

said. You always come." As I took his sweet face into my hands, I whispered to him that Jesus loves Him and that He will always show up, always come, always be there to help him.

This story reminded me that several weeks ago, Gwen's son, Elijah, was looking at pictures of some sweet Ugandan children on her computer. In an effort to teach him to be thankful for all that he has, Gwen explained to him that these children were hungry, sometimes not eating for days, some having no mommy or daddy, some unable to take a bath or drink clean water.

Elijah looked up at her with no doubt, "Mom, don't worry, Katie will feed them. Katie will take care of them."

Over and over and over again God reminds me. I see these children's blind faith and I long for my faith in the Lord to be so trusting. He will come. I am waiting for Him. I know that He will come and bandage my wounds and bind up my brokenness. He will always show up, just as He says, bringing the medicine or whatever else is needed.

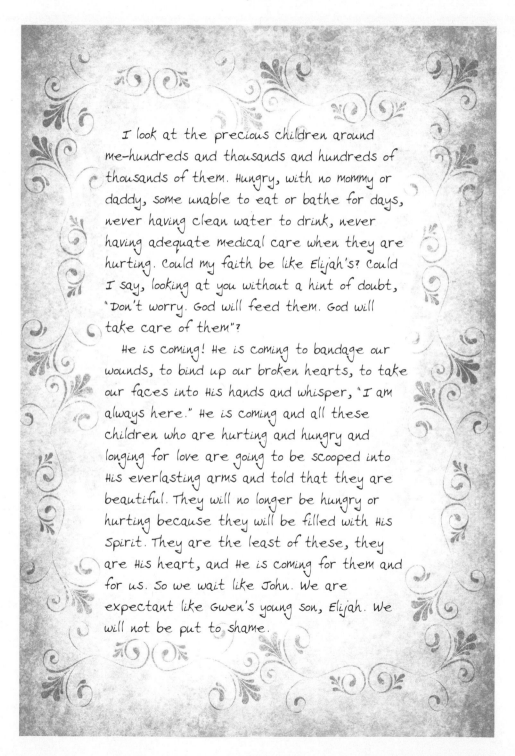

I look at the precious children around me-hundreds and thousands and hundreds of thousands of them. Hungry, with no mommy or daddy, some unable to eat or bathe for days, never having clean water to drink, never having adequate medical care when they are hurting. Could my faith be like Elijah's? Could I say, looking at you without a hint of doubt, "Don't worry. God will feed them. God will take care of them"?

He is coming! He is coming to bandage our wounds, to bind up our broken hearts, to take our faces into His hands and whisper, "I am always here." He is coming and all these children who are hurting and hungry and longing for love are going to be scooped into His everlasting arms and told that they are beautiful. They will no longer be hungry or hurting because they will be filled with His Spirit. They are the least of these, they are His heart, and He is coming for them and for us. So we wait like John. We are expectant like Gwen's young son, Elijah. We will not be put to shame.

Lord, we know You will come. We know You are here. Let us bring all our wounds and brokenness to You expectantly, without a doubt. Remind us that all the children we touch, and all the children we don't, are Yours. Yours in this broken life, and Yours in eternity. Come, Lord Jesus. We wait in hope.

NOTES

CHAPTER 3

1. http://www.theodora.com/wfbcurrent/uganda/uganda_people
.html.

CHAPTER 7

1. http://www.bread.org/hunger/global.
2. http://www.unicef.org/health/index_26163.html.
3. Margery Williams, *The Velveteen Rabbit* (New York: Simon &
Schuster), 14. There is no publication date on the copyright page
of the book, only a copyright date for the illustrations, which is
1983.
4. http://www.unicef.org/sowc06/press/who.php.

CHAPTER 8

1. Henri J. M. Nouwen, *Lifesigns: Intimacy, Fecundity, and Ecstasy
in Christian Perspective* (New York: Doubleday, 1986), 96–97.

CHAPTER 15

1. http://iconicphotos.wordpress.com/2009/11/19/famine-in
-uganda.
2. http://www.drt-ug.org/dev/publications//Understanding
%20Chronic%20Poverty%20in%20Karamoja.pdf.
3. http://www.unicef.org/evaluation/files/LL_Equity22Feb11
version_2.pdf.

Katie's journey in Uganda still continues. Read more at:

www.kissesfromkatie.blogspot.com

AMAZIMA
M I N I S T R I E S

To support the people of Uganda and Amazima Ministries, or to purchase magazine bead necklaces made by the Karimojong women of Masese, visit:

www.amazima.org